Pete Hill

ALSO BY BOB LUKE
AND FROM MCFARLAND

Bromo-Seltzer King: The Opulent Life of Captain Isaac "Ike" Emerson, 1859–1931 (2020)

Integrating the Orioles: Baseball and Race in Baltimore (2016)

Dean of Umpires: A Biography of Bill McGowan, 1896–1954 (2005)

Pete Hill
Black Baseball's First Superstar

Bob Luke

McFarland & Company, Inc., Publishers
Jefferson, North Carolina

LIBRARY OF CONGRESS CATALOGUING-IN-PUBLICATION DATA

Names: Luke, Bob author.
Title: Pete Hill : Black baseball's first superstar / Bob Luke.
Description: Jefferson, North Carolina : McFarland & Company, Inc., Publishers, 2023 | Includes bibliographical references and index.
Identifiers: LCCN 2022049939 | ISBN 9781476688770 (paperback : acid free paper) ∞
ISBN 9781476647814 (ebook)
Subjects: LCSH: Hill, Pete, 1882-1951. | Negro leagues—History. | Racism in sports—United States—History—20th century. | Segregation—United States—History—20th century. | United States—Race relations—History—20th century. | United States—Social conditions—1865-1918. | United States—Social conditions—1918-1932. | African American baseball players—Biography. | African American baseball managers—Biography. | BISAC: SPORTS & RECREATION / Baseball / History | SOCIAL SCIENCE / Ethnic Studies / American / African American & Black Studies
Classification: LCC GV865.H54 L85 2022 | DDC 796.357092 [B]—dc23/eng/20221026
LC record available at https://lccn.loc.gov/2022049939

BRITISH LIBRARY CATALOGUING DATA ARE AVAILABLE

ISBN (print) 978-1-4766-8877-0
ISBN (ebook) 978-1-4766-4781-4

© 2023 Bob Luke. All rights reserved

No part of this book may be reproduced or transmitted in any form or by any means, electronic or mechanical, including photocopying or recording, or by any information storage and retrieval system, without permission in writing from the publisher.

Front cover: Outfielder Pete Hill as a member of the 1916 Chicago American Giants (photograph courtesy of Gary Ashwill)

Printed in the United States of America

McFarland & Company, Inc., Publishers
Box 611, Jefferson, North Carolina 28640
www.mcfarlandpub.com

For Judy

Table of Contents

Acknowledgments   ix
Preface   1
Introduction   5

1. From Buena, Virginia, to Philly   15
2. On the Way to Chicago   25
3. The Hills Arrive in Chicago   37
4. The Rambling Giants   51
5. Racial Conflict On and Off the Field   68
6. Riots and the Noble Experiment   79
7. The Spanish Flu   88
8. President Wilson and the Suffragists   101
9. Pete Hill on His Own   109
10. Finally: A League for Black Baseball   121
11. Year Two in Detroit   133
12. On to Baltimore   143
13. Pete's Final Moves   154
14. Hall of Fame   162

Epilogue   169
Chapter Notes   179
Bibliography   201
Index   205

Acknowledgments

I could not have written this book without the substantial contributions of many people. Ron Hill, Pete's great-nephew and himself a historian of Pete's life, graciously invited me into his home where he shared many pictures, documents, and stories that have considerably enhanced this book. Ron read an earlier draft and made many helpful suggestions. Larry Lester, one of the nation's leading historians of Black baseball, edited the manuscript making many substantive and editorial suggestions.

Gary Ashwill, a nationally recognized authority on Black baseball's statistics, took time from his busy schedule of incorporating Negro League statistics with those of the major leagues to offer hard-to-find photographs, player identifications, and accounts of Hill's time in Buffalo. John Thorn, a prolific baseball writer, consultant, and the Official Baseball Historian for the Major Leagues, promptly answered e-mails with solid answers to questions.

Retired attorney, friend, and avid reader John Miles pored over a copy of the manuscript and made a multitude of insightful comments, suggestions, and edits.

Many people tracked down articles and documents including Ellen Keith at the Chicago History Museum; Susan Carlson at the Heinz History Center in Pittsburgh; John Egerston, County Administrator, Culpeper, Virginia; Kristina Donnally at the Virginia Department of Historic Resources in Richmond, Virginia; Cynthia Van Ness at the Buffalo History Museum in Buffalo, New York; Elizabeth Karcher, Executive Director, Woodrow Wilson House in Washington, D.C.; Stephanie Martin at the Lincoln Library, in Springfield, Illinois; Mindy Long at the Ida Library, Belvidere, Illinois; Rose Guerrero at the Historical Society of Palm Beach County; Cassidy Lent, John Horne, and Connie Robinson at the Baseball Hall of Fame in Cooperstown, New York; and Julie Bushhong at the Culpeper Virginia County Library.

Support and encouragement were generously offered by long-time friend, baseball historian, and mentor, Paul Dickson; and Negro League celebrant and founder of the Negro League Legends Hall of Fame, Dwayne Sims.

My wife, Judith Wentworth, and daughters Jennifer Morgan and Allyson Frusciano cheered me on. A special note of thanks is due to Deborah Patton, a skilled indexer and proof reader.

To all I am deeply appreciative and grateful. Any errors are mine alone.

Preface

Not a household name on the order of fellow Hall of Fame outfielders Babe Ruth, Ted Williams, and Mickey Mantle, but every bit as good, John Preston "Pete" Hill, known to all as Pete, ranks as one of the greatest outfielders of all time, Black or White. He is also the least known of the early Black players with a bronze plaque in Cooperstown. His career stretched from 1900 to 1925 during which time the foundation for organized Black baseball, featuring such better-known stars as "Satchel" Paige, Josh Gibson, Buck Leonard, Willie Wells, and Monte Irvin, was put in place. By bringing the game to cities large and small, Pete Hill and his fellow players built a fan base that would prove critical to the growth of Black baseball until the majors finally allowed Blacks into their ranks during the 1940s and 1950s. This book is the story of Hill's little-known baseball career and the times in which he lived and played.

Many contemporaries and historians have compared Hill to Ty Cobb. Cobb's career overlapped most of Hill's and spanned 24 years, 1905–1928; 22 with the Detroit Tigers and two with the Philadelphia Athletics. Cobb was one of the first five players, all White, inducted into the Hall of Fame's inaugural class in 1936. The Georgia Peach received more votes than any of the others inducted that year: Babe Ruth, Honus Wagner, Walter Johnson, and Christy Mathewson. Tris Speaker, another White Hall of Famer to whom Hill is frequently compared, also enjoyed a 22-year career (1907–1928) in the majors primarily with the Boston Red Sox and the Cleveland Indians. He entered the Hall the following year, 1937, but with fewer votes than Cobb.[1] Hill was in good company, but his induction, which had to be repeated to correct his name and birthplace, was delayed until 2006, 55 years after his death.

The Virginia-born Hill played for and managed professional Black teams in Cuba, Philadelphia, Chicago, Detroit, Milwaukee, Baltimore, Florida, California, and many other cities and states during off-season barnstorming games. He was groomed by the Chicago-based American Giants' talented and wily Andrew "Rube" Foster, considered the Father of the Negro Leagues. A towering figure as player, manager, executive, and owner, Foster not only nurtured one of the best Black teams of all time, the American Giants, and the game's first sustainable Black league, the Negro National League (NNL), he was a central figure in Hill's career from 1903 to 1921.

Social Movements

Hill's career played out amidst some of America's most turbulent times. Racial tensions during the early twentieth century sparked lynchings and riots that led to the birth of the National Association for the Advancement of Colored People (NAACP) in 1909. The fight for women's suffrage, officially initiated in 1848, culminated in the ratification of the 19th Amendment to the U.S. Constitution on August 18, 1920. Thirteen months earlier the Volstead Act, which spelled out enforcement activities for Prohibition, had gone into effect on July 22, 1919. The infamously named "War to End All Wars" fell far short of its promise. The Spanish Flu devastated the United States and the rest of the world in 1918. In what has become known as the "Black Sox Scandal," eight players for the Chicago White Sox succumbed to gamblers' bribes, enabling the Cincinnati Reds to win the 1919 World Series and putting a nation-wide stain on the national pastime. Though these events have been covered in detail elsewhere, I have included excursions into each to give the reader a flavor of the times.

Terminology

Until 1920 no Black team was affiliated with a permanent league. Before 1920, Black teams played games where they could find them. That changed in 1920 when Rube Foster presided over the formation of the first Black league, the Negro National League (NNL). The league brought a measure of organization to a few of the plethora of Black teams then in existence. More leagues would follow, the principal ones being the Eastern Colored League, the Negro American League, and the Southern Negro League. Only member teams could truly be called Negro League teams though the term is widely used to refer to African American players and teams who played professional baseball prior to 1920.

A Note on the Statistics

The Seamheads Negro Leagues database proved an essential resource during the writing of this book. Under the leadership of baseball historian and statistician Gary Ashwill, it has in fact become the leading authority on statistical information for Black teams and the Negro Leagues. Their mission "as an in-process statistical encyclopedia covering Black professional baseball players, teams, and leagues during the era of segregation" is to continue to be "the most authoritative record of Negro League statistics ever assembled"—a status Bryant Gumbel of HBO's *Real Sports* says they have already achieved. Rob Manfred, Commissioner of Major League Baseball, commended the organization's work when he announced the Negro Leagues would be recognized as major leagues.

"We are," Ashwill states, "always uncovering and adding new seasons, leagues, games and other information to our database which is built from the ground up." Box scores, newspaper articles, and score sheets are the primary information sources. "Everything," Ashwill says, "is verified from contemporary accounts of individual games."

To learn more about the database and explore its extensive contents, Google "Seamheads Negro Leagues Database."

Introduction

Black Baseball: An Overview

Blacks, with very few exceptions, were banned from White baseball teams as early as 1867. The National Association of Baseball Players, the country's first formal baseball organization, published a written statement that year barring any team with one or more Black players from membership in the association. The stated rationale? "If colored clubs were admitted, there would be in all probability some division of feeling. Whereas by excluding them, no injury could result to anybody."[1] At least, not to any White body.

Four years later, in 1871, baseball's first professional association, the National Association of Professional Base Ball Players, did not issue a written prohibition, but a tacit agreement existed among the teams' owners that Blacks were to be excluded.[2] Most, but not all, were.

William Edward White, born the son of a White slave owner and his mixed race servant, appeared in one game as a first baseman for the National League's Providence Grays on June 21, 1879.[3] Catcher Moses Fleetwood "Fleet" Walker, the second African American to play on a White professional team, appeared in 42 games for the Toledo Blue Stockings in 1884. The Toledo team was in the American Association and considered a major league team at the time. His brother, outfielder Welday, appeared in five games for the Blue Stockings. Blacks' participation in professional White baseball peaked in 1887 when five players—Moses Walker, second basemen Frank Grant and Bud Fowler, and pitchers George Stovey and Robert Higgins—played on International League teams, a circuit one step below the majors. In mid–1887 the league explicitly forbid the signing of any more Blacks but did not release those already on its payrolls. By 1900, however, all five were out of White organized baseball and played for Black independent teams. Many White players were happy to see them go. Chicago Cub infielder Ned Williamson spoke for many when he said in 1891, "Whites did not mind to permit darkies to carry water to them or guard the bat-bag, but it made them [Whites] sore to have one of them in the line-up."[4]

Perhaps the last Black team in the minor leagues during the nineteenth century was the Acme Colored Giants, which represented Celoron, New York, in the Iron and Oil Leagues in 1898.[5] By 1900 the color bar was firmly in place. There it stayed until Branch Rickey signed Jackie Robinson to a Brooklyn Dodgers organization contract in 1945.

Playing Conditions

Independent Black and Negro League teams were financed by men, sometimes White, who had the requisite passion and money. Many teams traveled extensively (barnstormed). They played against both Black and White teams wherever they could find paying spectators. In 1913, for example, Hill, as an outfielder for Rube Foster's American Giants, played in over 200 games thanks to a lengthy post-season barnstorming tour that included stops in California, the Northwest, Canada, the South, and Cuba. Teams relied heavily on base steals, bunts, and line drive singles. Home runs were a rarity.

As impressive as the action on the field could be, the White press often described Black teams in racially insensitive terms. The *Harrisburg Daily Independent*, for example, labeled the Philadelphia Giants, a team Hill played for from 1904 to 1908, "the dandies of Coonville," in an account of a September 1905 game in Pennsylvania's state capital. Such appellations were usually also accompanied by an acknowledgment of a team's prowess. In this case, the same article noted, "The mere announcement that the Philadelphia Giants were to play at Island Park (the Harrisburg ballpark) was enough to draw a large crowd."[6]

Teams carried twelve to sixteen players in contrast to the majors' twenty-five-man rosters. Few Blacks had the luxury of specializing in one position as did most major leaguers. Pitchers often played in the outfield or perhaps first base when not on the mound. Infielders who developed a reputation as a standout at shortstop or one of the bases often filled in at other positions when the need arose. Catchers tended to be an exception. Enduring long car, bus, or train rides, sometimes in sweaty uniforms; grabbing sandwiches from the back doors of restaurants that would not seat Blacks; sleeping, sometimes two to a bed, in Black hotels teeming with bed bugs, or in boarding houses or private homes—all were commonplace. All brooked racist taunts from White fans.

Foster paid his players well and took good care of them. While most Black teams got around on team-owned buses in various states of repair and, in some cases, private automobiles, Foster's teams traveled, at times, in a private Pullman car. Often staffed with several cooks and waiters, the car was hooked on to the back of White-owned trains. While far from the norm, other Black teams, notably the Indianapolis ABCs and the Page Fence Giants, also traveled by private rail car.

It was the steam age of railroading. Chris Skaw, owner of Trains and Travel International, gave this description of a steam engine that players who rode the rails became all too familiar with: "A steam engine has smoke coming out of the stack, the steam shooting out the sides, the wheels turning, the rods turning ... hundreds of moving parts all interlinked—it's a beast that snorts back at you."[7]

The Games

African Americans liked their baseball. The best Black teams drew large crowds. Hill's primary teams, the Chicago-based Leland Giants and later the American Giants, often outdrew the city's major league clubs, the Cubs and White Sox.[8]

Black games offered both entertainment as well as a haven for Blacks from the insults and discrimination of everyday life in segregated America. Sunday afternoon games, played soon after church let out, were the week's social highlight in many Black communities. People dressed to the nines and brought picnic baskets, beer, wine, spirits, and enough cash to make wagers on anything from the game's winner to whether the next pitch would be a ball or a strike. Adding to the action on the diamond were fights among players on the field, often sparked by an umpire's call, and dust-ups among spectators.

The games were brief by today's standards. Most were completed in two hours or less. The average length of a major league game in 2021 was 3 hours and 10 minutes.[9] Umpiring, a cost borne by the home team that selected the arbiter, was often done by one man, often White, in the early days. The lone arbiter had to call balls and strikes, plays at the bases, fair and foul balls, bear the brunt of criticism from players and fans alike, and occasionally find himself the target of a player's fists.

Record Keeping

Accounts of many games, but not all, appeared in newspapers, both African American weeklies and, less often, in White dailies. Some accounts consisted of just a few lines about the game; the respective batteries, and the runs scored by innings by each team. Other entries gave a full description of the game and a detailed box score identifying how each player performed. Such sporadic record keeping has made it difficult for historians to compile complete accounts of players' and teams' performances.

Robert Peterson, author of the classic book on Black baseball *Only the Ball Was White*, said in 1992, "Tracing the course of the organized Negro Leagues is rather like trying to follow a single black strand of spaghetti. The footing is infirm, and the strand has a tendency to break off in one's hand and slither back into the amorphous mass."[10] Much progress has been made in the years since Peterson's book appeared, but, for the reasons above, it is unlikely we will ever have a complete statistical record. The sleuthing continues, nevertheless. See Appendix A for a discussion of the well-respected Seamheads Negro Leagues Database.

Varying, incomplete, and even conflicting records do not detract from the greatness of Black and Negro League teams and their players. Many, save for their skin color, could have played and starred in the majors. Major League Baseball, buoyed by the vast increase in research since Peterson's comments and the Black Lives Matter movement, has acknowledged the caliber of play in the Negro Leagues by taking the monumental step in December 2020 of elevating the 1920–1948 Negro Leagues to major league status. The records of those players will be merged with the records of major league players.

As thorough and painstaking as the current research is, "to accept them as official at this point," cautions John Thorn, MLB historian, "would be premature. They now include postseason play and some doubtful foreign leagues. Major League Baseball (MLB), however, has no problem with the stats being fluid and subject to further research," Thorn added. The same "fluidity," he pointed out, is the case with MLB statistics before the Second World War.[11]

Motivation

Because pay for even the best Black players was considerably less than that commanded by White major leaguers, some have attributed Black players' motivation to their pride and love of the game. That was true in large part for some. Leon Day, a Hall of Fame pitcher whose Negro League career with the Baltimore Black Sox, Newark Eagles, and Baltimore Elite Giants spanned 1934 to 1950, said of his playing days, "We were a good bunch of guys traveling down the highway. One guy would start telling lies; then another and another. Then we'd start singing 'Sweet Adeline,' play cards, get to the ballpark, play the game, and get right back on the bus."[12] "We didn't make too much," remembered James "Red" Moore of his five-year career, 1936–1940, with the Atlanta Black Crackers and Newark Eagles, "but we traveled around and made some money. My dad liked to be talking about his son."[13]

Theodore Roosevelt "Double Duty" Radcliffe—so nicknamed by Damon Runyan, a famous short story writer, for pitching the first game of a doubleheader and catching the second, or vice-versa, during his 23-year career (1928 to 1950)—told a reporter for the *Detroit Free Press* in 1992 that playing ball "wasn't about the money. Playing ball back then was like being on vacation all your life."[14] Hall of Fame infielder Ray Dandridge said of his career (1933–1949), "I've enjoyed it, and I think I've been a lucky fellow. Didn't make no money, but I think I went a long ways. I have no regrets, none at all."[15]

Money, though, make no mistake, was also a motivator and a big one. Negro League historian Leslie A. Heaphy notes that while Black players in 1905 made less, at $450 a year "if lucky," than minor leaguers at $500, and far less than an average major league salary of $2,000 a year—they did as well as or better than many other Blacks. A plasterer could make $2.50 a day, a bricklayer 52 cents an hour, and a carpenter 40 cents an hour. Players added to their income by barnstorming or taking off-season jobs. They also enjoyed a measure of psychic income unavailable to most other African Americans.[16] Thousands of people did not turn out to see bricklayers, carpenters, and plasterers ply their trade. For most players, motivation was a blend of money and the psychic rewards.

Many players boosted their pay by summarily leaving ("jumping") one team, even in the middle of a season, for another that offered more money. One of the best-known Negro Leaguers, pitcher Leroy "Satchel" Paige, defended his decision to jump to Argentina in 1938. "Say you are getting a salary of six hundred dollars a month and somebody comes along and offers you three times that amount. Wouldn't you take it?" he asked a reporter for the Black weekly *Pittsburgh Courier*.[17] Hall of Fame shortstop John Henry "Pop" Lloyd, who played for thirteen Black and Negro League teams between 1906 and 1932, was considered by many the best shortstop in the Negro Leagues. Babe Ruth called him the greatest baseball player of all time. Lloyd, after his career was over, told an interviewer, "Where ever the money was, that's where I was."[18]

Many players besides Paige "jumped" to teams in countries outside the United States: Cuba, Mexico, Argentina, Venezuela, and Haiti. There they found less discrimination, a more relaxed game schedule, and better living conditions, in addition to fatter paychecks. Team owners, of course, opposed jumping but were powerless to stop it. Fines and threats of banishment deterred no one.

The Exception That Proved the Rule

The All-Nations team was a notable exception to segregated baseball. White Kansas City, Missouri, businessman J.L. Wilkinson owned the team from 1912 to 1918. Born in Algona, Iowa, he pitched for the town's sandlot team before joining the Hopkins Brothers Sporting Goods team in 1904 as a shortstop and later manager. When the team disbanded in 1908, he fielded an all-women's team, the Bloomer Girls, until 1911. He kept a supply of wigs on hand to use as needed.[19] Based in Des Moines, Iowa, the All-Nations team got its name from its roster: Native Americans, Asians, Latin Americans as well as Black and White Americans (all men) played for the team.

When the team's stars—Black pitcher John Donaldson, who averaged close to 20 strikeouts per game; Cuban-born pitcher José Méndez, who Hall of Fame New York Giants manager John McGraw said would be worth $30,000 a year to a major league team were he White; and outfielder Cristóbal Torriente, another Cuban-born player—were in uniform, the All-Nations were one of the best and most colorful of the day.

They barnstormed throughout the Midwest in a $25,000 Pullman car, carried bleachers for fans, slept in tents pitched on the field before games, featured a dance band and professional wrestlers to entertain before games. They used a portable lighting system making night games possible. The All-Nations demonstrated that ability was a better predictor of success than skin color.[20]

In 1916 the team "played the Indianapolis ABCs, off their feet" and, during a Sunday doubleheader at Chicago's Schorling's Park in the Windy City, inflicted two losses on the American Giants. The losing teams were two of the best Black teams in the country. The exceptional caliber of play exhibited by all three teams prompted a sportswriter for the Black weekly the *Chicago Defender* to admonish the city's two major league clubs, the Cubs and White Sox, for not signing the likes of Pete Hill, several of his mates, and All-Nation's pitchers Donaldson and Méndez. To do so, the reporter argued, would relieve the city's fans from another depressing winter spent wondering why no World Series games had come to the Windy City since the Cubs lost the 1910 Fall Classic to the Philadelphia Athletics.[21] The reporter was no doubt pleased when Chicago's major league teams appeared in three successive Series, 1917–1919, the last of which is talked about to this day.

World War I draft calls forced the All-Nations team to fold in 1918 but, at the same time, gave rise to one of the most prominent Black teams. Wilkinson, using some players from the All-Nations who were not drafted, five Blacks from the army's 25th Infantry Wreckers suggested to him by major league manager John McGraw and Kansas City native Casey Stengel, then playing for the Pittsburgh Pirates, and several others, founded the Kansas City Monarchs in 1920.[22] The Monarchs would remain a Negro League powerhouse for the next 30 years. In addition to "Satchel" Paige and Jackie Robinson, Monarch players Willard Brown, Andy Cooper, Wilber "Bullet" Rogan, and Hilton Smith went to the Hall of Fame in 2006; more than from any other Black or Negro League team. The Hall also inducted Wilkinson in 2006.

John Preston "Pete" Hill

The multi-talented 5'8", 180-pound outfielder could lay down a bunt as easily as he rapped out line drive singles, extra base hits, and the occasional homer. A favorite play of his long-time manager Rube Foster involved the batter dropping a short bunt toward third base with a man on first. If the infielder picked the ball up and threw to first, the runner on first raced on to third, perhaps skipping second base if the umpire's attention was directed elsewhere. If the third baseman held the ball, the Giants had two men on. Pete and others practiced for hours bunting the ball to spots on the infield marked by Rube.[23]

Hill had speed. He dashed around the bases with the best of them, once timed in 14.4 seconds.[24] Byron Buxton, an outfielder for the Minnesota Twins, set the major league record at 13.85 seconds in August 2017.[25] It was often said, tongue in cheek, of James "Cool Papa" Bell—a flashy outfielder who played with three of the Negro Leagues' strongest teams, the St. Louis Stars, Pittsburgh Crawfords, and Homestead Grays—that he could flick off a light switch and be in bed before the room turned dark. The fastest of all players, he is said to have rounded the bases in 12 seconds flat.

When on base, Hill was always in motion; darting back and forth from the base, jumping up and down, all in an effort to distract the pitchers' concentration. Hill was, in the words of Negro League historian James A. Riley, a "nervy runner ... a restless sort always in motion trying to draw a throw from the pitcher."[26]

While the stats for Hill and other Black players may not be complete, the consensus among those who knew or knew of Hill attest to his greatness. Riley, writing in the 1990s, described Hill "as the first great outfielder in Black baseball history." Riley's nominations for the three best outfielders in all of baseball during the dead ball era, which ended in 1920, were major league stars Tris Speaker and Ty Cobb complemented by Pete Hill.[27] Cumberland "Cum" Posey, who had a 35-year career with the Homestead

Grays from 1911 to 1946 as player, manager, and owner, and wrote a column, "Posey's Points," for the *Pittsburgh Courier*, anointed Hill in 1933 "the greatest hitter of all time."

Smooth-fielding third baseman Dave Malarcher, who played for and against Hill during a 16-year career, agreed. "Pete Hill," Malarcher said, "was the greatest hitter there ever was. Oh yes, better than [Oscar] Charleston. Charleston was the greatest all round ball player, but as a hitter, Pete Hill was the greatest hitter."[28]

In a similar vein, Seward Hayes "See" Posey, Cum's brother and officer of the Homestead Grays from 1911 to 1948, slotted Hill into the cleanup position, traditionally reserved for a team's best hitter, on his 1943 all-star lineup of Black players. See had "the incomparable Charleston" batting third.[29] Six years earlier Hill, as a right fielder, joined Cristóbal Torriente (left fielder) and Oscar Charleston (center fielder), considered by many, in addition to Malarcher, the best Black player of all time, on Cum Posey's 1937 list of "All-Time Immortals of Negro Baseball."[30]

Jeremy Beer, in his exhaustive 2019 biography of Charleston, cites "new statistical analyses" that show the top Black position players (players other than pitchers) during 1915–1920 "included the Cuban outfielder Cristóbal Torriente, John Henry 'Pop' Lloyd, 'mammoth' slugger Pete Hill, catcher Louis Santop, and infielder and manager James 'Candy Jim' Taylor."

Hill was also renowned for his play in the field. Lewis Means, an infielder and catcher whose Negro League career lasted from 1920 to 1928, put Hill in the same elite category as had Cum Posey. In 1939, Means told a reporter for the *Atlanta Daily World*, a Black weekly, "Every manager who knew Hill accords him the greatest arm in Negro baseball. He had no peer in fielding."[31] The *Pittsburgh Courier's* 1952 All-Time-Negro League All-Star Team, composed of nominations by former Negro League stars, included Pete Hill as one of the six outfielders. The others were Monte Irvin, Oscar Charleston, Cool Papa Bell, Cristóbal Torriente, and Chino Smith.[32]

Hill spent the bulk of his career with Rube Foster's American Giants, one of Black baseball's strongest teams. His stellar play, sharp baseball mind, loyalty, and ability to manage both rookies and veterans led Foster to name him the Giants' captain in 1911, a position he held for eight seasons. Foster also chose Hill to manage the Detroit Stars, a team Rube founded in 1919. After three years as the Stars' player/manager, Hill would go on, in a similar capacity, to the Milwaukee Bears, the Baltimore Black Sox, and, after his Negro League career ended in 1925, to several lower-level Black teams in Buffalo, New York.

Hill was as subdued off the field as he was boisterous on it. Not one to boast of his accomplishments, pick fights, drive a flashy car, talk to reporters, or frequent bars, he was married and divorced and the father of two sons, one of whom, John Jr, tragically died in Philadelphia in 1907 at age four days. His second son, Kenneth Preston Hill, born in 1909, often accompanied his father to the ballpark. On one occasion in 1915 the six-year-old saw his dad belt two home runs, albeit in a losing cause.[33] The few pictures of the senior Hill often show a relaxed and, sometimes, smiling demeanor.

In addition to his mastery of baseball, Pete proved adept with pen in hand. Letters from him to the *Chicago Defender* appeared occasionally. He wrote a column for the *Baltimore Afro-American* titled "Kinky Questions" in which he answered readers' questions and made predictions.

1

From Buena, Virginia, to Philly

The Family

Researching African Americans in the late 1800s often yields less than clear-cut findings, given the lack of official records such as birth, marriage, and divorce certificates. As a result, there are things we know about Pete Hill as a child and things we do not know. We are confident that Pete Hill was born October 12, 1882, though 1884 occasionally shows up as his birth year. He had two older brothers: Walter Vaughn (March 10, 1881–March 17, 1948) and Jerome Bryant (March 30, 1879–August 17, 1940).[1]

Pete Hill's paternal parentage and that of his brothers is shrouded in some uncertainty. Records displayed at FindaGrave.com for the Maple Park Cemetery in Bluefield, West Virginia, where a Ruben W. Hill is buried, show him to be the father of the three brothers. Pete Hill, however, listed his father as "Ike" on his Social Security application. Nothing more definitive could be found for an Ike or Isaac Hill. Ron Hill, Pete Hill's great-nephew, has indicated that recent family discussions have surfaced the possibility that not all three brothers had the same father. We do know that all three took the Hill surname, and that Elizabeth "Lizzie" Seals Hill was the mother of the three brothers.[2]

The three were born in Buena, Virginia, a rural, African American hamlet located two miles north of the village of Rapidan in Culpeper County, Virginia. The village emerged in the late 1860s as an enclave for the area's newly-freed slaves. Both "Lizzie" Seals Hill, born 1859, and Reuben W. Hill, born 1854, were most likely slaves as children. Journalist Allison Brophy Champion, a reporter for *McClatchy-Tribune Business News*, said after her search of census records, "I cannot find her [Elizabeth's] father or Pete's paternal grandfather living as freemen in the 1860 census. If they were free, they would have been listed."[3] Certainly free by the 1870s, the Hills joined other families—among them Fryes, Strothers, Prices, Graves, Porters, and Moores—to found Buena.[4]

Cedar Mountain

The boys spent their formative years on the side of Cedar Mountain in "upper" Buena where little of note had happened until August 9, 1862. On that day Union and Confederate soldiers clashed in the Civil War battle of Cedar Mountain. Confederate general Thomas "Stonewall" Jackson narrowly avoided defeat at the hands of Union general Nathanial Banks, who was leading his troops into central Virginia. A reinforcement of Confederate soldiers, led by Major General A.P. Hill, who also called Culpeper County home, arrived just in time. Many historians consider the Battle of Cedar Mountain the first of the Second Manassas Campaign, giving General Robert E. Lee's Army of Northern Virginia the initiative and pushing the war north from Richmond.[5]

Second Lieutenant Robert Gould Shaw, a member of the 2nd Massachusetts Infantry, in an August 29, 1862, letter to his father, wealthy abolitionist Francis George Shaw, cited "a total lack of discipline" among the Union troops as a reason for their defeat. "I shouldn't say men skulked out of battle if I hadn't seen it myself," he wrote. "We [the Union army]," he continued, "will never do much until the government finds it is worth their while to get competent officers and attend themselves to the organization of the army."[6]

It was a costly encounter for both sides. Union causalities amounted to 2,381 killed, wounded, or missing. The Confederates lost 229 killed, 1,047 wounded, and 31 missing.[7]

Shaw's competent service as a second lieutenant and later captain at the battle of Antietam made a favorable impression on Massachusetts governor John A. Andrew. Appointed by Andrew as commander of the 54th Massachusetts Volunteer Regiment, the first official regiment of African Americans, Shaw earned lasting fame for leading his Black troops in an unsuccessful assault against the Confederates' Fort Wagner on Morris Island near Charleston, South Carolina, on July 18, 1863. The 54th, though losing the fight, gave the Union its first demonstration that men of color could and would fight as valiantly as any White soldier. Shaw, the first to scale the Fort's walls, lost his life as he urged his troops forward.[8]

By war's end, crops in Culpeper County had been decimated, livestock killed or confiscated, and the tracks of the Orange & Alexandria Railroad, which ran through Buena, destroyed by Union troops. Recovery came slowly. By 1872 the railroad had been re-established and merged with two other lines to form the Virginia Midland Railroad. By 1880 most Culpeper businesses were owned and run by Whites even though the majority of residents were Black. Not so in Buena. All enterprises there, including the post office, established in 1892, the lone school, and the Baptist Church were controlled and operated by African Americans.[9]

The war-damaged house that Confederate general Charles S. Winder used as his headquarters and where he was killed during the Battle of Cedar Mountain (Library of Congress).

From Buena to Pittsburgh

Following a separation from Reuben, Lizzie found herself the struggling single mother of three growing boys in an area holding out little promise. By 1889 she had gathered up her three sons, courage, and belongings to join the growing exodus of Blacks boarding northbound trains. Expanding jobs in steel mills, coal mines, and related industries were attracting African Americans from the rural South to northern cities like Pittsburgh where she settled. The family's new home was in Homewood, a community in Allegheny County across the Allegheny River east of Pittsburgh.

Industrialists Andrew Carnegie and George Westinghouse had built massive estates there. But as the twentieth century approached, these wealthy magnates and their families left. Their land was sold or converted into smaller plots. German, Italian and Scots-Irish immigrants came to work in the city's manufacturing sector, attracted by the flat land, cheap housing and easy access to transportation. Around the same time, Black families began to move in and establish themselves. The community was mixed racially in public spaces, but still segregated in commercial places like pools and theaters.[10]

Little is known about how Lizzie provided for her family until 1893, when she married John T. Reynolds, 33, a barber, with whom she lived in a rented house at 7221 Susquehanna Street in the Homewood section of town.[11] Pete, still known as John Preston, completed the seventh grade by about 1895, found work as a day laborer, and played ball on the neighborhood sandlots in his spare time.[12]

After Reynolds died, Lizzie married John Kelly, also a barber, with whom she lived in Pittsburgh until her death. The headline of the *Pittsburgh Courier*'s front-page article announcing her passing in 1931 read, "Mother of Well Known Citizen Passes Away." The "well known citizen" was not Pete, who by this time was retired from Negro League baseball and living in Buffalo, New York. It was his brother Jerome, a well-respected post office executive and an officer of the Pioneer Building and Loan Association. Pete's other brother, Walter, also lived in Pittsburgh. Pete is referred to in the article as "Johnnie." A small item in the *Courier* of the same day notes that Pete was in town visiting family.[13]

Early Baseball Days

By 1898–99, Pete had established himself as a phenom on the Steel City's sandlots with his bat, glove, and arm. How and when he got his start in Black baseball are also matters of conjecture. Several accounts, including one on the Baseball Hall of Fame's Pete Hill page, cite the Pittsburgh Keystones as his first team, as does baseball historian James A. Riley.[14] The *Afro-American,* a Baltimore-based Black weekly, in a brief sketch of Hill when he joined the Baltimore Black Sox in 1924 as manager, also credits Pete with breaking in with the Keystones in 1896 at third base.[15] That account would make Hill 13 years old at the start of the 1896 season, an unusually young age for a rookie. *Afro* sports editor G.L. Mackey gives the year as 1898, a more likely possibility if true.[16]

On the other hand, baseball historian Gary Ashwill, whose baseball research blog Agate Type is a major source of information on Black and Latin American baseball, believes Hill could have played for the Keystones, but he has no proof.[17] Researcher Phil Williams, in an article for the Society for American Baseball Research (SABR), also casts doubt on a Hill connection with the Keystones. None of the scant references to the Keystones in that era makes mention of him. More likely, Williams suggests, is that Hill debuted in 1901 with the Golden Slides or the Barnes Colored Americans, the latter a Pittsburgh-based team organized by Bud Fowler.[18] An early professional Black baseball player, Fowler played on several White teams until the color bar was enforced. A well-traveled player, who by his own account played on teams in 22 states and Canada from 1877 to 1899, also organized and managed several Black barnstorming teams—the best known of which was the Page Fence Giants.[19]

A Mr. Barnes, owner of the city's Crampton Hotel, engaged Fowler to field "a first class colored baseball club." "The local club," the *Pittsburgh Daily Post* said, "would be made up of a few of the Keystones" (but no names given). Hill could have been one of them. Several brief accounts in Pittsburgh newspapers of Barnes Colored Americans' games in 1901 make no mention of players other than pitchers and catchers. References to the Golden Slides could not be found.[20]

Baseball historian Jerry Malloy offers another possibility of Hill's rookie year. In his introduction to Sol White's classic book *Sol White's History of Colored Baseball,* Malloy puts "rookie Preston 'Pete' Hill, one of the finest outfielders in the pre–Negro Leagues," on the roster of the 1903 Cuban X-Giants. Consulting the page in White's book cited by Malloy, however, yields the mention of a John Hill, not a John Preston "Pete" Hill, as a member of the 1903 Cuban X-Giants.[21] The Seamheads Negro Leagues Database likewise shows a Johnny Hill, not Pete, on the 1903 Cuban X-Giants and has Pete Hill on the 1904 Philadelphia Giants roster.[22] Sol White, an infielder with a variety of black teams from 1887 to 1901 and captain and manager of the Philadelphia Giants from 1902 to 1911, in a 1931 article in *The New York Age* includes Pete Hill on the Philadelphia team's 1904 roster but not the 1903 aggregation.[23] Historian Robert Peterson wrote that Hill began his career in 1904 with the Philadelphia Giants.[24]

Other baseball historians, John Holway and Jorge Figueredo, also place Hill on the 1903 Cuban X-Giants. Holway notes that "rookie Pete Hill" along with Grant "Home Run" Johnson "landed in the arms of the delighted Cuban X-Giants" in 1903. Figueredo includes "Pete Hill" as a member of the Cuban X-Giants who lost 7 of the 9 games the team played during the Cuban American Series, December 1 to December 9, 1903, in Havana, Cuba.[25] The last two accounts make it likely that Pete Hill got his professional start with the post season 1903 Cuban X-Giants.

How he got to the Cuban X-Giants remains a mystery. Since there were no minor leagues for Black players, Hill might have simply presented himself for a tryout, a frequent occurrence at the time, or he may have impressed the Giants with his play for an opposing team during an exhibition game. As to his nickname, "Pete," he found himself with a teammate on both the Philadelphia Giants and the Cuban X-Giants, the aforementioned John or Johnny Hill, a third baseman. Perhaps the presence of another John Hill prompted John Preston Hill to adopt the nickname "Pete" to avoid confusion. Why he chose "Pete" is not known.

Philadelphia Giants

Hill's baseball career comes into clearer focus in 1904 in Philadelphia, two years after the Philadelphia Giants were founded. Philadelphia's growing Black population and a heavily attended 1901 game between the Cuban X-Giants and the American League Philadelphia Athletics in the A's newly-built Columbia Park caught the attention of two men. Harry Smith, a sportswriter for the *Philadelphia Tribune*, a Black weekly, and H. Walter (Slick) Schlichter, White, sports editor for the *Philadelphia News Item*, a White daily, sensed an opportunity.[26]

Together, Schlichter and Smith founded the Philadelphia Giants in 1902. Schlichter, in April 1902, proudly announced in the *Item*, "For the first time in the history of base ball in this city a star team of colored players will wear a Philadelphia uniform. The Philadelphia Giants ... is composed of some of the best players in America today, and were it not for the fact that their skin is black, some of them would to-day be drawing fancy salaries in one or the other of the big leagues."[27] The Giants were not the first Black team to call Philadelphia home, but it was the first to feature top-flight players.

Schlichter, everyone called him "Slick," had his finger in many an athletic pie. As a youngster he competed in swimming meets, handball tournaments, 100-yard dashes, and 220-yard hurdle races. As an adult, sports editor and baseball team owner, he found time to sponsor professional wrestling matches, serve as timer for 12-mile runs, and manage "pushmobile" races. A pushmobile race was the forerunner of the soap box derby in which a homemade wooden cart, constructed by a child with the help of a "mechanic," often a dad, was pushed by the builder around a track in competition for prizes and trophies. As co-manager of the Lancaster (Pennsylvania) Athletic Club, 80 miles west of Philly, "Slick" paired Jack Johnson, soon to be (1908) the "colored" heavyweight champ, with Jim Jeffords, a White heavyweight boxer, in November 1906 for a six-round bout. Johnson won going away.[28]

Sol White joined the founding duo as the newly-formed team's manager and shortstop. Recalling their first meeting, White said of Schlichter, who served as the team's business agent when the two joined forces in 1902, "He was a keen-minded sportsman, as shrewd as you make 'em." "'We will see this thing through,' says he. 'I am with you,' says I. And so we went from there."[29]

Going from there included a wholesale raiding of players from the Cuban X-Giants. By the start of the 1904 season, Schlichter had acquired many players compliments of the Cuban X-Giants. Notable among them were Bill Monroe, who could play every infield position "with grace," Charles Grant, a superb second baseman whom John McGraw unsuccessfully tried to sign for his major league Baltimore Orioles team, Rube Foster, Hill, Danny McClellan, a southpaw pitcher whom many considered the peer of Foster, hard-hitting Grant (Home Run) Johnson, and stellar outfielder Mike Moore. Not surprisingly, Schlichter's raids resulted in the Philadelphia Giants' eventual supremacy over their Keystone State rivals.[30]

By 1903 the Cuban X-Giants and the Philadelphia Giants were the country's two best Black baseball teams. The Cuban X-Giants had defeated their Philadelphia counterparts for the 1902 and 1903 championship series. The 1903 championship was due in large part to Rube Foster's performance on the mound. A sportswriter for the *Philadelphia Item* described the team's ace "as a man of huge frame. His arms are like those of a windmill. He would swing them like the pendulum of the clock, looking awhile about the diamond. Suddenly he would twist up like a Missouri grasshopper to make a spring and the ball would shoot from the pitcher's box. Time and again he would strike out his man."[31]

Starting in 1904, the Missouri grasshopper led Schlichter's aggregation to three straight seasons in which the Philly Giants took the championship of eastern Black teams by whipping a depleted Cuban X-Giants team. Schlichter managed to win a fourth championship with Hill on board but without the services of Foster and many of the players Schlichter had purloined from the Cuban X-Giants. They, as we will see, left Philadelphia for Chicago for the 1907 season. Defections of other players and disagreement between Schlichter and White led to the Philadelphia Giants' demise in 1916.[32]

Another player of note for the 1903–1904 Philadelphia Giants, though he played only occasionally, was first baseman Jack Johnson. Johnson's baseball aspirations exceeded his abilities, but he would go on to gain fame and notoriety as the first Black heavyweight champion of the boxing world, a title he held from 1908 to 1915 while flaunting social norms. His three wives were White, and he had numerous run-ins with the law.[33]

Hill's Mentors

Two players from Philadelphia 1904 squad would have a lasting influence on Hill: the most important, Andrew "Rube" Foster, was three years older than Hill. Grant "Home Run" Johnson, a shortstop and eight years Hill's senior, was the other.

Universally acclaimed as the Father of the Negro Leagues, Foster excelled as a pitcher, manager, and executive from 1902 to 1926. At age 22 he joined the 1902 Chicago Union Giants for the start of his rookie season. The following season Foster, now a member of the Cuban X-Giants, defeated the Philadelphia Athletics' ace "Rube" Waddell as a member of Nat Strong's Murray Hills, a mid-town Manhattan semi-pro team. To hide his identity, the *New York Sun* reported Waddell pitching under the name of "Wilson." The Giants and Foster outscored Waddell's Murray Hills club 6 to 3. Foster acquired his nickname "Rube" from that game.[34]

Elected to the Hall of Fame in 1946, Waddell posted a 21–16 record in 1903 and led the League in strikeouts each season from 1902 to 1907. He went on to baffle hitters, White and Black, in America, Canada, and Cuba with blistering fastballs, sharp breaking curves, and unpredictable screwballs.[35]

A man as big as his vision, Foster stood a stout 5 feet 9 inches tall,[36] though his height is often incorrectly stated as over 6 feet. He tipped the scales anywhere from 210 to 290 pounds. Always in fashion, he favored three-piece suits, from the vest pockets of which dangled a chained watch. A "big apple cap" and a pipe completed his outfit. He adored his wife, Sarah, whom he lovingly called "Smoochie," and their two children, Sarah Watts, who took her middle name from her mother's maiden name and tragically died at age 5 of toxic poisoning, and son Earl Mack.[37]

The son of a Methodist minister, Andrew Foster, and a gospel-singing mother, Evaline, Rube was born on September 20, 1879. His birthplace is often given as Calvert, in Robertson County, Texas. While no birth certificate is available, the 1880 census, enumerated in May of 1880, shows the family, including an eight-month-old male child named "Bishop," living in the unincorporated town of Winchester in Fayette County, Texas.[38] The name "Bishop" may have been used to prevent confusion from there being two Andrews in the family or a nick name reflecting his father's role. Evidence points to the Fosters working as sharecroppers in 1880 on a 200-acre farm owned by a J.L.T. McKinny. Like many small towns in rural Texas at the time, Winchester supported hotels, saloons, rooming houses, wheelwrights, barbers, and seven mercantile stores.[39]

By the time of the 1900 census, the Foster family had moved to Calvert, 127 miles northwest of Houston. The future all-star was a middle child at the time with an older sister, Christina, and a younger brother, Johnson. A thriving segregated community of 3,000 residents, Calvert, 48 percent Black, was a railroad center and the county seat of Robertson County. The town boasted 52 businesses and Presbyterian, Baptist, Methodist, and Catholic Churches. Cotton was king until the boll weevil decimated the crop. Floods in 1899 and a 1901 fire in the business district further dampened the town's prosperity, causing many to move out.⁴⁰ Among them was Andrew "Rube" Foster.

The star pitcher for sandlot teams in and around Calvert set off for Waco, Texas, 35 miles northwest of Calvert. There he hurled for the Waco Yellow Jackets, a semi-pro Black team, before heading to Chicago for the 1902 season and Frank Leland's Chicago Union Giants. A Memphis, Tennessee, native and graduate of Fisk University in Nashville, Leland was a staunch Republican and former county commissioner. He had played the outfield for several teams including the Washington Capital City entry in the National League of Colored Baseball Clubs in 1887. The league, which lasted only two weeks, was an early, but not the last, attempt to form a circuit of Black teams. He soon decided his talent lay more in organizing and managing baseball teams than in playing. He shed his bat and glove for a seat in the dugout to manage the Chicago Unions, Chicago Union Giants, Leland Giants and the Chicago Giants, all of them among the best Black teams in the Midwest.⁴¹

A rarely seen portrait of Andrew "Rube" Foster, the father of Black baseball, in formal attire. Note the cigar (courtesy of Hake's Auctions).

Following a game with a White club in Otsego, Michigan, late in the 1902 season, Foster, for reasons unknown, left the Leland Giants to stay in Otsego and pitch for the local team. Fellow teammate and second baseman Dave Wyatt joined him, making the Otsego club a rare example of an integrated team. Thinking Otsego to be a town friendly to Blacks, Foster was soon disillusioned. A publicity poster referred to him as a "coon." Walking down the town's main street one day he heard a child exclaim to his mother, "there's a big nigger."⁴²

He and Wyatt finished the season and quickly moved on to Philadelphia to join the 1903 Cuban X-Giants. Wyatt, who had starred as a middle infielder and right fielder for Leland's Chicago Unions and Chicago Union Giants, retired from baseball after the 1903 season. He turned to journalism as a sportswriter. Over the course of his career he wrote for the *Illinois Chronicle*, the *Indianapolis Freeman*, the *Chicago Defender*, and the *Pittsburgh Courier*, all Black weeklies.[43] He was best known for his articles in the *Defender*. Robert S. Abbott, an attorney, founded the *Chicago Defender* in 1905. A Black newspaper with a national distribution, it opened the door for coverage of all Black teams and contributed to the Leland Giants—and, later, the American Giants—becoming an icon in Black communities throughout the country.[44]

Foster quickly established himself as the star he would be for the rest of his life.[45] On the mound for the 1903 Cuban X-Giants, he lost his first game but proceeded to win his next 54 including four playoff victories over the Philadelphia Giants with a sparkling earned run average of 1.50.[46]

People took note. There is an oft told story that John "Muggsy" McGraw, then in his second year managing the major league's New York Giants, engaged Foster in early 1903 to teach the screwball to two of his pitchers, Christy Mathewson, who famously called the pitch a "fade away," and Joe "Iron Man" McGinnity.[47] Some claim the account of Foster tutoring Mathewson is a well-worn myth, but the timing of Mathewson's sudden improvement adds credence to the story.[48] He went from striking out 159 batters in 1902 to setting down a league-leading 267 in 1903. He led the National League in strikeouts for the next four out of five seasons. He improved his 1902 won-loss percentage from .452 to .698 in 1903. The percentage never fell below .600 for the next 11 seasons. "Matty" ended his Hall of Fame career in 1916 with 373. This tied him with eventual fellow Hall of Famer Grover Cleveland Alexander as the major leagues' third winningest major league pitcher as of 1930. McGinnity won 31 games in 1903 and a league-leading career-high 35 in 1904. Both have a plaque in Cooperstown.[49]

Grant (Home Run) Johnson

Johnson hailed from Findlay, Ohio, forty miles south of Toledo and a prominent stop on the Underground Railroad during the Civil War.[50] The 5'10", 170-pound right-handed batter earned a reputation as the best shortstop in Black baseball before John Henry "Pop" Lloyd suited up. Johnson's nickname sprang from his reported 60 homeruns for his hometown Findlay Sluggers at age 20 in 1894. His reported batting averages were well above .300 for most of his career. Johnson and Hill were teammates with the Philadelphia Giants, Leland Giants, and American Giants. The two also played together in Cuba, the California Winter League, and on several Florida hotel teams. Hill and Johnson spent many of their later years together in Buffalo, New York, working on separate railroads as red caps and organizing lower-level semi-pro Black teams.

2

On the Way to Chicago

The Florida Connection

Following the 1903 championship game, a team composed of players from both teams, the Cuban X-Giants and the Philadelphia Giants, left the chilly confines of the mid–Atlantic states for sunny Palm Beach, Florida. They spent six weeks playing for the Royal Poinciana Hotel team against the Breakers Hotel's team, similarly composed of Black players.[1] The games became known as the Coconut or Florida League, but *league* is a misnomer given that only two teams played. Hill, Foster, and Johnson made the trip and made similar trips in the years to come.

The games served one of the many diversions offered to the hotels' White, well-heeled guests. Henry Morrison Flagler, a railroad and real estate tycoon in the Sunshine State, who made his initial fortune with John D. Rockefeller in the oil business, built both hotels, separated by a golf course and baseball diamond, in the 1890s. By 1901 the Royal Poinciana was the world's largest resort hotel, with three miles of corridors and rooms for 2,000 guests. The hotels served as the center of Palm Beach's winter social scene for such glitterati as the Rockefellers, Vanderbilts, Morgans, Astors, a U.S. president, and the occasional European nobility.[2]

The games began in 1897 when Flagler hired the best Black players he could find to suit up in the uniforms of the hotels to play a dozen or so games against each other between late January and mid–March. He contracted only with Blacks since he could also employ them as waiters. Games were played on Tuesday and Friday afternoons starting at 3:00 so players could get to their evening duties on time. The men lived in segregated barracks near the hotels.

Games were well attended by, in the words of reporter Stuart McIver, "elegantly clad socialites sipping tea or scotch in the grandstand, who cheered for and bet heavily on players who would have moved immediately into the Big Leagues if not for the racial barriers of the day."[3] White elites cheering Black players holding servile jobs set an enduring pattern for race

The Royal Poinciana Hotel as it looked circa 1910 (author's collection).

and sport for years to come.[4] The games were so popular they continued into the early 1930s.

Each year *The New York Times* printed the names, titles, and plans of guests at both hotels and kept readers apprised of the bevy of social activities with weekly articles.[5] Hundreds of employees arrived each year by train around Christmas time. The weather, of course, was a big draw. "We know it is hard to convince our friends in the north just at this wintery time," one guest from Philadelphia wrote, "but we are enjoying ocean bathing, wearing straw hats and other summer apparel, but such is the fact."

In addition to baseball, Flagler filled his guests' days and evenings with imported bands and orchestras from New York City and Atlantic City, dances, plays, golf outings, track meets, tennis matches, evening balls, meetings of the literary society, masquerade dances, concerts,[6] and cake walks—a dance first performed by slaves in the presence of their masters.[7] While these and other diversions had their devotees, the *Philadelphia Tribune* explained, "all meet on one common ground when the great American game of base ball is on."[8] Spectators enjoyed the games immensely. An observer of a 1907 game wrote, "The crowd would yell themselves hoarse, stand up in their seats, bang each other over the head, and even the girls would go into frenzy as if they were in a Methodist camp meeting."[9]

An aerial view of the complex Flager built. The Breakers Hotel (upper right) fronts the Atlantic Ocean while the Royal Poinciana is in the foreground. The ballpark is visible in the left center surrounded by the golf course (Historical Society of Palm Beach County).

Other Resort Teams

Flagler was not alone in forming teams of Black players to entertain White guests at a luxury resort. Frank Thompson, the headwaiter at the Argyle Hotel in Babylon, Long Island, created a similar diversion for Argyle guests. In August of 1885, he hired the best players from the Philadelphia Keystones, the Manhattans of Washington, D.C., and the Orions of Philadelphia, ostensibly as wait staff, but really as ballplayers. The team, which went by the name the Black Panthers, played nine games in Argyle Hotel uniforms against local amateur White teams from the Long Island–New York City area on the hotel grounds. The Panthers won six, lost two and tied one in their inaugural season. After the tourist season, the team added several more players, adopted the name Cuban Giants to downplay the Black/White racial tensions, and toured the country. Sol White, infielder and author of the first book about the history of Black baseball, credits Thompson with organizing "the first colored professional baseball team in the world."[10]

The Eastland Hotel in Hot Springs, Arkansas, fielded a similar team made up of Black hotel employees in 1901. Among them was a light-skinned bellboy, Charlie Grant, whose play at second base caught the eye of vacationer John McGraw, then manager of the Baltimore Orioles, a major league team in the American League. McGraw tried unsuccessfully to sign Grant. The infielder, at McGraw's urging, claimed to be a Native American with the concocted name of Chief Tokahoma. Chicago White Sox owner Charles Comiskey got wind of the ruse and nixed it. Grant continued his career with the best Black teams of the day.[11]

Rube and Hill Change Teams

Back in Philadelphia, Schlichter was impressed with Foster after losing the 1903 championship to him. At some point Slick lured the star hurler to "jump" to his team, the cross-town rival Philadelphia Giants, for the 1904 season. Hill accompanied him. Grant "Home Run" Johnson joined the two a year later.[12] The year 1904 turned out to be a good season for Schlichter's charges.

Among those who took note of the Philadelphia Giants' stellar play during the 1904 season was E.B. Lamar, Jr., manager of the Cuban X-Giants, which had defeated Schlichter's men for the championship just the year before. In a stinging August 23, 1904, letter to the sports editor of the *Philadelphia Tribune*, Lamar lambasted Schlichter for not playing his team in 1904. Such a state of affairs, Lamar complained, can lead the public to only one conclusion: "the Philadelphia Giants are afraid to play the Cuban X-Giants, the colored champions of the world, a series of games."[13]

Schlichter took up the challenge. Rather than respond in kind, Schlichter arranged a three-game series between the two teams to be played on neutral ground, Inlet Ball Park in Atlantic City. In game one, played on September 1 before 4,000 spectators, Rube Foster struck out 18 of Lamar's players on his way to an 8–4 win. Game two, played the next day before a slightly diminished crowd of 3,000, went to Lamar's charges 3–1. So excited were many in the stands that several hundred left their seats in order to watch the game from the field. A passed ball and two errors by the Philly crew made the difference.[14] The third and final game, to be played the next day, September 3, would decide what the *Philadelphia Inquirer* christened "the colored baseball championship of the world."

The game was a typical thriller. Five thousand spectators filled the grandstand and bleachers. Others spilled onto the field behind police-held ropes along the sidelines. Tempers ran hot. The Cubans' catcher, Clarence Williams, a native of Harrisburg, Pennsylvania, who had jumped from the

Philadelphia Giants to the Cuban X-Giants two years previously, twice objected to an umpire's call. Both times the catcher threatened to "clean up the umpires (these games had two) and the remainder of the field." Police restored order each time, "to," according to the *Inquirer*, "the great disappointment of the crowd which appeared willing to have the game turned into a free-for-all fight." Even with the two outbursts, the game took only one hour and 50 minutes. Foster's two-hitter won the contest, 4–2.[15] Hill had an uncharacteristic showing, failing to get a single hit.[16] No more was heard of Schlichter's being afraid.

After winning the 1904 championship, a number of Schlichter's Giants, including Hill, again returned to Palm Beach in January 1905. Records could be found for only four games of which the Poinciana nine, to the pre-game accompaniment of a brass band of talented waiters, won three behind Foster's pitching.[17]

1905

Back in Philadelphia for the 1905 season the Schlichter's Giants played spectacular baseball. They beat at least seven White minor league teams. Among them were games against the Newark International League Team managed by Ed Barrow, who subsequently served as secretary and Board member for the New York Yankees for 25 years. The Giants compiled a reputed .848 winning percentage.[18] Hill led the team in hitting, amassing a reported 198 hits including 37 doubles, 11 triples, and 10 round-trippers. Ten dingers may not sound like a lot to twenty-first-century fans, but Hill's output was only two behind that of the year's major league's leader, Harry Davis of the Philadelphia Athletics, who belted a grand total of 12. No player, Black or White, hit more than 14 in one season until Babe Ruth connected for 29 in 1919. Hill was credited with pilfering 30 bases.[19]

The team again won the 1905 championship by beating the Brooklyn Royal Giants in three straight playoff games. Hill got three hits in Game 1 to lead Philadelphia to a 2–0 win. Foster won the second game, a squeaker, 7–6. Pitcher Danny McClellan made it three in a row, thanks in large part to Hill's four hits and Foster's two. Rube played right field that day.[20]

Cuba Beckons

Following the 1905 championship game a combined team of Cuban X and Philadelphia Giants, including Foster and Hill, descended on Cuba for ten exhibition games during the American Series. The American Series,

The 1905 Philadelphia Giants. Standing (L to R): Grant Johnson, Rube Foster, Emmett Bowman, Walter Schlichter, Sol White, Pete Booker, Charlie Grant Seated (L to R): Danny McClellan, Pete Hill, Tom Washington, Harry "Mike" Moore, Bill Monroe (courtesy of Gary Ashwill).

usually starting after the World Series and ending before the late January start of the Cuban season, began in 1879. The extra games often meant the difference between a financially successful season and a loss for the Cuban teams. The first American Series featured a roster of White Americans in "All Americans" uniforms, including third baseman John McGraw.

Games between Cuban teams had flourished since 1878. The professional teams played largely in Havana. The rest of the island supported all manner of teams. Billy Evans, an American League umpire, writing articles for *The New York Times* in addition to calling balls and strikes in Cuba, noted, "On every corner lot in Havana and on every vacant plot of land in the suburbs a ball game is always in progress."[21]

The 1905 combo team, going by the Cuban X- team name posted a 6–4 record. The wins and two of the losses came against amateur teams. An all-star squad of Cuban players easily beat their visitors in the series last two games: 7–0 and 4–1. A bright spot for the Americans was Hill's .351 average at the plate.

American players liked Cuba. The tropical weather was a welcome reprieve from the winter weather in the States. They played only two to three games a week, leaving ample time for sightseeing, casinos, and some tasty Cuban delicacies. Some players brought their wives. The extra money was also appreciated.

Cuban Pride

Cuban players and fans had another take on the games. After the end of the Spanish-American War in 1898, Cuban players and citizens took a special interest in games against Americans.[22] By 1902 many Cubans felt under the thumb of the United States, even though the U.S. Army and Navy had driven the hated Spaniards from the island as a result of the 1898 four-month war. The Platt Amendment, introduced to the U.S. Congress by Senator Orville Platt (R–CT) and passed in 1901, put conditions on Cuba's new-found "independence." The amendment allowed the American military to intervene in Cuban affairs at any time to "preserve Cuban independence." Under the amendment Cuba could transfer land only to the United States, had only limited authority to negotiate treaties, and transferred the rights to a naval base, now Guantanamo Bay, to America. To put an end to the U.S. occupation and attain the status of a Republic, Cuba's leaders reluctantly incorporated the amendment into its new constitution in 1901. The U.S. withdrew its troops in 1902.[23]

They would, however, return when threats to America's national interests were perceived. Between 1906 and 1922 the U.S. military intervened on three occasions; in 1906–09 to put down an armed rebellion, again in May of 1912 to suppress another armed rebellion by Afro-Cubans that threatened American property, and from 1917 to 1922 after a disputed presidential election sparked another armed uprising.[24]

The U.S. occupations fueled the pride Cubans felt each time one of their teams beat an American team, White or Black. Baseball historian Peter Bjarkman noted, "The soaring of such triumphs over the occupiers would soon become the highlight of many a Cuban baseball season." Bjarkman added that the occupations "set the stage for Cubans to look to baseball as a level playing field to test themselves against the colonial power of the much-admired if also much-resented neighboring United States."[25]

All conditions of the Platt Amendment save for the rights to Guantanamo Bay, were withdrawn in 1934.

1906

Before the season got underway, Schlichter sent his team, with Hill, Foster and Johnson on board, against major league competition. They faced the second stringers, referred to by the press as "Yanigans," on Connie Mack's Philadelphia Athletics in Atlantic City, New Jersey, on April 15. The game ended in an inglorious 13–13 tie after 10 innings. Hill, playing left field, tripled and singled off pitcher Bill Bartley.[26] Bartley, a major leaguer but far from a famous one, compiled a 0–1 record in three major league seasons. Neither team felt vindicated.

Failure to overcome Mack's second-stringers didn't deter Hill and his mates from a stellar 1906 campaign. They finished the season with a 108–31–6 record and edged the Cuban X-Giants 3–2 in the championship game of the Independent League before 12,000 fans at Phillies Park. *The Philadelphia Tribune* took credit for the large turnout, pointing to its intensive publicity for the game two weeks before game day. Those who made their way to the Labor Day doubleheader, in which the morning game was the championship game, were treated to a stellar performance by Foster. Twice he struck out a batter with the bases loaded and two outs. At the plate he connected for a double and a single and scored two runs. He and his mates took home the Freihofer Cup, named for league president William F. Freihofer. The league, one of a number of Black circuits with short life spans, disbanded at the end of 1906, its sole year of operation, and consisted of only four teams which played a total of 32 games in 1906.[27]

Schlichter, in a rare show of generosity, was so pleased with the 1906 season that he outfitted his players with new white uniforms with "Worlds Champions" splashed across the front.[28]

Two Notable Losses

One of the Giants' few losses in 1906 came in a game against the Scranton Miners, a White team from Scranton, Pennsylvania. Knowing how infrequently the players from Philly lost a game, Miner's Manager Edward Ashenback, who had described the Giants as "the strongest aggregation of colored players in the world," took particular pleasure in the 15–8 drubbing his men delivered to Foster's nine on April 30. "With Foster away from the rubber" (he played first base that day), the sportswriter for *The Scranton Truth* crowed, "The Giants were the easiest sort of Proposition." Such, however, had not been the case two days earlier when the Giants won 7–3. That game, Ashenback observed, "Was an inglorious occasion for the locals." Hill was the only player on either team to collect a triple in each contest.[29]

Schlichter, confident that the Giants were of major league caliber, issued a best three games out of five challenge to the New York Giants, winner of the 1905 World Series over the Philadelphia Athletics, to determine bragging rights for the world's best team. He received no reply.[30] Connie Mack, however, again agreed to an exhibition game, this one on October 12. The Giants met the A's at Seaboard Park in Chester, Pennsylvania. This time the A's starters provided the opposition. The Giants put up a grand fight but lost the hard-fought game, 5–4. Giants pitcher, Emmett "Scotty" Bowman, renowned for his versatility that enabled him to play every day either as pitcher or infielder, held the major leaguers to a mere three hits, all singles, and contributed a homerun. However, he gave up eight walks, three of which resulted in runs. Eventual Hall of Fame pitcher Eddie Plank held the Giants to five hits and yielded only two passes. Hill got two of the Giants' hits, both singles. Rube Waddell shed his pitcher's glove for an umpires' chest protector and mask for the hour and forty-five-minute affair. It had been a close call for the major leaguers.[31]

Greener Pastures

The Giants' performance against big league opposition enhanced the high esteem in which Sol White held his 1906 roster. "This was a nice little team," he recalled 25 years later. "They could do more little things on a ball field than any team we ever managed. They could bunt nicely, place hit, make home runs and worked the bases to a queen's taste. We certainly liked those boys of 1906."[32]

The "boys" agreed. Foster and others felt entitled to a raise. The players' meager salaries consisted of splitting a hundred dollars for every Sunday game and splitting a lesser amount for weekday games. Schlichter didn't agree to a raise. The team was so good, Schlichter complained, he couldn't book enough games with top teams that would attract enough spectators to substantially increase his revenue. Instead of giving players a raise or finding ways to attract better teams, he chose to cut costs. Players' per diem was now reduced by a dime, to fifteen cents a day to cover two meals. Players had to buy their own uniforms. Payment of salaries was delayed for a full month after the games were played.[33] "In spite of the fact we were the best colored team in baseball," Rube, while enjoying a two-filet-mignon lunch at a Pittsburgh café in 1926, told *Pittsburgh Courier* sportswriter Rollo Wilson, "that's all Schlichter could or would pay us."[34]

"Could" might be the operative word. The Philadelphia Giants, Cuban X-Giants, Cuban Giants of New York, the Cuban Stars of Havana and the Royal Giants of Brooklyn banded together in October of 1906. They met at the Lions' Club at 87 Fleet Street in Brooklyn. There, in an attempt to improve their balance sheets, the owners formed the National Association of Colored Baseball Clubs of the United States and Cuba. The owners elected Schlichter president. All had lost money in 1906. Exorbitant salaries as well keen completion, both of which Schlichter had alluded to, were, they all agreed, the main culprits. Exorbitance may have been in eyes of the beholders. In any case the owners wanted to stop players from jumping from team to team and protect "colored" teams from White independent teams known to schedule a game and then cancel it at the last minute. The league appears to have operated from 1907 through the 1909 season with probably little effect, but its objectives would form the bedrock of Rube Foster's successful efforts in establishing the Negro National League in 1920, which did achieve some permanence.

Foster, believing his salary came nowhere close to exorbitant, envisioned greener diamonds back in Chicago. He convinced six players to bid farewell to Philadelphia and join him on a trip to the Windy City and Leland's Giants for the 1907 season. Accompanying Foster were the husky catcher James Booker; Dangerfield Talbert, whose consistent infield play earned him the nickname of "Old Reliable"; shortstop Nate Harris, known as "the bright star," for his judgment and skills; George Wright, who played an impressive second base; outfielder and power hitter Andrew "Jap" Payne; and slugger Henry "Mike" Moore, who played every position but catcher.[35] Hill would wait a year to join them.

Cuba Once Again and a Wife

Immediately following the 1906 season, a team of players drawn from the Philadelphia Giants, Cuban X-Giants, and the Leland Giants, including Hill but without Foster, again using the Cuban X-Giants name, traveled to the island for the American Series. The Americans easily took the measure of the Habana team, winning all seven games between the two teams but floundered against the Almendares, often Cuba's leading team, losing three of four games.[36]

Once the American Series ended, Rube, accompanied by Hill, "Home Run" Johnson and Bill Monroe, signed on with the Cuban Fé team in Cuba in late January 1907 for 30 games ending on April 4, giving them enough time to make it back to the States for their Opening Days. The Fés team finished in second place behind the Almendares and ahead of the Habana crew. Foster, who signed on for the extended games, pitched 15 complete games, winning 10. Hill, referred to as Preston Hill by the Cuban press, managed a less than magnificent, for him, .264 average at the plate, garnering 24 hits of which, unusually for him, only one, a double, was for extra bases.[37]

By then the 24-year-old Hill was a married man. Little is known about the date and place of his marriage other than it may have taken place before August 1906. A social notice in the *Republican-Northwestern* of

2. On the Way to Chicago

Belvidere, Illinois, reported on August 10, 1906, that Hill's brother-in-law, John Lawson, Jr., had returned from Philadelphia where he had been visiting his sister, "Mrs. Preston Hill of Philadelphia."[38] The possibility that the knot may have been tied a bit later is raised by ship manifests showing him arriving in New York from Havana on November 30, 1906, after leaving Cuba when the American Series concluded, as a single person. Returning to New York from Cuba on April 18, 1907, after his contract with the Fés was over, a ship's manifest shows Hill was accompanied by his wife "Gerty."[39]

The union was his first and her second. A native of Belvidere, Illinois, where her father, John Lawson, had worked as a custodian at the Pearl Street School following his service in the Union army during the Civil War, Gertrude was in her mid-twenties and divorced from a Gordon Diggs. How Pete and Gertrude met is a mystery, but baseball had a prominent place in the Lawson family.[40] John Jr. had a brief tryout with the Leland Giants in 1909. He took the mound for two games with his brother-in-law's team, winning both. Lawson accompanied the Giants on their 1910 tour of the South and, according to his home town newspaper, the *Belvidere Daily Republican*, received an offer from the Philadelphia Giants, by then declining precipitously from its former greatness. Lawson may have received an offer, but there is no evidence he made the team. He pitched several years for local teams, including the Fuqua Giants, the Majestics, and an independent Black team in Rockford Illinois. Gertrude's sister, Lulu, traveled the country with The Tennessee Ten, one of the finest early jazz bands and vaudeville shows. In 1914, the famed jazz singer Florence Mills joined the group as its lead performer.[41]

Gertrude, who had joined Hill as he played for the Fé team, was two months pregnant and expecting their first child in December 1907.[42] While in Cuba she saw her husband's team play well. The Fés, composed of both American and Cuban players, faced the all-Cuban Almendares, who prevailed once again in the close-fought series to win the championship by a single game. Foster, relying on his screwball that darted back and forth, crafted a 10–5 record, but only two Americans, Johnson and Bill Monroe, hit over .300 against Cuban pitching.[43]

By now Cuba was a familiar post-season destination. Many of the same players, including Hill but without "Gertie," returned to Cuba in October 1907 as members of a Philadelphia Giants team, this one made up of all American players, for two sessions, one in October and one in December. The American team went 5–7–1 in October and split 10 games in December. They missed Foster, who begged off these fall festivities. All games were again against the Habana squad and the Almendares. The latter won another Cuban League championship. Hill upped his average to

.343 and led the league in hits and runs scored during the October series, after which he returned home to Philadelphia.[44] Hill, along with Grant Johnson and pitcher Bill Holland, both now with the Brooklyn Royal Giants, who had joined the Giants for the Cuban series, and Dan McClellan, a pitcher and outfielder for the Philadelphia Giants, returned to the States on the S.S. *Havana* on November 5. Gertrude and Pete were expecting their first child in December. Tragically, the four-day-old baby boy, John Hill, died suddenly in a Philadelphia hospital on December 7, 1907, of inanition, lack of nourishment.[45]

3

The Hills Arrive in Chicago

When Hill and Gertrude did get to Chicago in early 1908 they were greeted by a city in the midst of a population explosion fueled by waves of Europeans and Southern Blacks. The city's population quadrupled from 1880 to 1910. The Black population more than doubled, from 14,582 to 30,150, during the years 1900–1910. Black churches increased in number from 12 to 24. Housing and other sectors of the city became increasingly segregated. By 1915 the majority of Blacks lived in enclaves in South Chicago's "Black Belt" where crowded conditions, high rents, and few jobs forced many to turn to gambling and prostitution. Smoldering racial tensions, fueled in part by movies like *The Clansmen*, later retitled *The Birth of a Nation*, which portrayed Blacks as sex-starved imbeciles and the Ku Klux Klan as heroes, became a constant undertone to daily life.[1]

1908

In the midst of increasing population and racial tensions, Rube, now the Leland Giants' manager, got the team off to a fast start in 1908. He wasted little time in installing Hill in centerfield. The Giants' starting lineup now included all seven of the former Philadelphia Giants whom Foster had brought to Chicago.

With the help of Hills' reported sizzling .392 batting average, the Leland Giants handily outplayed the competition, winning the Chicago City League pennant in the process. The league consisted of five White teams and the Giants—a typical example of an integrated league with segregated teams. The White teams were the Gunthers, Logan Squares, Milwaukee White Sox, West Ends, and Anson's Colts. The Colts took their name from owner Cap Anson, a Hall of Fame first baseman for the Chicago White Stockings from 1876 to 1897 and the owner of an abiding dislike of Blacks. He refused in 1887 to play in an exhibition game against the Toledo Blue Stockings because Moses Fleetwood was the team's catcher.[2] In another exhibition game, this one against the Newark Little Giants, he refused to take the field if George Stovey, the team's Black pitcher, started. Stovey didn't start.

References to Blacks in Anson's autobiography, first published in 1900, include "the little darky," "the chocolate covered coon," and "the no-account nigger." A change in Anson's comportment became evident after his retirement and several failed business ventures. Anson found himself playing many games against Rube's Giants and even talking baseball strategy with him on occasion.[3]

The Gunthers, another well-established White team in the league, also took their name from the team's owner, Charles Gunther. A German immigrant in 1842 who had opened a confectionary store shortly after the Civil War, he became wealthy from his store and his later involvement in banking. Gunther built his own park, which hosted many a game against the Leland Giants.[4]

During 1908 the Leland Giants defeated a minor league White team, the Minneapolis Millers, and downed the South Chicagoans, another White team, behind the no-hits, no-runs pitching of their player/manager. Indicative of Hill's importance to the team was a July game against the Cuban Giants in the Leland Giants' home grounds, Auburn Park. He played his usual errorless game and led all batters with four hits; a triple, double, and two singles. With characteristic braggadocio Rube claimed a 108–11 record for the season. Recent research credits the team with a more modest but still not to be sneezed at 64–21 record. Either way, Rube was happy.[5]

On their way to a winning season the players had a brief brush with politics in June of 1908. The Republican National Convention was in town and would nominate William Howard Taft as the Republican Party's presidential standard bearer. William's brother, Charles, took in a game. He rooted for the Leland Giants to beat the Gunthers. They did decisively, 11–4. In return for Charles' support the Giants' players promised to back his brother's presidential run. Their support plus that of millions of others elected Taft to become the nation's 27th president.[6]

Following the successful 1908 campaign Pete, with "Gerty" along, joined the Brooklyn Royal Giants, for whom Grant "Home Run" Johnson played that year, for a return jaunt to Cuba in the fall of 1908. The Royal Giants won seven and lost five. Hill led the way at the plate with a .326 average.[7] Pete and Gertie made it back to Chicago just in time for the start of the 1909 season.

1909

Before the season got underway, the Leland Giants, without Hill, embarked on what would become a post-season staple, barnstorming.

3. The Hills Arrive in Chicago

More games meant more money and they kept the players in shape. On March 16, 1909, the team and several players' wives, boarded their private railroad car, complete with three waiters and two cooks, hooked onto cars of the Illinois Central Railroad, for a month-long journey through Missouri, Iowa, Kansas, Oklahoma, Arkansas, Texas, Louisiana, Tennessee, and Alabama. The sleeper car was both a luxury and a convenience in an era when Jim Crow laws prohibited Blacks from traveling in the same rail car as Whites.

Among other opponents the Leland Giants met on this trip were the Memphis Giants, Birmingham Giants, Fort Worth Giants, the Black Bronchos of San Antonio, Texas, and in New Orleans, the "Creoles." Many Black teams, as was evident on this trip, used the name "Giants" in their team title as a signal that the team was composed of African Americans.[8]

The broadside for a game in Austin, Texas, on April 21, 1909, against the Samuel Huston College (now Huston-Tillotson University), illustrates the special meaning of such games for the local populace. Scheduled on San Jacinto Day, commemorating the last battle of the Texas Revolution giving Texas its independence from Mexico, the placard announced that Foster, the "greatest pitcher in the world," would pitch for the Giants. Hoping to draw spectators from beyond Austin, the game's organizers arranged for railroads to offer half-fare tickets to members of groups larger than 14. The promoters, the notice said, had to put up more than a hundred dollars "to get This Great Team to come to Austin and we trust the lovers of this great American Game will turn out." As was often the case when a largely Black turnout was expected, part of the grandstand, where the price of admission was 50 cents, had been reserved for Whites. The Giants won that game and 14 others without a loss before returning home for Opening Day.[9]

The practice of reserving a portion of seats for Whites attending games featuring Black teams was not uncommon. Three years earlier, in 1906, the *Baltimore Sun's* notice of a game to be played by the Cuban X-Giants and the Havana Giants in Baltimore's Oriole Park included the statement that "a portion of the grandstand will be reserved exclusively for white persons who wish to see the game."[10]

Back in Cuba

Hill, as noted above, again opted for Cuba over barnstorming with the Giants in 1909. Along with John Henry "Pop" Lloyd, then with the Philadelphia Giants, and Grant "Home Run" Johnson with the Brooklyn

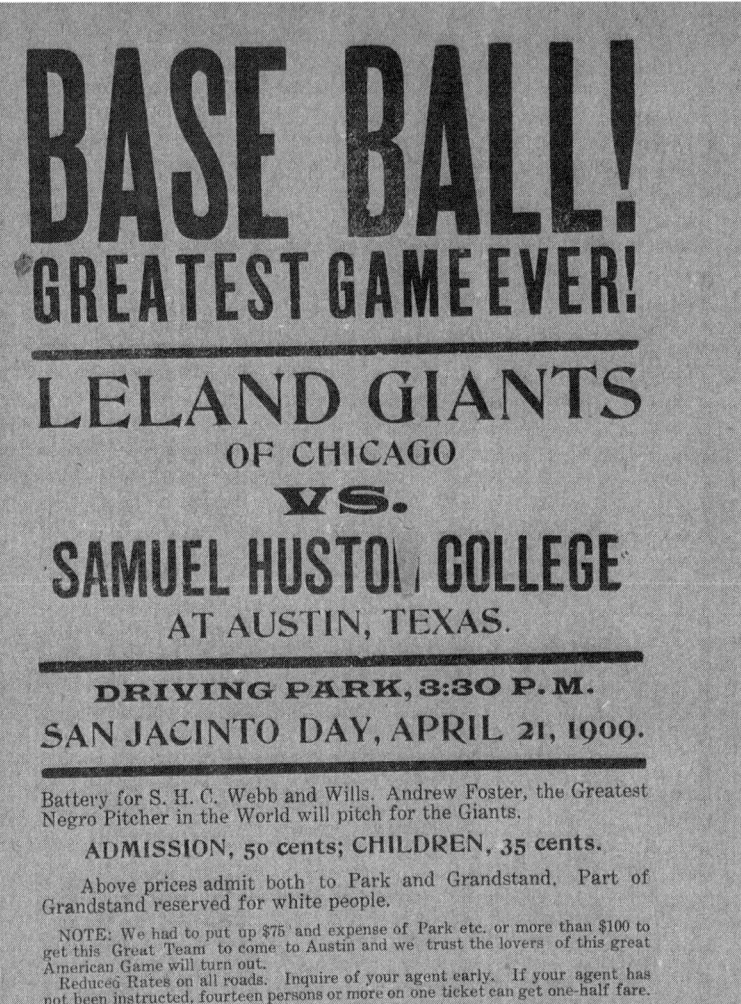

Broadside announcing the 1909 barnstorming game between the Leland Giants and the Sam Huston College nine. Note the reference to a seating section for Whites (courtesy of Heritage Auctions, HA.com).

Royal Giants, Hill joined the Habana team for 43 games between December and April. He would have played close to the same number of games had he gone barnstorming, but he didn't have to travel from town to town in Cuba. All games were played in Havana. Habana took the pennant in the four-team league, nudging the Almendares out by a single game. Hill managed a .246 average on 35 hits, which included a double, three triples, and two homers. He led the league in runs scored with 36.

Hill Shines at Home Also

During the 1909 regular season, the Leland Giants played both an independent schedule on weekdays against a variety of teams and again participated in the Chicago City League on weekends. Hill's contribution to the team was never more apparent than in two early July games. A reporter for the *Chicago Daily Tribune* glowingly wrote that "the stock centerfielder of the Giants, put on a dazzling performance," in a July 5 game against the Gunthers. In six trips to the plate the centerfielder connected for as many hits; a double and five singles. He took a triple away from the Gunther's first baseman, Harry White, with "a magnificent one-handed catch."[11] In another July outing, during the deciding game in a five-game series against the Cuban Stars, Hill again led the way at the plate with a triple and three singles, accounting for most of the Giants' seven runs in its 7–4 win.[12]

He could, on rare occasions, be less than dazzling. In a performance a month later against the Anson Colts, Hill was "drawn in" to play second base. In the fifth inning an error and a failure to complete a double play by the usually sure-handed outfielder led to five runs for the Colts. In spite of Hill's miscues, the Giants eked out a 6–5 win, sparing Hill the goat's mantle. On another occasion when Hill was tapped for a non-outfield position, he performed as expected. He threw four no-hit innings against the Cuban Stars during a July game. Hill finished the season by smashing the ball for a reported .354 average to lead Foster's team to a 31–9 record in the City League to again claim that pennant. The team's record in independent play that year reportedly stood at 54–18–1. Foster, again throwing modesty to the winds, called his team "The Greatest Colored Team in the World." The absence of an organized Black league, however, left the door open for similar self-acclaim by other teams. Three Black teams, the Kansas City Giants, St. Paul Gophers, and Birmingham Giants, each announced themselves to be the best team in the West.[13]

A Class Act

Regardless of the competing claims, the 1909 Leland Giants' roster laid the foundation for a team that would dominate Black baseball for the next decade. Players would come and go as Rube continually attracted top talent to his Giants. Foster was a dominating force on the mound and had surrounded himself with pitchers Walter Ball, Pat Dougherty, and "Big" Bill Gatewood. Standing six feet tall and tipping the Toledos at 195 pounds, the right-hander Gatewood intimidated batters with a nasty spitball and a rocket thrown at those willing to crowd the plate. Bill also employed the spitball. He started 25 games for Leland in 1909, losing only one and winning the rest. Dougherty, for whom 1909 was his rookie season, proved his mettle in the championship series against the St. Paul Gophers. With Foster sidelined by injuries, Dougherty stepped in to win two games. Unfortunately, the Gophers, in the pre-eminent achievement of their short, four-year existence, won the other three to claim "the championship."

In addition to Hill, Leland had a stellar group of position players, notably right fielder Andrew "Jap" Payne. Payne's many talents proved invaluable. Lloyd, in 1953, named Payne as the right field on his all-star team. Infielder Dangerfield Talbert, and, for a short time, John Henry "Pop" Lloyd at shortstop also starred. Lloyd possessed in abundance all the skills a baseball player needed. Baseball historian James A. Riley considered Lloyd to be the greatest Black player in the first two decades of the twentieth century. Babe Ruth cited the shortstop as the greatest baseball player of all time. Lloyd was a consistent hitter, an excellent fielder with a strong arm and a knack for stealing bases. Another major contributor was third baseman Dangerfield Talbert, credited with a .309 average in 1909. Talbert spent almost his entire career playing for teams owned by Leland. With this cast it's easy to see why Foster made the claim he did.[14]

Major League Competition

At season's end Rube, ever looking for games with major league teams, challenged the neighboring National League Chicago Cubs to meet his Leland Giants in a three-game series in October of 1909. Featuring the legendary double-play combination of Tinkers, Evers, and Chance, the Cubs had won the National League pennant in 1907 and 1908 and finished second in 1909. Two prominent Cubs did not play against the Leland Giants. Chance was out with an injury and served as manager. Evers had gone home to Troy, Illinois, to be with his wife and new baby boy. Foster beefed up the Giants with first baseman Bobby Marshall, from the St. Paul Gophers. The Leland Giants went down to a respectable defeat, 4–2, in game one played on October 8, 1909. Marshall's two errors didn't help.

Rube's players also lost the second game, played four days later, but under protest. With the pride of Calvert, Texas, on the mound, only three months after breaking his leg on a slide into third base on July 12, the

Giants had built a seemingly comfortable 5–2 lead going into the ninth inning of game two. The Cubs promptly tied the game, scoring three runs and had a man on third. Realizing that the injury and subsequent layoff were taking their toll, Rube took himself out of the game. Moving, in the words of one reporter "about as fast as a hippopotamus on skis," he walked to the Giant's dugout, ball in glove, to ask Pat Dougherty to relieve him. Thinking Rube was stalling, both umpires joined the discussion as did several players. Cubs' right fielder Frank Schulte looked on from third. Realizing no one had called time, Schulte streaked for home with the winning run. The Giants protested but to no avail.[15] A day later, the Leland Giants, with Dougherty replacing Foster on the hill, lost the best-played game of the three to future Hall of Famer Mordecai "Three Finger" Brown, 1–0. Brown had finished the 1909 season with a league leading 27 wins against 9 losses and a stingy earned run average of 1.31.[16]

An umpire's miscue may have cost the Giants a win in game three. In the bottom of the first inning, Hill, whom Rube always called a "money hitter," and "a pitcher's worst nightmare," approached the plate with two out and two on base. A single would bring in both runners. Hill fouled off the first, swung and missed on the second, and took the third pitch for a called strike three. The ball, a reporter said, "would have cut off his toes had he not hopped out of the way."[17]

Foster's Leland Giants, even though they lost all three games, showed they could play with the best of major leaguers. Cubs manager Frank Chance said afterwards Foster "was the most finished product I've ever seen in the pitcher's box."[18] Foster, of course, agreed. The following year Rube let it be known he had $5,000 that said his Giants "could beat any baseball team in the world, white or black."[19] No record of any team taking up his challenge could be found.

Leland Branches Out

With Foster taking over Leland's managerial duties, Leland was able to give full rein to his managerial talents beyond baseball. In 1907 he formed a business consortium, the Leland Giants Baseball and Amusement Association, with attorneys Beauregard F. Moseley and Major Robert R. Jackson. Moseley, a prominent Chicago attorney with an interest in baseball, would replace Leland as president of the Leland Giants in 1909 as Leland's health began to fail. Moseley developed a close relationship with Foster when Rube and Leland parted ways in 1910.

Moseley's endorsement was sought by White entrepreneurs as well as Blacks. An example of the former, two White developers of a resort community for Blacks, Idlewild, in central Michigan, included testimonials from Moseley in their sales literature. Jackson attained the rank of major in the U.S. army during the Spanish-American War, rose from humble origins to positions of leadership in Chicago's Black community including managing the Chicago Unions baseball team in 1889, won election to the Illinois General Assembly as an advocate for equal rights, and would serve as president of the Negro American League from 1937 to 1939.[20] Together the threesome financed and built a restaurant, resort, skating rink, bowling alley, opera house and movie theater in addition to owning the Leland Giants.

All enterprises were a response to the blanket discrimination that barred Blacks from similar White establishments. Leland used segregation as a selling point in his solicitations for start-up capital. In a March 1908 notice in Black newspapers offering shares of stock to the public at ten dollars per share, he wrote, "**You Squander More** than this amount **Any Holiday** around Amusement Parks and Public Places where you are not wanted and never welcome." As a further inducement to potential subscribers Leland pointed out "The Public is Base-Ball mad and amusement Crazy.... **Millions** can be made by those **Who Take Stock in This New Enterprise**." The three men sponsored a contest to pick a name for their amusement creation. "Chateau de la Plaisance" (House of Pleasure) won.[21] Their fundraising success led to, in addition to the amusement facilities, a new baseball park, Leland Giants Park, ready on Opening Day in May of 1910.[22]

Just two days after Opening Day, Leland held a reception for his Giants at his newly opened Chateau De La Plaisance at 5324 State Street. Featured speakers were B.F. Moseley, the team's secretary and treasurer, and of course Rube Foster, identified in *The Defender* as both manager and team captain. On the podium with the speakers were 13 players; infielders James Booker, Grant (Home Run) Johnson, "Pop" Lloyd, Wes Pryor and Fred Hutchinson; "outer gardners," as outfielders were called, Hill, Payne, and Frank Duncan; catchers Bruce Petway and Tim Strothers; and Rube's compatriots on the mound, Pat Dougherty and Frank Wickware. The event had three purposes. To show off Leland's new facility, introduce the team to attendees, and sign up those interested in becoming members of the Leland Giants Rooters Club.[23]

Florida Calls Again

While the new stadium was going up Rube had his Giants back in Palm Beach as an entire team wearing the colors of the Royal Poinciana Hotel. The Brooklyn Royal Giants, in the Breakers' uniforms, provided the competition. Foster won the season opener 4–1, played on a Wednesday, January 26, supported by a stunning one-handed catch by Hill on a dead run in right field in the ninth inning that brought the crowd to its feet and assured the victory. *The Palm Beach Daily News* accorded Foster the distinction of being "the colored champion ball pitcher of the world, who added grace and dignity to his title." He allowed only three hits while striking out four. Both teams' first baseman, Al Robinson for the Breakers, and George (Chappie) Johnson, who would connect with Hill in later years, for the Poincianas, were credited with crowd-pleasing "humorous catches." The Poinciana's winning ways continued as they claimed the "championship" of the Coconut League.[24]

Friction between Foster and Leland

As the 1910 season started in Leland's new ballpark, the partnership between Rube and Leland disintegrated. Foster had taken exception to Leland, now facing financial difficulties, not fully sharing all gate receipts from the 1909 season with his players. At the same time, Beauregard Moseley claimed that the team owed him $10,000 for shares of stock he had sold. In the face of pressure from Foster and Moseley, Leland sold his team to Moseley, who re-appointed Foster as team captain and manager of the Leland Giants. Leland formed another team. He recruited eight players from the 1909 Leland Giants, three from the St. Paul Gophers including pitcher "Steel Arm" Johnny Taylor, one of the four Taylor brothers who starred in Black baseball, and catcher Bill Pettus from the Kansas City (Kansas) Giants for his new aggregation which he named Leland's Chicago Giants. A court battle over naming rights ensued as Foster kept the name Leland Giants for his roster. In addition, Foster claimed ownership of the 1909 City League flag won by the team then known as the Leland Giants of which Foster had been manager and Leland the owner. Leland took Foster to court. Because Leland's now Chicago Giants had a majority of players from the 1909 Leland Giants, Cook County Judge Jesse Baldwin gave Leland the right to fly the pennant flag. Baldwin granted Foster the right to continue to use the Leland Giant team name, which he did for the 1910 season.[25] He renamed the team American Giants in 1911.

The court episode prompted David Wyatt, a former teammate of Foster, to opine in *The Freeman*, a Black weekly serving Indianapolis, that Chicago's White baseball establishment thought there was "a war in Negro baseball." Wyatt's editorial drew a sharp rebuke from Major R.R. Jackson, now Leland's club secretary. Seeking to downplay the rift between Leland and Foster, Jackson dismissed Wyatt as a "has been" and "attempting to discuss a situation that he does not know the inside facts of." Jackson adamantly denied any perception of a war on the part of "the oldest and most influential baseball men in the White association." To the contrary, Jackson said the White Park Owners Association and the Inter-City Association members recognized the Chicago Giants as a legitimate and viable enterprise. Both teams, Jackson pointed out, will pursue their own schedules so, he asked, "Where is the war?"[26]

Wyatt's comments may have caused Foster's—up to this point pro-forma—application for membership in the City League to be denied, even though Foster's team would play games against City League teams throughout 1910.

Leland retained use of Auburn Park, forcing Foster to use another venue, Normal Park, at 69th and Halsted streets, which had been refurbished. The *Chicago Defender* described it as, "One of the swellest and best-equipped ballparks in the city. It is clean and accessible to the street car lines and a credit to the race." Box seats at Normal went for fifty cents.[27]

With a new park came a new roster. In addition to keeping the star players from the 1909 Leland Giants, Foster "recruited" three players from the Philadelphia Giants; catcher Bruce Petway, a light hitter but the owner of an arm that kept runners hugging their bases; shortstop John Henry "Pop" Lloyd, whom historian Riley called the greatest Black baseball player between 1900 and 1920; and outfielder Frank Duncan, a consistent hitter with skills just a notch below Hill's. Duncan and Petway stayed with Foster for the 1910–1919 seasons. Lloyd wore the Giants' uniform for five of those seasons, making intermittent stops with other teams.[28]

An Auspicious Debut

With the legal entanglements sorted out, Foster's 1910 Leland Giants, featuring not only Hill but also the three "recruits," put together a season never equaled before or since. They began with 35 wins in a row. Not until early June did they lose a game, to the Gunthers. It was another month before they lost again, this time to the Stars of Cuba 15-7 at Normal Park. Hill reportedly led all Giants hitters that year with a hard-to-believe .511 average. Known for his prodigious output of singles and doubles, he could also hit the long ball. In an August Sunday afternoon against the Gunthers, "Hill," a writer for the *Englewood Economist* wrote, "bobbed up with his familiar home run." To be known as a producer of "familiar home runs" was high praise in an era where few players, White or Black, hit as many as ten in a season.

Rube's charges were credited with a 128–6 record by one account, 123–6 by another. They were depicted in the local media as the Colored Champions of the West and the Colored World's Champions.[29] Hill's performance earned him the accolade of being "the best field captain that covers the Normal Park field." "Quiet, gentlemanly, and a hustler. Everybody likes him," wrote one sportswriter.[30]

A Game for Charity

The Giants interrupted their juggernaut 1910 season with a game against the Gunthers on August 18, all proceeds going to the city's Provident Hospital, an integrated facility organized in the 1890s after Emman Reynolds, a Black woman, was denied admission to the city's all-White nursing schools. Provident's founding and continued existence relied on donations from wealthy citizens, both White and Black, and work performed by citizen volunteers.[31]

Efforts to attract a large crowd included White Sox owner Charles Comiskey donating his White Sox Park for the day, Mayor Fred A. Busse donating the balls for the game, a band "to keep things lively," and an invitation to Heavyweight Boxing Champion Jack Johnson to umpire. Johnson attended but did not umpire. The Giants bested the Gunthers 9–4 before "a large crowd."[32]

In addition to Johnson, another notable attraction at the Provident Hospital game was six-term Republican Congressman William Lorimer, known as Chicago's "Blond Boss." He supplied the bats. He had challenged incumbent U.S. Senator Albert J. Hopkins, whose term had expired, at the May 1909 joint assembly of the Illinois legislature in Springfield. At the time, state legislatures elected a state's two U.S. Senators. The session quickly deadlocked. Neither man could attract the 102 votes required by the state's constitution. It took 95 ballots before Lorimer was elected with 108 votes by a coalition of Democrats and Republicans. Hopkins delivered a gracious concession speech. Lorimer took his seat in Washington, D.C.

Soon after the vote, reports of bribes, some as much as $1,000 (about $30,000 in 2021), surfaced. Charges, counter charges, and denials, many by Lorimer himself, were detailed in the pages of the nation's newspapers in Chicago, New York, Baltimore, the nation's capital, and elsewhere. Lorimer's case was a national cause célèbre for three years until July 13, 1912, when the U.S. Senate, by a vote of 55–28, after listening to Lorimer's three-day speech claiming his innocence, for the first time in its history expelled a member. Other senators facing sure expulsion had resigned before a vote was taken. South Carolina Senator Benjamin Tillman, once censured for fisticuffs on the Senate floor and one of only three senators swayed by Lorimer's three-day exposition, wept as did many in the gallery. Lorimer's case helped obtain ratification of the 17th Amendment to the U.S. Constitution on April 8, 1913. The amendment replaced the election of U.S. Senators by their state legislatures with election by registered voters.[33]

Johnson and Baseball

The heavyweight champ, as we have seen, had an interest in baseball. Johnson, with his Black significant other at the time, Clara Kerr, a Black prostitute, had spent the summer of 1904 in Philadelphia. There he played an occasional game at first base for the Philadelphia Giants to—as his biographer, Geoffrey C. Ward put it—"back his friend and fellow Texan, the pitcher Andrew 'Rube' Foster."[34] The extent of Johnson's involvement with the Giants at that time is uncertain. Foster, in a 1926 interview with W. Rollo Wilson of the *Pittsburgh Courier,* said, "Jack Johnson, yes THE Johnson played first base for the Phillies for two years after he came out of Texas in 1903–04."[35] While it's quite likely Johnson played a few games with Rube in 1904, a busy travel schedule in constant search of bouts would have made it impossible for him to have put in two full seasons. In addition, Ward did not document his assertion, making the picture even blurrier.

Three years later, on August 24, 1907, he umpired an exhibition game between the Philadelphia and Cuban Giants in Philadelphia's Athletic Park. Johnson's presence was of more interest to fans than the game. As players left the field after the game, won by the Cubans 7–4, Johnson remained at home plate awaiting the adulation he expected. Fans, Black and White, didn't disappoint him. They rushed him, grabbed his clothes and hands, told him he was the Black race's greatest representative, and vied with each other to praise him. Several players had questioned some of his calls during the game. They were silenced "by either a deprecatory wave of the hand or a significant look," as the *New York Times* reported. Things went no further. The players knew better than to put up any physical shows of displeasure with this umpire.[36]

He had at least one other encounter with Rube and the American Giants. For reasons that are unclear, Johnson refused a reporter for the Hearst papers permission to enter his training camp where he was preparing for "the fight of the century"; a fight against Jim Jeffries scheduled for July 4, 1910, in Reno, Nevada. Jeffries, White and a former heavyweight world champion, had been called out of a six-year retirement in hopes of returning the title to a White boxer. Johnson won the bout. The rebuffed reporter discovered Johnson had sent a $200 money order to a White woman, Belle Schrieber, after she had called Johnson in San Francisco from Pittsburgh asking for money. It was well known that the two had been engaged in a romantic relationship. Johnson was brought to trial in Chicago in 1912 on charges of violating the Mann Act, which prohibited bringing a woman across a state line "for immoral purposes." Schrieber testified against him. Johnson denied the charge. He was, nevertheless, convicted by an all-White jury, sentenced to a year and one day in prison, and temporarily freed on a $15,000 bond (about $420,000 in 2022 dollars), after assuring the judge he had no intention of going anywhere. After thinking it over and being urged by his mother to depart, Johnson left

Jack Johnson circa 1900 (Library of Congress).

town even knowing he would forfeit his bond. He slipped out of Chicago with Rube's help.[37]

Details about how he did it differed. As Johnson told it in 1920, he claimed to be headed to New York and offered his private rail car to Rube gratis for the team's scheduled trip to Gotham if Rube's car would travel through Toronto, Canada. Rube, ever the savvy businessman, accepted. Carrying a bat case, Johnson boarded the train one stop after the team had and avoided being recognized by any of the porters. While the drawing room in the car had been reserved for him, he gave his ring and the drawing room to a player who looked like him. If stopped by the police, he hoped they would mistake the player for him. Johnson got off the train in Toronto.

His biographer, Geoffrey Ward, gives a slightly different account. Ward cites an interview with a British reporter in 1919 in which Johnson said he and his nephew, dressed as if they were going fishing, boarded a train along with the Giants while carrying bats and gloves. The White policemen patrolling the station were unable to tell one tall Black athlete from another and failed to recognize one of the best-known faces in America. Johnson and nephew departed the train in Hamilton, Ontario, 43 miles south of Toronto. In this telling Johnson occupied the drawing room and locked the door. "I am not a coward gentlemen, but I can assure you I trembled every time the train stopped," he told his British audience.

Whatever the details of the trip, Johnson did make it to Canada. He and his second of three White wives, Lucille Cameron, who had reached Canada on a separate train, went on to Montreal and from there to Paris. Johnson spent eight years in Europe before returning to Chicago and serving his sentence.[38]

4

The Rambling Giants

Back to Florida and Cuba

Immediately after the 1910 season ended, the Leland Giants traveled to Florida for several non–Coconut League exhibition games before heading to Cuba as an intact team for the American Series. There they beat the Habana team five straight, then fell to the Almendares Blues 0–4–1.[1]

Following these games, most of the Leland Giants returned home, making it back to Chicago in time for a gala tribute to the team hailed by the *Defender* "as the greatest ball team on earth." Formally known as *The Reception Ball and Banquet to Rube Foster and the Leland Giants*, the late–November event finally broke up at 1:00 a.m. after sumptuous dinners had been enjoyed and twelve speakers had lauded Foster, who spoke last. He ended the evening with promises of more great baseball to come.[2] The stars of the team, Lloyd, Hill, Petway, and Johnson, missed the festivities. They remained in Havana as members of the Habana club.

Ty Cobb Takes a Licking

Of particular interest to Cubans this year were the upcoming games against the barnstorming major league Detroit Tigers and Philadelphia Athletics. The latter were fresh off winning the World Series from the Cubs. Detroit had finished in third place after winning the American League pennant from 1907 through 1909 but falling short in each World Series.

Toward the end of the American Series, the Tigers played six games against both the Almendares and the Habana squads. Ty Cobb was the Tigers' mainstay. The "Georgia Peach" had taken the American League titles in batting, runs batted in, homers, and stolen bases in 1909. In 1910 he again led the league in hitting but had slipped to second place in homers, RBIs and stolen bases. To the disappointment of many Cubans, Cobb appeared in only five of the games. The Motor City team won four of those five games, but three of the Giants' players on the Habana roster out-played Cobb. Petway, Johnson, and Lloyd outhit him. Petway nailed him twice attempting to steal second. Cobb stuck out his last time at bat, causing the fans to gloat after the game, "Did you see Ty Cobb punch out?" So embarrassed was Cobb that he refused to ever again play against Blacks.[3]

The foursome extended their stay in Cuba by continuing with the Habana team for the Cuban American Series 27-game season, Christmas Day 1910 to April 2, 1911. The Almendares continued their championship ways, finishing in first place ahead of the Habanas by three games and the Fés by a resounding 19½ games. Hill, now referred to as Preston Hill by the Cuban press, had a standout season. He led all players on the three teams in triples with 5, hits with 35, and batting with a .365 average.[4]

To California

A week before the banquet, Leland took his newly formed team, now known as the Chicago Giants, to San Diego, California, for a precedent-setting series of games in the California Winter League (CWL). By the end of the nineteenth century, baseball was flourishing up and down the state with a multitude of teams and leagues. Reflecting the social conditions of the day, most leagues were integrated—containing both Black and White teams—but teams remained segregated. The CWL, previously known as the Southern California Winter League, based in San Diego and one of the few all-White leagues, eventually emerged as the most prominent of the leagues. San Diego's warm climate and the league's ability to entice many major leaguers, most notably Walter Johnson for several seasons, and Black stars like Rube Foster, Pete Hill, Bruce Petway, "Cyclone" Joe Williams, "Bullet Joe" Rogan and later "Satchel" Paige, "Turkey" Stearns, Willie Wells, and "Mule" Suttles, gave the CWL a skill level well above that of any other league in the state.[5]

The Giants' arrival marked the integration of the CWL, which that year consisted of the Giants and three White teams—the Doyles, San Diego Bears, and the McCormicks. The Giants, whom the CWL magnates referred to "as the crack colored team of Chicago," won out over a local team, "the Occidental colored club," for the right to integrate the league.[6]

The season consisted of three games a week for about twenty games between late November and mid–January. Before the Giants' arrival, the CWL was a mediocre roster of little interest beyond San Diego. That changed in a hurry when the men from Chicago took the field. The novelty of highly skilled Black players did not go unnoticed. "Leave it to those [Chicago] Giants to bring some uphill ball players," opened the *Los*

4. The Rambling Giants

Angeles Herald's coverage of the inaugural doubleheader between the Giants and the Doyles. Attendance at the game was so much better than anticipated that a newly built grandstand couldn't accommodate everyone. Fans, half-a-dozen deep, lined the outfield. According to the *Herald*, "All the money in Darktown was staked on them [the Giants]." Each team won one game, and in the process the Giants proved their worth to the CWL.[7]

A month into the season, the *Los Angeles Herald* reported that the "Winter league has met with unusual success," due in large part to the "Giants throwing in a dash of color that helps a lot at the gate." "So satisfied were the league magnates that they extended play from three games a week to four."[8]

The Giants finished in second place, just a hair behind San Diego. Two games were particularly notable. The first, in early December, resulted in a Giants loss to San Diego. The teams were tied, 1–1, in the bottom of the ninth inning. San Diego's leadoff batter had reached first. The next batter worked the count to three balls. After the next pitch, Giants' pitcher Bill Gatewood stormed off the mound insisting that his pitch was a strike and not ball four as called by umpire Longnacker. Longnacker held firm and called San Diego's next batter to the plate. Gatewood refused to pitch, even over the entreaties of his teammates. Longnacker called four balls and the batter took first base. The scenario was repeated twice more, forcing in a run to give San Diego a 2–1 win.[9]

The second game of note, played a month later, featured "Cyclone" Joe Williams of the Giants fanning 19 Doyles "with a blazing fastball and an effective 'floater.'"[10]

Williams had come to Leland's attention during a barnstorming game in San Antonio on the Giants' way west. Not only did these games contribute to the team's and players' coffers, but they were also, in the absence of Negro minor leagues and professional scouts, a primary source of new talent. An unheralded player who caught Leland's eye often ended up on the Giants.

Williams, Leland's biggest find, was discovered in a game against the San Antonio Black Broncos. The tall fellow mowed down the Giants one after the other on his way to shutting them out, 3–0. "What's your name?" Leland asked him after the game. "Just call me Cyclone," the 25-year-old hurler answered.

Before the 1911 season got underway, Leland introduced his new player to Chicago fans by telling a reporter, "If you have ever witnessed the speed of a pebble in a storm you have not even seen the equal of the speed by this wonderful Texas Giant."[11]

"Cyclone" came to be better known as "Smokey" Joe Williams. He left the Giants before the 1911 season started for the New York Lincoln Giants and a variety of other teams, including the 1914 American Giants, before retiring in 1932. The Hall of Fame belatedly inducted him in 1999.[12]

Rube scheduled a five-game series against the McCormicks after the CWL season ended. The Giants won the first contest, but lost the following four. The die, nevertheless, had been cast. The Giants proved that a powerhouse Black team from the Midwest could compete in the otherwise White CWL and attract many spectators. Many other Black teams would winter in San Diego in the years to come.

Then it was back on the Pullman car for games against amateur and semi-pro teams in Northern California, Washington, Oregon, and Canada before heading back to Chicago.[13]

A Major League–Styled Park

As the Giants' 1911 season got under way, Foster had a new ball park. Due to a rent increase in 1910 at South Side Park where the White Sox played, owner Charles Comiskey built a new stadium for the Sox. He ordered his old stadium at 39th and Wentworth, torn down to prevent competition for spectators and their dollars. John M. Schorling, a White, wealthy tavern owner with a palatial mansion in Detroit, obtained the lease for Comiskey's abandoned site in January 1910.

Schorling is often inaccurately referred to as Comiskey's son-in-law. The two men undoubtedly knew each other, but Comiskey had only one child, a son named John Louis Comiskey.

Schorling had been associated with semi-pro teams in the city for 20 years. He developed his love for the game as a child, when he told those gathered for tribute to Rube and the Giants at Chicago's Odd Fellows Hall, "I was very sick, and I discovered that by playing base ball I had found a sure cure for consumption and the thing was so inevitable to me in developing my physique that I was convinced it would save the day for other boys and girls."[14]

Schorling owned Auburn Park where the Leland Giants had played. He had once again leased the park to Leland for his 1910 Chicago Giants games. Foster's Leland Giants, as we have seen, had moved its operations to Normal Park for the 1910 season. Schorling was initially undecided about what team he would contract with to play in his new park. The *Suburban Economist* predicted "it would be a colored team, as it is within easy walking distance of the 'Black belt.'" He was not undecided about what the new park would look like. "It would," he promised, "be the finest semi-pro plant in the country, the parlor home of baseball." He kept his promise.[15]

4. The Rambling Giants

At the cost of $15,000 (about $470,000 in 2021 dollars), a new grandstand and set of bleachers, both made of wood, appeared, adding 4,000 seats for a total capacity of 18,000 seats. Each seat offered its occupant an unobstructed view of the field, a noticeable improvement over the seating in most ball parks of the day. Sixty-two boxes comfortably accommodated eight persons in seats placed so high that ladies didn't have to remove their hats for the gentlemen behind them to follow the action. The boxes had free ice water for all, lavatories, and two rooms for the players, each with showers and hot and cold running water. Ushers were instructed to find seats for ladies. The refurbished field was of major league dimensions; 450 feet to dead centerfield, and 350 and 360 feet down the lines.[16] "Dusky" Rube, the *St. Louis Times and Star* reported, was assembling a team for the new stadium "that will make last year's Leland Giants look like bush semi pros."[17]

The *Economist*'s prediction proved to be spot on. Schorling invited Foster to call Schorling's Park home for the American Giants. Foster accepted. The two men agreed to split the game revenues 50–50.[18] "You run the team, Rube," the spirits dispenser told him. "I don't want anything to do with it. I have enough worries."[19] That suited Rube just fine.

Back on the Road

While the new stadium was going up, Rube left the confines of Normal Park and again went south for exhibition games which also served as spring training. In Jacksonville, Florida, at the end of March, Rube's Giants faced off against the Brooklyn Royal Giants, one of the most powerful Eastern teams. They had claimed eastern championship titles in 1909 and 1910 and would do so again in 1914 and 1916. Following a successful 1911 series in Palm Beach, the team's "portly" manager, John W. Conner, challenged Rube's roster to three games. Foster eagerly accepted, but the team did less well than expected. The Brooklyn players took two of the three games, including a 3–0 shutout in game three.[20] Then it was on to Hot Springs, Arkansas, to face a team of local players of noticeably less talent than the Royal Giants. The locals went down to defeat, 11–1, as the American Giants garnered 22 hits in the process. In another blowout, Hill and the American Giants took the measure of a local team in San Antonio, Texas 12–0, amassing 20 hits. In one of the last games before returning home the Giants squeaked by the Fort Worth (Texas) Giants, an independent team, which provided stiffer opposition but, nevertheless, lost the game 5–3 when Hill and company pushed across two runs in the ninth inning.[21]

1911

By Opening Day 1911 in Schorling's Park the Giants, including Hill, were in fine fettle. During the second game of a July doubleheader against the Chicago Giants, now run by Leland, Hill outdid his consistently stellar glove work with what *Defender* sportswriter J.H. Wright called "one of the most sensational catches seen on a semi-pro diamond." After a long run to deep centerfield, Hill leapt as high as he could against the wall with arm outstretched to snag a ball in his glove's webbing just as it was about to clear the fence for a home run. "Honestly," Wright continued, "if that boy Hill keeps up the rough stuff he will be passing for a Cuban next year and playing on Clark Griffith's Cincinnati Reds."[22]

Rube's players competed in many venues in 1911. On two occasions they were the main attraction at Wisconsin Fairs. Publicity for "Fennimore's Two Big Days," August 3 and 4, featured the American Giants (Champion Colored Team of the World) vs. the Chicago Gunthers (Best Independent Team in U.S.). Other activities included the "World Famous Comedy Colored Ragtime Trio Thomas, McDonald & Thomas," speeches, including one by Wisconsin's governor F.E. McGovern, and music performed by the "Celebrated Lancaster and Boscobel Dutch Band."[23] Two weeks later the Giants and the West Ends headlined the three-day Mineral Point Fair. Horse races, a performance by the Royal Ishakawa troupe from Japan, and a talk by Robert Henry Hendershot, also known as the Drummer Boy of the Rappahannock, recounting his Civil War experiences, completed the program. The Mineral Point Band regaled the crowds with tunes throughout the day.[24]

Some Important Games

A major highlight of the 1911 season was a five-game series with the Cuban Stars. By the end of August the *Standard Union* of Brooklyn announced that the "American Leland Giants [some confusion over the team's name remained] champions of the West will hook up with the champion Cuban Stars" in American League Park at 168th Street and Broadway in New York City to determine "the independent professional championship." Two of the best pitchers in Black baseball at the time, Rube Foster and Jose Méndez, went the distance in Game 1. Méndez won in a 1–0 shutout. Hill was credited with "cutting off many well-meant hits by his sensational running catches." The third game also ended in a 1–0 shutout but with Foster's team the winner. Foster won the game but not as a pitcher. His pinch-hit RBI single with two men on in the 12th inning carried the day, giving the Giants a 2–1 lead in games. The Stars evened the series with a 5–4 win in game four, helped by the Giants' three errors, one, "a costly one" by Hill. The fifth and deciding game, played the next day, September 9, saw the Giants best the Stars 5–2 and take home the championship. A record crowd, estimated at 8,000, saw every game.[25]

In the midst of the series, the Lincoln Giants, founded in New York City in 1911 by White businessman and sports promoter Jess McMahon and featuring such names as John Henry Lloyd, Smokey Joe Williams, Cannonball Dick Redding, Spot Poles, and Louis Santop, arrived at American League Park for a Labor Day doubleheader against the Giants in the morning and the Stars in the afternoon. The Lincoln Giants took both contests, leaving them feeling "very chesty."[26] They were credited with a 108–12 record in 1911 and became the winner of the first of three straight eastern championships.[27] Before formation of the Negro National League and the Eastern Colored League in the 1920s, "championship" was a loosely used term.

A Split Squad in Cuba

Following its first season in Schorling's Park, the Giants once again embarked for Cuba and the 1912 Cuban Winter season, January 14, 1911, through April 29, 1912. In an unusual arrangement, the Giants did not play as a team. Some played for Habana and some for the Fé team. Hill, Homerun Johnson, Lloyd, Petway, and Williams, on loan from his New York team, suited up for Habana. American Giants Rube, Jess Barbour, Bill Pierce, Leroy Grant, and Pat Dougherty were among the Black Americans who wore the Fé team colors. The Fés fared so poorly against the Habana team that the Fé directors, in another unusual move, by late February had released most of the Americans on the team, including all the Giants players, and sent them sailing for the States. Cuban players replaced them. This year the Habana team finished in first place, beating out the Almendares by five games. The Fé team finished in third and last place. Hill played in 32 of the 34 games but fell short of his spectacular performance in 1910. In 1911 he managed a mere .284 batting average with 30 hits, with only one, a triple, for extra bases. He did steal 13 bases. Teammates Johnson, Petway, and Williams clinched first place respectively in hits, 43; stolen bases, 20; and complete games pitched, 12.[28]

1912

Midway through the 1912 season, criticism of the 50–50 arrangement between Foster and Schorling surfaced in the *Chicago Broad Ax,* a

Pete Hill

1—Gonzalo Sanchez, catcher. 2—Sam Lloyd, short stop. 3—Ricardo Hernandez, outfielder. 4—Preston Hill, outfielder. 5—Grant Johnson, short stop y second base. 6—Luis Padron, right fielder. 7—J. H. Magrinat, outfielder. 8—Carlos Moran, third base. 9—Camilo Valdes, mascota.

JUGADORES DEL "HABANA."

4. The Rambling Giants 59

Black weekly. Schorling's share, the paper argued, "should be received by the Race to whom the patrons of the game belong." Foster, ever the clever administrator, muted the discontent by masking Schorling's role, so that by 1915 most believed Foster, not Schorling, owned the park. The criticism died down and the deal between the two men remained intact.[29]

How Rube managed to mute the criticism could not be determined, but Schorling, though he didn't want to run the team, continued to play a key and visible role in the team's affairs. For openers, the new stadium carried his name, Schorling's Park. In January of 1913 the *Suburbanite Economist* informed its readers that "John Schorling has again contracted with Rube Foster to manage his baseball team for the coming year." A year later the same paper reported that "John Schorling's basebase [sic] park ... is drawing as good crowds as the major league parks. His team, the American Giants, are certainly meeting the best teams and playing mighty good ball." In November 1918, the same paper said "Johnny [Schorling] has made a world's championship team out of these colored boys, and done much for the advancement of clean baseball." Foster listed Schorling as his supervisor when filling out his draft card during World War I. And in February 1921 *The Courier* in Waterloo, Iowa, reported that it was John M. Schorling who ended negotiations between "his team" and the Boston-based New Continental Baseball League.[30]

Rube remained pleased with his relationship with Schorling. In a letter to the *Chicago Defender* in January 1924, Foster wrote "Mr. Schorling is one of the best and most honorable men I have ever come in contact with.... In our 12 years together there has never been a difference of opinion. He has never asked me why I did anything or censured me for any steps taken."[31] Their relationship was a long-standing demonstration that shared interests could trump racial differences for the benefit of many.

In spite of Schorling's active role, the games continued without a hitch. In one of the first games played at Schorling's Park in 1912, an early May clash against the West Ends, Hill once more served notice of what fans could expect from him. His four hits—two singles, a double, and a triple, paced the Giants to a 7–3 win.[32]

After a good start to the 1912 season, the Giants' winning ways hit a snag, compliments of the New York Lincoln Giants. Just as the American Giants were the best Black team in the Midwest from 1910 to 1919, so the

Opposite: **Portraits of Cuban and American players on the Habana team circa 1911. Players by their numbers are (1) Gonzalo Sanchez, catcher; (2) John Henry Lloyd, mis-identified as "Sam," SS; (3) Ricardo Hernandez, OF; (4) Pete Hill; (5) Grant "Home Run" Johnson, 2nd base; (6) Luis Padron, OF; (7) J.H. Magronat, OF; (8) Carlos Moran, 3rd base; Camilo Valdes, mascot-batboy (Library of Congress).**

Lincoln Giants was regarded as the best team in the East for the same time. Foster's Giants lost a 12-game series to the New York squad that ended on August 13, 1912, to give the Lincoln Giants seven wins and claim their second consecutive title of "Colored World's Champions."[33] Rube was not happy.

He was in a better mood when midway through the 1912 season he received an unsolicited application for a tryout with the team as a first baseman. The applicant was his friend Jack Johnson, then midway through his reign as the nation's first Black heavyweight boxing champion of the world. Rube invited the champ to report to morning practice for a couple of weeks.[34] It's not known if Johnson did. There's no evidence that Johnson made the team.

A Championship Awaits Out West

After the 1912 season ended in the Midwest, Foster, without declaring anything about a championship this year, took his squad on a grand barnstorming tour beginning in a return visit to San Diego. This season, 1912–13, the CWL competition consisted of three White teams whose players were drawn from the Pacific Coast League and the majors. Major leaguers included such names as Dave Bancroft, Chief Myers, Fred Snodgrass, and Fred Merkle. The Giants had Hill on board this time. All four teams in the estimation of baseball historian William F. McNeil were of AAA caliber, just a notch below major league status. Tufts-Lyons' manager Walter Nagle claimed his roster "was the strongest club in the league." When told of Nagle's claim, Foster responded with a "scornful grunt."[35]

The Giants got off to a good start when the season opened in December. The *Chicago Defender* lauded the team's performance, saying, "Never before in the history of baseball has a colored team accomplished ... what the American Giants have accomplished on their present trip to the Pacific Coast."[36]

One game between the Giants and the San Diego Bears on December 16, 1912, gained notoriety for several players' behavior. Following a close call at first, visiting Giants' first baseman Bill Pierce, usually a catcher, disagreed with umpire McCafferty's call. After much complaining and whining, calling McCafferty a "vile name," and refusing to leave the field when ejected by McCafferty, a police officer led the disgruntled player "to the visitors' habitation." Later in the contest, Hill was the victim of a straight right to his jaw delivered by the Bear's left fielder Walker. Stunned, but still standing, Hill declined retaliation and led the Giants to an 11–5 win with three singles and two runs scored.[37]

The *Defender* later awarded the CWL championship to the Chicago

4. The Rambling Giants

Pete Hill looks on as the San Diego Bears make a pitching change during the contentious November 16, 1912, California Winter League game (courtesy of Gary Ashwill).

team, but baseball historian McNeil's research shows a third-place finish for the Windy City crew behind the San Diego Bears and Tufts-Lyons with the McCormicks finishing in last place. The *Fresno Morning Republican,* on the other hand, sided with the *Defender.* In any case, the Giants performed well enough in the rubber match of a three-game series against the Tufts-Lyons for a fan to opine, "If these brunette babies had been on John McGraw's staff, the world's championship would be reposing in Gotham instead of in Boston." (McGraw's New York Giants had just lost the World Series to the Boston Red Sox four games to three.) Nothing was heard from Tufts-Lyons' manager Walter Nagle. Hill, usually a .300 and better hitter, managed only eight hits, though five were doubles, in 10 games for a .235 average.[38]

From San Diego the team moved on to Visalia, California, where they won four out of five games from a White team, the Portland Beavers, a Portland Coast League team. The local papers extolled the Giants' performances. One scribe, enthusing over a Giants' victory, proclaimed the team had "applied the kalsomine brush" (one that Amazon touts as the perfect brush to apply water paints, or wallpaper paste to rough or flat surfaces) to the Portland Coast nine. Walter Henry (Judge) McCredie, owner, manager, and player at different times for the Portland Beavers, and who had spent 1903 as an outfielder for the Brooklyn Dodgers, noted that the PCL "is made up of major league stars and the negroes are fully as good as the average Coast League team. If I had my way," he exclaimed, "the African Americans would be welcomed inside the fold."[39]

The Giants also made an impression on *San Francisco Examiner* sportswriter Al C. Coy, who had covered the five games at Visalia. He came away writing "Sakes alive man, but them brunette gentlemen suttingly kin play baseball." McCredie would sign the whole team, Coy said, "if only they were whitewashed." Coy was particularly impressed with the players' speed, saying "these sons of Ham can tear over the ground at the gait of the Overland Express." Coy noted that while his readers may not be too interested in the Giants' abilities, his praise for them was intended "to furnish a satisfactory alibi for the Beavers and to explain that the defeats ... have not brought any woe to the heart of Walter McCredie."

McCredie was confident his Beavers would do well during the upcoming PCL campaign because they would not face a team as talented as the Giants.[40] Rube's roster continued their train trip seeing Northern California and travelling as far north as Victoria in British Columbia, Canada before returning to Schorling's Park for Opening Day, April 23.[41] The "brunette gentlemen" had played 88 games since leaving Chicago on October 12, and had lost only 10.

Hill and his cohorts also earned praise for their gentlemanly behavior off the field. Players avoided bars, and tended only to their own business, "an example" a reporter pointed out, "lots of White clubs can take pattern from."

1913

On the team's return to Chicago, Foster learned that Dangerfield Talbert, an infielder for Leland's Chicago Giants who had earlier played for Foster when he managed Leland's Leland Giants and had played with Foster in Philadelphia, was sick with tuberculosis. Saddened by the news, Rube immediately set about raising money for the ailing player. Contributions came from players, fans, Charles Comiskey, B.F. Moseley, and Leland's manager, Joe Green. All proceeds from the May 17, 1913, benefit game against Joe Green's Chicago Giants went to Talbert. Rube, in a tribute to Talbert, pitched for the Chicago Giants and was beaten by his own team 6-0. He gave Talbert about $300 ($8,000 in 2021 dollars) to help with his recovery. Unfortunately, Talbert died just months later at age 34.[42]

Another Championship Claimed and One Lost

Six weeks later Foster adopted the *Defender*'s version of which team captured the 1912–1913 CWL pennant. A cream-colored banner with a

4. The Rambling Giants 63

border of blue and white stars and red lettering—spelling out "Champions of the California Winter League for the Season of 1912–1913 American Giants"—appeared in Schorling's Park on Independence Day, 1913. Both the Giants and their opponents for the day, the West Baden Sprudels, an Indiana-based independent Black team, provided the action. Hill and his mates sported new cream-colored uniforms trimmed in blue. The Sprudels spoiled the celebration by winning the game 7–5. The *Defender*'s reporter assuaged his readers' disappointment by saying, "The Giants were beaten, but we shouldn't worry. A team of their own color did it."[43]

The loss to the Sprudels interrupted a winning streak which was quickly resumed. The Giants again played the Cuban Stars. The Stars went down to defeat in mid–June 12–6 in game three of the series on their home field. The Giants attacked Star's pitchers for 20 hits. Hill led all Giants' batters, banging out two doubles and two singles.[44] In another notable game Foster and Hill teamed up to lead the Giants to an 11–6 win over the St. Louis Stars in early September. Rube pitched like his old self. Hill again led all Giants' batters, collecting five hits in as many trips to the plate.[45]

The Giants' strong finish to the 1913 season did not, however, impress the Lincoln Giants, who again won a playoff series against them to claim their third straight world colored championship. The third game, won by the Lincoln Giants 6–4 and played in Schorling's Park in mid–August, featured plenty of action: 22 hits in all. Hill chipped in two singles. Foster had a chance to win it with his bat, but his line drive over-the-fence clout with two on was a couple of feet foul.[46]

Back to Palm Beach

Hill spent little time licking his wounds. By mid–January 1914 he had joined four fellow Giants and five members of the champion New York Lincoln Giants in the warm and sunny embrace of Palm Beach, this time in a Breakers Hotel uniform. The games against the Royal Poinciana squad began January 22. The *Palm Beach News*, a White paper, promised Flagler's guests that both squads are composed of "all stars, selected from the leading colored baseball aggregations" ... and that "ripping good baseball ... should be presented during the season."[47] Fans were not disappointed. Four future Hall of Famers—"Cyclone" Joe Williams, Hill, John Henry Lloyd and Louis Santop, a catcher who could throw a ball over the centerfield fence and whose bat, named "Big Bertha" after the Germans' long-range artillery gun—all produced tape-measure homers. The Breakers came out on top of a hard-fought series, 8 games to 6. Hill played well but without the usual accolades coming his way.[48]

California Beckons Again

The rest of the Giants returned to California in the fall of 1913, but not to the CWL. Instead, "Judge" McCredie scheduled four Games between his PCL Beavers and Rube's Giants. Injuries to Rube, other pitchers, and catcher Petway put a crimp in the team's play. The Beavers took three of the four games. The first two games were played in Santa Maria, the third further up the coast in Santa Cruz, and the final game a few miles south of Santa Cruz in Watsonville. The Giants continued their barnstorming to Chico, California, and Grants Pass and Medford, Oregon, before finishing in Portland.[49]

Jim Crow in Oregon

Jim Crow beliefs often accompanied the Giants. In Medford, Oregon, on their way to Portland, every White-owned hotel and restaurant refused to serve them. Only through entreaties to a Japanese restaurant were Hill and his mates able to obtain something to eat. The main dish was cheese and crackers. The team fared better in Portland's thriving black community. Lodging and meals were found at the Black community's finest hostelry, the Golden West Hotel. Lew Hubbard, a Black promoter, amateur boxer, one-time second baseman for a local team, and owner of the city's Hubbard Giants, feted the Giants in grand style with a "smoker" at Portland's Eschel's Hall on the evening of April 10. The term "smoker" signaled that boxing, then struggling for legitimacy, would be on the program. The smoker also featured "singing, dancing, ragtime piano playing, and wrestling." A local pugilist, Bud Anderson, known as the "Pride of Medford," was invited to be the headliner. A good time, as they say, was had by all.[50] The players also had time for baseball while in Portland. Perhaps invigorated by the smoker, they won both two-game series against the Portland Colts and the Portland Beavers.[51]

From Portland, it was on to Montana for a game in Butte's Columbia Garden. Larry Duggan, an undertaker and embalmer, had seen Rube's men play in Chicago and promised the local populace that they would never see a better team in action. The Giants proved Duggan right.[52] Next stop: Lewiston, Idaho. Rube threw a three-hit shutout at the Lewiston nine, putting to rest a popular rumor, in the words of *Defender* sportswriter Frank Young, "that Rube's pitching days are over and that he is all in."[53] From Lewiston it was a return to Chicago for the April 29, 1914, Opening Day game.[54]

Praise from the Defender

While most of the Giants were touring the West, the *Defender*, in looking ahead to the 1914 season, outdid itself in heaping accolades on the team. The big news was that Black baseball's consummate shortstop of the day, John Henry "Pop" Lloyd, had "left" the Lincoln Giants for another stint with the American Giants, demonstrating once again that Rube paid his players well. After touting the rest of the roster, including Hill as one of the "outer gardeners," the paper went on to assure its readers that few games would be lost because they (the American Giants) "will be the equal of the White Sox or the Cubs, or the Athletics or New York Giants."[55]

Whether or not the Giants were the equal of the four major league teams, they were an exceptionally strong club that fared well against the independent Black teams of the Midwest and East during the 1914 season. In early June the squad split a six-game series with the strong Cuban Stars at Schorling's Park. Had it not been for a single by the Stars' Cristóbal Torriente, Foster, who proved not be slowing down even at age 35, would have had a no-hitter to his credit in the series' last game won by the Giants 1–0. A week later Foster threw a three-hit game against the ABCs, winning 2–1.

A week after that game, against a White team from Benton Harbor, Michigan, Foster dueled a pitcher with a familiar name, "Cy" Young. Not *the* Cy Young, who holds the record for both the most major league games won (511) and games lost (313), but former major leaguer Irv Young, who had pitched for the Boston Beaneaters, Pittsburgh Pirates, and Chicago White Sox from 1905–1911. He carried the nickname "Young Cy." Off to a rocky start giving up three runs in the first inning, Rube settled down, giving up only one more. The Giants narrowly prevailed 5–4 on the strength of Hill's game-winning run scored following a Hill specialty, a double, in the seventh inning.

Fans who attended a mid–September game at Schorling's Park against the Gunthers were treated to one of many examples of Pete's clutch hitting. His bases-loaded, game-winning triple assured the Giants of a 6–2 victory.[56] In bringing the 1914 season to a successful close, Hill and his teammates subdued the Brooklyn Royal Giants by making a clean sweep of their four-game September series to win what Frank Young of the *Defender* called "the world series."[57]

A Ferry Expels Jim Crow

Following their "world series" championship, the Giants bypassed Palm Beach during the winter of 1914–1915, but the games continued with players from a variety of Black teams. During the games, the issue of segregation appeared in the local paper. Just as Flagler's hotels were segregated, so was the rest of Florida. One exception was the ferry which carried people from West Palm Beach across the Lake Worth Lagoon (now the Atlantic Intracoastal Waterway) to Palm Beach before bridges were built. People could sit anywhere they liked on the ferry.

This arrangement sparked an anonymous letter to the editor of *The Daily Tropical Sun* bemoaning the open-seating practice. "Blacks," the person wrote, "invariably sit alongside the white passengers ... which is certainly offensive to the average white man." The writer proposed that the same Jim Crow laws that apply to railroads and street cars be applied to the ferry. The editor replied that it would be a blessing if people such as the writer could serve in the war (World War I which the U.S. had not yet entered) "with its terrible list of killed and wounded." We would not wish them to be wounded, however, the editor said, "for the wounded sometimes recover."[58] While the editor's position is clear, it's not known if the exchange of views had any impact on the ferry's seating policies.

Back on the Road

The Giants did not have the entire 1914–1915 winter off. Late February of 1915 found the Giants' private Pullman car pulling out of Chicago attached to the *Daylight Special*, a luxury train of the Illinois Central Railroad with service between Chicago and St. Louis, eventually bound for spring training in New Orleans. Three limos whisked the players from the train to St. Louis' Keystone Café. John Slaughter, a Chicago real estate mogul, and Noah Warrington, a majority stockholder in the St. Louis Giants Black baseball team, both Black and friends of Rube, treated the team to a festive four-hour "elaborate spread."

St. Louis Giants star shortstop, Dick Wallace, introduced Rube to Harry Bauchman, an infielder then with Leland's Chicago Giants and a native of Omaha, Nebraska. At 11:00 p.m. the team caught another "rattler" out of St. Louis bound for the Crescent City. Bauchman went along. His play during the upcoming exhibition games, and the untimely death of Bill Monroe, created the opportunity for Bachman to play second base for the Giants for the next six seasons.[59]

Spring training continued as their Pullman car carried them through the Gulf Coast, Southern California, the Northwest, Montana, and the Dakotas for 36 games before arriving back in Chicago for Opening Day on April 25 against the Milwaukee White Sox, champions of the White Lake Shore league. While in the Pacific Northwest the Giants wore black armbands in memory of Bill Monroe, who died of tuberculosis on March 16, 1915, at his parents' home in Chattanooga, Tennessee. A teammate of both Foster and Hill with the Philadelphia and American Giants, Monroe was variously called the "king of second basemen," "idol of all the ladies," and "the most sensational player on the American Giants team."[60]

Of the 26 games on the West Coast, Rube's team won 20. Hill missed several games due to a severe cold. Otherwise, he pounded the ball as usual, cementing his moniker in the press as "Demon Hill."[61]

It was not all work on this trip. The players visited San Francisco's Panama Fair on March 29. The Fair celebrated the completion of the Panama Canal, completed a year earlier, and showcased the city's recovery from its devastating 1906 earthquake.[62]

The 1915 season was unremarkable. Seamheads, a Black baseball database, credited the Giants with a 29–25–3 record, good for third place among Western independent teams. A particularly forgettable game occurred in August at Schorling's Park. The Giants took a 13–0 drubbing from the New York Lincoln Stars, a splinter team of the New York Lincoln Giants, for their worst loss in many a year. The game was part of another championship series. With the teams tied at five games apiece, the deciding game was called in the fourth inning, because of a deluge, with the Stars ahead by one run. Play never continued.[63]

5

Racial Conflict On and Off the Field

Baseball, like the rest of America, remained solidly segregated throughout Hill's career. White fans sometimes joined their Black brethren in the stands. At other times they sat in a section of the grandstand reserved for Whites. Games between an all-Black team and a team of "pale faces" were commonplace, but in no case, with the notable exception of the All-Nations team, did Whites and Blacks play on the same professional team in the first two decades of the twentieth century.

There was, of course, more to segregation than separation. An emotional cauldron bubbled not far below the surface most of the time. At times the feelings erupted into acts of violence both on and off the field.

Off the Field

Brutal White-on-Black riots were not uncommon. A particularly heinous one occurred on August 14 and 15, 1908, in Springfield, Illinois, Abraham Lincoln's hometown, 200 miles south of Chicago. A White mob lynched two Black men. One, William Donnegan, owner of a shoe repair shop in the city for 50 years, was set upon in the early evening hours of April 14 in front of his house. The mob dragged him from his front steps by a clothesline around his neck to a nearby tree close to the state capitol building where they hanged him. The hardworking shoemaker was lynched, the town's police chief told a reporter, because he was living with a White wife. Donnegan's terrified family, seeing what was happening but feeling helpless, barricaded themselves in their house. The mob set fire to the modest dwelling. Only the fire department's timely arrival saved the family from being incinerated. The frenzied mob also torched the homes of 40 other Black families. Now homeless, they took refuge in the State Arsenal. A few moments later an excited crowd of 2,000 gathered

5. Racial Conflict On and Off the Field

at the undertakers where Donnegan's body had been taken. They jeered at the soldiers of the Seventh Calvary that Governor Charles S. Deneen had called in to enforce martial law. Confronted with soldiers brandishing fixed bayonets, the crowd dispersed.[1]

The vengeance-seeking throng, led by a White 250-pound woman with an avowed hatred of Blacks, Kate Howard, then descended on a cafe owned by Harry Loper, a White man, who had helped a "negro" escape the mob's murderous intentions. Several of the men overturned and burned Loper's car. The car, with Loper's permission, had been used by the sheriff to spirit George Richardson, a "negro ex-convict" accused of accosting Mrs. Earl Hallam, a White woman, out of Springfield before the mob could get to him. Others piled furniture, decorations, fixtures, tableware and dishes onto a fire that destroyed the entire building. Loper and his family managed to escape to an undisclosed location in Michigan. The riot, his insurance company later informed him, voided his policy and those of others whose properties suffered similar damages. Restitution, the company claimed, was the responsibility of the city and county. It took five years, but in August 1913 the city council of Springfield allocated $45,000 from city funds to settle riot-related claims. The largest share, $8,350, went to Loper. The amount was less than the $11,276 which Loper had agreed to

Tents pitched on State House grounds for militia members called in by the governor to quell the Springfield, Illinois, riot (Library of Congress).

in February 1909 as a compromise from his initial claim for property damages of $15,034.[2]

Once the rioting ended, a military court of inquiry set about identifying the rioters. The group turned its evidence over to a Sangamon County special grand jury. On August 20 the jury charged Abraham Raymer, a Russian Jewish peddler, with murder for the lynching of Donnegan and with cases of "malicious mischief" for the destruction of Loper's café. Kate Howard was initially charged with several counts of looting—she took linens and silverware from Lopers—and aiding in the wrecking of the cafe. A week later, the grand jury added a murder charge against Howard for the lynching of both Donnegan and Scott Burton, a barber and the second Black lynched. Loudly protesting her innocence, proclaiming, "I am not guilty of the murder of anyone," she nevertheless swallowed a fatal dose of cyanide of potassium, purchased just days before "to kill rats," in her home just as sheriff's deputies arrived to arrest her. On the same day, the panel indicted six others on 20 separate counts, after which Assistant State's Attorney Wines promised, "we have only made a fair start."[3]

The trials started in September. They were preceded by the trial of a Joe James, a Black drifter accused of murdering Clergy Ballard, a White mining engineer, in July. Ballard, awakened by his daughter's screams, had chased a man from her bedroom, caught him, or so he thought, and was stabbed to death by the unidentified man. The next day a group of Whites saw James asleep on a bench and beat him until police arrived to prevent a probable lynching. An all-White jury deliberated just three hours before convicting him in mid–September of first-degree murder. No physical evidence or eye-witness account tied James to Ballard's murder. The judge sentenced James to the gallows. James had no connection to anyone in Springfield. He had a reputation for drinking and gambling, and had spent a month in jail for vagrancy. James maintained his innocence, telling his mother just before his October 23 execution that the only thing he was guilty of "was having lived a sinful life."[4]

Immediately after James' trial ended, State's Attorney Frank Hatch proceeded to try those indicted for rioting. First up on September 19 was Raymer on the charge of murdering Donnegan. Circuit Court Judge James A. Creighton instructed the all-White jury that it was not necessary to determine that Raymer personally aided in the lynching, his presence in the mob, which Raymer admitted to, was enough to convict him. After taking only one ballot the jury returned a not guilty verdict. Raymer faced three more trials; for taking part in the destruction of Loper's café, rioting, and petty larceny. Convicted only of the petty larceny charge, he spent a month in jail and paid a 25 dollar fine. The bulk of the remaining cases, including a few against Blacks, were dismissed.[5]

Several days after the Springfield riots, accounts of the violence sparked antagonisms between White and Black dock workers on the Western Transit Company's Chicago wharves. Some Whites said they would refuse to work unless the Blacks quit. Fisticuffs erupted. A melee involving bricks and clubs followed. Louis Hawkins, Black, stabbed Hugh Brady, White, in the neck and arms. A nearby group of Black and White laborers for the Lehigh Valley Transportation Company heard the ruckus, came running, and took sides. Two patrol wagons filled with Chicago's finest quickly arrived. The police subdued the fighting and arrested Hawkins. With revolvers drawn and threats to shoot the first person who might attempt to free Hawkins, the men in blue departed with Hawkins in tow.[6]

Birth of the NAACP

Out of the ashes of the Springfield riot emerged the National Association for the Advancement of Colored People (NAACP). While riots and lynchings were common in the South, this one took place in Illinois. And not just any place in the Land of Lincoln, but in the very city where Lincoln had practiced law and where he was buried. City officials in Springfield, as seen by their tepid response to the rioters, did not express much concern. Others, however, did. Many White northerners, seeing that racial conflict was not confined to the South, felt if actions to defend Blacks were not taken soon, the cancer of Jim Crow could quickly metastasize throughout the North.

An article by journalist William English Walling, "Race in the North," described the Springfield events in lurid detail and raised the specter of more such riots in the North. His article lit a fire under many people, including Mary White Ovington. A White settlement worker, activist, and author of the book *Half a Man*, she spoke throughout the country in support of Blacks' rights. She wrote a column for the *New York Amsterdam News* titled "Book Chat," where she reviewed books dealing with Black issues throughout the world. Her most important achievement was a meeting of like-minded people she convened in New York City on February 12, 1909, the 100th anniversary of Lincoln's birth.[7]

Headquartered in New York City, the organization held its first formal session in May. With the exception of W.E.B. DuBois, a sociologist and activist who edited the organization's groundbreaking newsletter, *The Crisis*, the group's leaders were White. Ovington and others felt funding would come from Whites since they had caused much of the racial unrest, and they thought that Whites would be better fundraisers than Blacks. Some Blacks initially opposed the paternalistic attitude of its leaders, but the nascent group grew quickly. By 1914 6,000 members had joined 50 branches. By 1920 the number of branches had shot up to 400.[8]

Even as the NAACP grew in members and chapters, racial tensions continued to simmer in Chicago. In February of 1911 about 75 Whites, including some women, attacked 15 Blacks who had moved into a house in an all-White neighborhood. Using clubs, stones, and revolvers, the Whites plundered their belongings and bludgeoned the Blacks into submission, warning them, "If you try to live in this house or neighborhood, the house will be burned down in the next hour, and you will be stoned to death and lynched." The Blacks quickly retrieved what was left of their belongings and fled the neighborhood.[9]

Similar episodes prompted the *Chicago Defender* in 1913 to urge African Americans to seek protection directly from Chicago's chief of police and "apply for permits to carry fire arms or any other engines of war used in self-protection." Should the chief not be responsive and applications for guns be denied, "You should," the editorial continued, "immediately supply yourself with sufficient implements of war and ammunition to withstand a siege of reasonable duration.... Allow no quarter."[10]

Two years later, in 1915, the Illinois General Assembly got involved. The body launched an effort to protect Blacks from the intimidations rampant in the movies and plays of the day. Major R.R. Jackson, one of two "colored" members, both from Chicago, sponsored the bill titled *An Act to Prohibit Acts Tending to Excite the Feeling or Prejudice to Ridicule or Disparage Others on Account of Race*. If passed, the bill would prohibit the exhibition in Illinois of any art form "representing or presenting any hanging, lynching, or burning of any human ... like that portrayed in current movies *The Niggers* and *Birth of a Nation*." Jackson said the bill would benefit Jews and the Irish, as well as African Americans. Following what the *Chicago Defender* touted as a "rousing speech" by Jackson, the bill sailed through the Assembly 111–2. It failed by one vote in the Senate, because two senators, both White and from Chicago, refused to vote.[11] Disappointed, Jackson nevertheless continued to press the case for racial equality and maintained his involvement with Black baseball.

On the Field

Violence on the diamond usually involved an umpire. Umpires have long been the target of catcalls, boos, and invectives, mild and otherwise. In Pete Hill's games things got physical. It was not unusual to see the umpire, usually White, escorted off the field by police officers after a game to avoid not only cascades of verbal taunts but barrages of bottles and other projectiles.

5. Racial Conflict On and Off the Field

Defender sportswriter Frank A. Young, also known as FAY, lamented such an instance occurring in one of the playoff games between the American Giants and the Brooklyn Royal Giants in September 1914. In an effort to promote civility in the stands he went on to implore the police to remove "men who insist on making foul and insulting remarks in the presence of ladies."[12] No accounts of such actions by Chicago's finest could be found.

In a not uncommon fray, the Stars' Cristóbal Torrente kicked umpire Neill Kelly to signal his displeasure with being called "out" on his attempted steal of third during a game between the Giants and the Cuban Stars (West) in July 1915. Giants' pitcher Sam Crawford rushed to the Kelly's defense and landed a haymaker on Torrente's jaw. The Stars' players threw bats and balls at the Giants until police arrived on the diamond. "Five coppers," the *Defender* reported, "joined the fray with an immodest use of their night sticks." The fight spilled outside the ball park where the combatants availed themselves of bricks being used by workmen to repair a broken water main. After play resumed, the Giants won 3–1, but only because, as reported in the *Honolulu Advertiser*, "they had more reinforcement in the shape of bricks." Crawford and Torrente went at it on the street after the game until Foster separated the two.[13]

Umpires learned to come to games prepared, some packing heat. Hill was the victim of one such arbiter. In the midst of an argument between Hill and the umpire at home plate during the seventh inning of a game between Foster's players and the Indianapolis ABC's (also in July of 1915), the ump slammed Hill on his nose with his revolver—breaking Hill's nose. A fight erupted. Several players were hurt. The umpire awarded the game to Indianapolis. The reporter for the *Defender* called the scene "a disgrace." He predicted no more games between Black teams would be played at Federal Park, the home stadium for the White Indiana Hoosiers in the short-lived Federal League. The contrast between the "gentlemanly playing of the Federal teams and the riot scene was," he opined, "too great."[14] The scribe proved not to be a great prognosticator. Games between "colored" teams continued to be played at Federal Park though not always peacefully.[15]

Another example of violence on the field occurred in an October game, also at Federal Park, between the host ABC's and a team of all-stars assembled by Detroit Tigers' shortstop Donie "Ownie" Bush. Elwood "Bingo" DeMoss, the ABC's second baseman, took exception to umpire Jimmy Scanlon's call of "safe" for Bush's fifth-inning attempt to steal second. DeMoss and Scanlon started sparring. Oscar Charleston raced in from centerfield. With one punch he knocked Scanlon out, leaving "an ugly wound." Spectators bolted from their seats to join the fray. Police finally restored order and took DeMoss and Charleston to jail where they were soon bailed out. The game continued. The All-Stars won 3–1. The ABCs left for Cuba the next day.[16]

The ABCs, a dominant Black team during the 1910s, took its name from the initials of the American Brewing Company. Opened in the 1890s in Indianapolis, the company fielded a Black baseball team to advertise their product. Kegs of beer accompanied the team to every game, providing free libations to spectators. The company soon turned the team over to a "colored saloon keeper," who kept the name but stopped the gratis distribution. By 1914, the team, under new owner Thomas Bowser, an Indianapolis businessman, and manager C.I. Taylor, considered by many the equal of Rube Foster, began laying the groundwork for what would become one of Black baseball's strongest teams by 1916.[17]

Back on the Road

With the brisk Midwest fall coming on, the Giants made another trek to sunny California at the end of the 1915 season; first stop Omaha, Nebraska. There they faced what the *Defender* called "the strongest ball club ever to be gathered west of the Mississippi." A large crowd, excited by the local press hyping the game for two weeks, saw major league pitcher Pat Ragan, who made his home in Omaha, lead a barnstorming group of minor leaguers, The All Professionals, to a hard fought 2–1 victory. Neither team made an error. Hill had the sole stolen base of the game. Ragan held the Giants to a mere two hits, both by Hill, who singled early in the game and homered in the bottom of the ninth inning to prevent a shutout.[18]

While en route from Omaha to the Golden State, Foster contemplated scheduling games in Hawaii. In letters to friends there he promised to bring "the greatest colored baseball team in the world, the wonderful, marvelous, and fleet footed Giants of the diamond," for the not-so-trifling sum of $3,500 (about $90,000 in 2021 dollars). The money would cover first-class passage over and back, living expenses for three weeks, and $1,000 in "gold coin of the United States." The *Honolulu Advertiser* took a dim view. If Rube really wanted to come he'd have to "shave his offer." The paper also questioned the Giants' manners, citing the ruckus in recent games.[19] Lengthy negotiations over the course of several months between Rube and his Hawaiian counterparts followed to the point where the *Advertiser* reported, "The Windy City aggregation will, in all probability, come during February 1916." In the end, no agreement was reached. The Giants never got to the Paradise of the Pacific.[20]

Once in California, Pete Hill and the Giants again took on teams in the CWL. In a November game against the Cline-Cline nine, an all-White team from Los Angeles, the Giants' Frank Wickware, often called the Black Walter Johnson on the strength of his two exhibition game victories over

5. Racial Conflict On and Off the Field

the "Big Train" in 1913 and 1914 when both were in their prime, hurled a masterpiece three-hit, 4–0 shutout in late November. Hill's fourth-inning homer was all that was needed.[21] Hill led the Giants to another victory, this one against the San Diego–based Pantages in mid–December. His triple off the centerfield wall and a sharply slashed single to right brought home three runs to lead the Giants to a comfortable 7–3 win.[22] Hill and the other Giants continued their mastery of the White teams to win a Winter League pennant, this one with no dissenting claims.[23]

Racial Tensions Surface in the Golden State

Even though the Giants' presence in the CWL increased attendance and revenue as more people turned out to witness a quality of play few had

Members of the 1915 Breakers' Hotel team. Note the relaxed, smiling Pete Hill in the front row sporting a hat much like the one Rube favored. Back row, L to R: Jesse Barbour, Dick Redding, John Henry Lloyd, Jude Gans, Louis Santop, Leroy Grant Middle row, L to R: Sam Mongin, Dicta Johnson, Joe Williams, Bill Pettus, Bill Francis, Spottswood Poles. Front row, L to R: Pete Hill, William "Knucks" James, Dick Wallace (courtesy of the Baseball Hall of Fame and Museum).

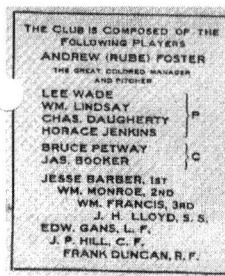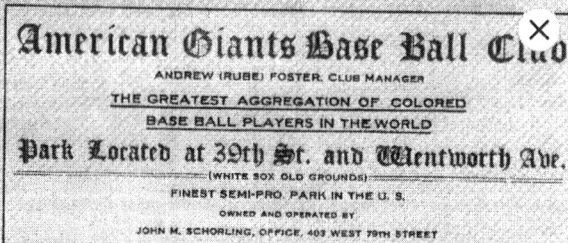

A typical letter from Rube making arrangements for a game. Note the team's name in 1915 as American Giants, not Chicago American Giants, and Rube's claim of "the greatest" (courtesy of Heritage Auctions, HA.com).

seen before, racial tensions become more public. Dan Long, manager of the PCL San Francisco Seals from 1908–1912 and a scout for the Chicago White Sox in 1915, turned down a request for the Sox to face the Giants. "Colored players," he explained to reporter Joe Murphy of the Black weekly, *San Francisco Call*, "are barred in organizational baseball and I see no reason why white players should even meet them in exhibition games…. Baseball is a sport that must be elevated, and it is up to the managers and players to keep it free from criticism." He continued, "I never arranged or played in any games with colored players."[24]

A year earlier, in 1914, PCL president Allen T. Baum formalized the growing resentment of African American players on the part of many California baseball officials. He issued two edicts in April. One banned PCL teams from playing exhibition games with Black teams. The second banned Black teams from PCL ballparks. It took several years for the edicts to be fully complied with—one reason being a manager or owner could simply ignore them during games not played in the regular season, as Baum himself grudgingly acknowledged. "I have no jurisdiction in the matter, but my sentiments are strongly against it. I am sure there is not another manager in the league who would consider playing with the Chicago [sic] Giants." But there was. Portland Beavers' manager Walter McCredie, as we have seen, welcomed the Giants to play the Beavers more than once. He told the *Defender* in 1915, "I don't think the color of the skin ought to be a barrier in baseball."[25]

The Trip Continues

The CWL ended in time for Hill to re-visit Palm Beach in January of 1916 and the rest of the team to again play in Cuba.

This year Flagler invited what he touted as "teams of all stars selected from the leading colored base ball aggregations of America." Pete Hill, playing for the Breakers Hotel team, joined other players from several of the top Black teams for a leisurely 12-game schedule. When not on the diamond, the men again waited tables, at salaries well above that of other wait staff, and indulged in the luxuries at hand, while still living in segregated quarters.[26]

Following his time in Palm Beach, Hill rejoined the Giants in Cuba where they won seven and lost eight games against various Cuban teams. Then it was back to California for exhibition games throughout the Northwest. This foray consisted of 37 games against teams in California; Vancouver, British Columbia, Canada; Oregon; Washington; and Montana.[27] Rube supplied a comedic episode for Vancouver, British Columbia fans in the first game of a doubleheader on April 21 against the Vancouver Beavers. He attempted to steal second base. A reporter, who noted that Rube's build was similar to that of ex–President Taft, wrote "The idea of a lumbering Rube trying to steal second, at which he was caught some twenty feet away from the sack, was really funny."[28] Perhaps the batter had missed a hit and run sign.

In the last game on the tour, against the Tacoma (Washington) Tigers,

The 1916 American Giants at a barnstorming stop in Vancouver, Canada. L-R: Pete Hill, Harry Bauchman, Steven Dixon, Tom Johnson, Judy Gans, Bruce Petway, Rube Foster, Leroy Grant, Edgar Washington, unknown (possibly C. Bernice Wood), John Henry Lloyd, unknown (possibly Clarkson Brazelton), and Frank Duncan. C. Bernice (pronounced "Burnis") Wood was a Los Angeles White Sox pitcher who was released by Foster, along with Washington, and spent his baseball career on the west coast (courtesy of Gary Ashwill).

Hill led the way. "Hill who was always the batting sensation of the Giants," wrote the *Defender*'s reporter, "got his usual three safe drives." The Giants won 10–8.[29] By the time Opening Day arrived on April 30, 1916, the Giants had played 72 games since season's end, winning 57, while traversing more than 20,000 miles since leaving Chicago six months earlier. It was the longest barnstorming tour undertaken by any team, Black or White, to date.[30]

6

Riots and the Noble Experiment

Seeds of Prohibition

In the same year that Allan Baum was devising ways to ban African Americans from the PCL, efforts to ban alcohol from American bars and taverns were gathering steam. The Methodist Church–based Anti-Saloon League was leading the way. Its members attacked the "saloon evil" rather than the imbibing behavior of its patrons, who were overwhelmingly male and known for boisterous and disorderly behavior. While some states and regions within states were already "dry," many were not. Legislation had been introduced in Congress to create a national ban on the manufacture and transportation of alcohol for years. But it wasn't until 1914 that the issue gained some traction.

U.S. Senator Morris Sheppard (D–Tex) introduced a resolution in Congress in 1914 that would eventually become the Eighteenth Amendment to the United States Constitution. Sheppard's bill prohibited the manufacture, sale, import, and transportation of "intoxicating liquors." The resolution, curiously enough, did not make drinking such beverages illegal. Trying to explain what many saw as a contradiction, Sheppard told his fellow senators, in words strikingly similar to those of the Anti-Saloon League, "I am not a prohibitionist in the strict sense of the word…. I am fighting the liquor traffic. I am against the saloon. I am not in any sense aiming to prevent the personal use of drink."[1]

By the time of Sheppard's resolution the saloon had embedded itself in the lifestyle of many Americans, mostly men, many of them recent immigrants and members of the working class. By one estimate the country had nearly 300,000 saloons in 1900. San Francisco reportedly had 3,000 licensed dispensaries and perhaps another 2,000 lacking a license. The saloon meant different things to different people. A not uncommon draw was relief and respite from drudgery. Upton Sinclair, who had campaigned against the drink for years, in his classic muckraking book *The Jungle*, described why his "brutalized Lithuanian immigrant" Jurgis Rudkus, stopped by a tavern after a day's work in "the steaming pit of hell" that was his employer's meatpacking plant. "He could forget the pain, slip off the burden, see clearly again and be master of his own brain," wrote Sinclair. For author and liberal imbiber Jack London, the saloon offered a social and cultural diversion. "Life was different," he wrote. "Men talked with great voices, laughed great laughs, and there was an atmosphere of greatness."[2]

Noted Chicago reformer Episcopal priest Samuel E. Fellows thought perhaps the benefits experienced by so many could be achieved in a saloon setting without the booze. In 1895 he opened a bar with all the trappings—a bar, barmaids, and spittoons. He called his establishment on Washington Street a "Salon." He served no spirits, wine, or beer. The Salon closed shortly after opening.[3]

Whatever one's reason for seeking the comfort and companionship offered by a saloon or tavern might be, exactly how "the personal use of drink" would be dealt with would attract much attention and conflict in the next several years.

King Alcohol

The "personal use of alcohol" was an issue in Black baseball in general and with the American Giants in particular. On Saturday evening April 29, 1916, the Giants, returning from California, rode the *North Coast Limited* into the Windy City's Union Station only to be met by a thunderstorm causing Sunday's opener against the West Ends to be postponed a week. Eighteen-year-old pitcher Edgar "Blue" Washington, enthusiastically recruited by Rube in California, would not be a part of any Giants' games in the near future. Washington alighted somewhat tipsily from the train. Rube handed him his walking papers for "having too much King Alcohol under his belt." Rube gave his players who overindulged a choice. They could "part with their ways or with the American Giants."[4] After a four-year hiatus from baseball, Washington played one final year, 1920, as a first baseman for the Kansas City Monarchs. His son Kenneth became the first African American to sign a National Football League contract. The Cleveland Rams acquired his services in 1945, before their move to Los Angeles the following season.

Veterans who favored "King Alcohol" fared no better than rookies under Rube's abstinence policy. Star pitcher Tom Williams, who posted a 10–2 record in 1917, suffered the same fate as Washington. As the team was boarding a train to leave New Orleans in early April 1918, players tried to get a staggering Williams on the train before Rube saw his inebriated pitcher. The right-hander refused their help and truthfully answered "yes" when asked by Rube if he was drunk. Rube asked for his uniform there and then.[5] Williams caught on with several other Eastern teams before returning to the American Giants, presumably no longer drinking or at least not where Rube could see him, for the 1921, 1923, and 1924 seasons—posting a combined record of 27–12.[6] He may, however, have fallen off the wagon for a while in 1922. Immediately after a four-week spring training trip through the South with Williams on board, Foster released him just before Opening Day but re-signed him in time for the start of the 1923 season.[7]

Hill, as the Giants' captain, enforced Rube's policy about inebriated players even when it might be detrimental to the team's success. William (Dizzy) Dismukes, who spent forty years in Black baseball as pitcher, manager, and executive, noted in a 1923 column for the *Pittsburgh Courier* that Hill once benched a player who had just homered in a tight game. Asked by Rube "Why?" Hill answered, "He was drunk."[8]

Drunkenness was a condition Hill avoided. Al Monroe, sportswriter for the *Chicago Defender*, reporting on his 1935 interviews with Hill and boxing champion Joe Louis, said both were teetotalers. "Both enjoyed a cigarette," Monroe said, "but," Monroe wrote, "neither would consent to supplant those smokes with liquid stimulants." "Joe," the sportswriter continued, "has never tasted liquor while Hill has never learned to like its taste or after effect." Evidently, both men were adamant in their convictions. Monroe, who imbibed now and then, concluded that "trying to convince either that your taste doesn't necessarily have to run like theirs is a job that proved entirely too tough for this correspondent."[9]

Other players were known to imbibe but without suffering penalties. While Rube and the ABC's manager, C.I. Taylor, made no bones about dismissing an intoxicated player, other managers turned a blind eye to their players' drinking habits. As time went on, however, some thought changes were in order. Three years after Dismukes' article, in a plea to Black players, the *Courier* published a lengthy article, without a by-line, illustrating how alcohol shortened careers by diminishing abilities and subjecting fans to shoddy play. Pitcher Frank Wickware, who spent six seasons with the Giants, had, the writer said, "liquored himself out of big time baseball," by the time his career ended in 1925 at age 37 with the New York Lincoln Giants. His play in his last few years rendered him "almost forgotten."

Jimmie Lyons, pitcher and outfielder for many teams including the American Giants from 1921–1925, was also one whom the writer felt "should be in the game today." "Lyons," the writer said, "fell victim to 'Demon Rum' and now graces the sidelines." Infielder Morten Clark, who played seven seasons for the Indianapolis ABC's tee-totaling and strict disciplinarian manager, C.I. Taylor, was another felled too early by drink. Once applauded "for his uncanny ability to handle the most difficult chances and make them look easy, his long embraces of the wine when it was red, resulted in another star lost to Negro baseball before his bolt was shot."

Resisting the temptation to go on "almost indefinitely," citing players who lost their battle with booze and subjected fans to second-rate play, the writer turned to Oscar Charleston "who shuns liquor" and is "a fielder supreme the peer of whom is yet to be located. Oscar could not have," the writer insisted, "maintained such a remarkable record if he had been a drinker...." Dizzy Dismukes came in for similar plaudits. "Players who imbibe to excess," the writer concluded, "must give way to the clean players who build up instead of tear down the grand old game." This turnabout would, the writer predicted over optimistically, "be pretty well accomplished by the next year, 1927."[10]

Hill and Foster Lead the 1916 Giants

Having reinforced his abstinence policy, Foster led the team through the 1916 season without losing a series to any team save one season-ending series to the ABCs. Several games with Foster and Hill in prominent roles were notable. Hill, a left-handed batter, crushed an opposite field homer over Schorling's Park's left field fence for only the fourth time in the park's history as the Giants downed the Cuban Stars in May for the second time in as many games.[11]

Now 37 years old, definitely on the stocky side, and near the end of one of the finest pitching careers of any mounds man, Black or White, and having not pitched in more than a year, Rube attempted a comeback in a May game against a White team from La Porte, Indiana. A ripple of laughter spread through the crowd when the White umpire, Ed Goeckel, announced the Giants' battery of Foster and Petway. Many assumed Foster had retired from active play to manage the club. Talk had been circulating quietly for two years that the "gentle giant" was past his prime. The laughter soon turned to applause as the old master turned in five stellar innings on the Giants' way to a 13–1 rout of the visitors.[12]

An emboldened Foster was now game for one more challenge; this one in mid–July, at home, against the Kokomo Red Sox, a White team featuring pitcher George Mullin, just a year retired from a 14-year career with the Detroit Tigers and a year younger than Rube. According to the never-ending praise showered on the Giants by the *Defender*, the Red Sox would be facing "the best semi-pro team that has ever been gathered." The *Defender* did acknowledge that the Kokomos also had a good team, "having lost only three games this season."[13] At game's end the Kokomos still had only three losses. "Mullin," the *Defender*'s scribe reported the

6. Riots and the Noble Experiment 83

next day, "simply had too much 'stuff' on that little sphere…." He held the Giants to three singles, one to Hill and two to Grant "Home Run" Johnson, while on his way to a 5–0 shutout.[14]

Even after being blanked, Foster was not quite finished as a pitcher. In a midsummer game, witnessed by Charles Comiskey and members of his Chicago White Sox who had the day off, he threw a two-hitter at a White team. One of the hits gave Hill a chance to show off another of the tools in his arsenal, his arm. A Texas leaguer dropped in front of him in centerfield. Hill scooped it up on the dead run and pegged it on a line to catcher Bruce Petway in time for Petway to tag the runner trying to score from third. "How often does he do that?" an impressed Comiskey later asked Foster. Foster replied that Hill routinely rifled balls from the outfield on a line to the catcher or an infielder. "Whitewash his face and I'll buy him," Comiskey told Foster. Foster, with a half-smile on his face, replied, "I got a picture of that … they'd run you out of the league … besides, you wouldn't do it."[15]

Hill's throw recalled a 1910 contest against the Gunthers. Hill purposely dropped an easy fly ball with runners on first and second. The runners, sure Hill would make the catch, held their base. Seeing the ball on the ground they tried to advance. Hill's bullet to third nailed the lead runner. The throw to second completed the double play.[16]

Another 1916 highlight came in a game against the Cubans in early September. Two Giants' pitchers, Tom Johnson and Richard Whitworth, combined to throw a no-hit, no-run game that was called in the seventh inning due to darkness. Johnson gave up six walks, but stellar defensive work kept the Cubans away from the plate. Hill garnered two singles and a double, the only extra base hit of the game.[17]

Their 1916 performance to date earned them the title of World Champions, at least in the eyes of Edward R. Litzinger, a close friend of Rube's and a well-respected White Chicago attorney. Shortly after the no-hit, no-run game, he presented the manager with a championship banner. Each player received a "gold emblem." The *Defender* ran a photograph of the Giants above the caption "World Champions."[18] Rube explained in a November letter to the *Defender* that the banner was only in honor of the team's play that season against the Lincoln Giants.[19] The "championship" series, pitting the Giants against the ABCs, was six weeks away and would not be without its conflicts.

The series opened in Indianapolis on October 21. The park was crammed, betting was heavy and, given the high stakes of the contests, Indianapolis' manager C.I. Taylor had hired four umpires; one to call balls and strikes and one to cover each base.[20] By November 4, each team had won two games, one of which the ABCs won by a forfeit. In the seventh inning of game three, Rube, coaching at first base, picked up a glove laying nearby and put it on. ABC manager C.I. Taylor, for reasons unknown, asked the first base umpire to tell Foster to take it off. The umpire did. Foster refused. After some further discourse with the arbiters and Taylor, Foster took his team off the field. The umpires awarded the game to the ABCs. Removing one's team from the field was a seldom-used tactic frowned on by all associated with the game. Foster defended his decision in a lengthy, two-part letter to the *Defender,* citing Taylor's humiliation of him as the reason. Foster said he was breaking no rule. Only five games, out of an initially scheduled 12 to decide the championship, were played. Counting the forfeited game, the ABCs had won three and the Giants two. Taylor claimed the championship. Foster, saying the forfeited game should not count, strenuously disagreed but to no avail.[21]

Sunny Florida

The Giants had played such outstanding baseball during 1916 that Flagler invited the team to compete in the Florida Hotel League from late January through mid–March 1917. Rube added Oscar Charleston, Bingo DeMoss, and Dan Kennard from the ABCs to bolster his squad. Charleston bumped Hill to right field from his usual centerfield position for the opening game. Hobbled by two errors and mediocre hitting, Rube benched Charleston. Hill returned to centerfield. The Poinciana squad squeaked by the Breakers in an exciting series to claim the pennant 7–6–2.[22]

The easy living came to an abrupt end on March 18, 1917. Foster corralled his players back on their Pullman car for a month of barnstorming through the warm South. In a telegram to the *Defender,* Foster said he'd scheduled 31 games in 31 consecutive days in Florida, Georgia, Alabama, Mississippi, Louisiana, and Arkansas. He promised the Chicago loyalists, "We'll have a good team on our return."[23] His telegram was one of the many he sent to the *Defender* over the years to keep the paper's sportswriters apprised of the team's performance and whereabouts. The weekly showed its appreciation by carrying reports of games, praising the team and its players, and encouraging readers to come out to the ballpark.

1917

As promised, the Giants put forth a good team for the 1917 season. The pride of Buena, Virginia, now 35 years old, could still handle the bat. Hill slammed a grand-slam ninth inning homer at Schorling's Park in an early May tilt against the White Beloit, Wisconsin, nine to lift the Giants to a come-from-behind 5–2 win. In a June game against the Merchants of the Commercial League, Foster "played like one of his youngsters." Playing first base, which he often did when not pitching or coaching at first or third, he accounted for three runs batted in and relieved Dick "Cannonball" Redding, whose talent on the rubber had earned him his apt nickname. But even a "cannonball" couldn't pitch after being hit in the head by a batted ball. "Rube," the *Defender* reported, "showed plenty of his old-time stuff and the white boys were baffled."

The Chicago nine fared especially well against their first-rate nemesis, the Indianapolis ABCs. By the end of June, the Giants had copped six games from the Hoosiers without a loss. The teams clashed again in Detroit in late July. Playing before the then largest mixed-race crowd ever to see a semi-pro game in Detroit, the Giants prevailed 3–2. Hill accounted for two of the runs with a run batted in, a double, and a run scored.[24]

Not all games counted in the standings. Earlier in July Rube had organized a charity game for Harry Moore, who had played his last game in 1913 and was now suffering from consumption. Moore had been a teammate of Foster, Hill, and John Henry Lloyd with the Philadelphia and American Giants. He played several positions but excelled at first base. Moore's well-earned reputation generated contributions for the game from Charles Comiskey, Indianapolis ABC's manager C.I. Taylor, and many players and managers from other teams. Many who bought tickets did not attend. The American Giants with several other players formed two teams: Hill's Stars and Lloyd's Stars, managed by Pete Hill and John Henry Lloyd, respectively. Hill's Stars won 2–0. The benefit was deemed "much of a success" by the Defender. Moore died two months later on September 2, 1917, at age 40 of tubular tuberculosis at his home in Chicago.[25]

In a doubleheader a month later that did count in the standings, a team from the Lone Star State, the Texas Stars, dropped two games to the Giants at Schorling's Park. With Foster doing "the slabbing" the entire way in game 2, the Stars fell 16–2.[26] The season ended in late October with a game against another all-star team "made up of major leaguers," or so proclaimed the *Defender*. Only one, however, catcher Bob O'Farrell, who was at the start of a 21-year career as a catcher in the majors, could be considered a big leaguer. The Giants won, 9–7. Hill, as he often did, contributed a double and scored two runs.[27]

A Riot on Lake Shore Drive

While the Giants were in Detroit battling the ABCs in late July, temperatures in Chicago had soared into the high 90s for days. As the sun rose higher on Tuesday morning, July 31, 1917, several thousand sought relief at Lake Michigan's Oak Street Beach which fronted a fashionable section of Lake Shore Drive known as the "Gold Coast," home to many wealthy Chicagoans. A city ordinance limited swimming to the hours between 4 a.m. and 8 a.m. Bathers laughed at officers who arrived mid-morning at water's edge in their patrol wagons. Several officers commanded them to come ashore. One policeman grabbed a swimmer and dragged her ashore. The laughter suddenly turned to threats, taunts, and outright assaults on several officers. The police arrested eight people, including three women still in their bathing suits. The bathers, who substantially outnumbered the men in blue, won the day and remained in the waters of Lake Michigan until well after dark. The fate of those arrested could not be determined, but, in light of a three-day heat wave which had taken the lives of 19 people, the Lincoln Park Board decreed the beach open 5 to 9 in the mornings and again in the evenings. No one was seriously hurt this time, but more serious riots were not far off.[28]

Back to Palm Beach

On a calmer note, Foster informed the *Defender* in mid–January 1918 that the *Seminole Limited* had carried the team once again to the luxurious center of the state's winter social season. "The boys" he said, were "in short sleeves and some are bathing in the Atlantic and others doctoring frost bitten ears caused by the zero weather in Chicago."[29] This year the Giants, including all six soon to be drafted, would contest a team composed of players from the Lincoln and Royal Giants of New York, the Bacharachs of Atlantic City, two from the Cuban Stars, Pelayo Chacon, a flashy shortstop from Cuba whose skin color kept him out of the bigs, and Gervacio Gonzalez, the first great Cuban catcher.[30] So dominant had the American Giants been in previous years that Flagler felt it necessary to hand pick a team for the Breakers in "an effort to dethrone the American Giants." Once again, the American Giants played for the Poinciana Hotel, but this year without players from other teams.[31] Foster's Giants had been invited to play in Havana, Cuba again but, said Foster, "we will not take the proposition, and play the series out here."[32]

Unusually cold weather put a crimp in attendance for game 2. Those who braved the weather saw the closest contest of the series, a pitching duel between two of Black baseball's greatest hurlers, "Smokey" Joe Williams of the Breakers and Dick "Cannonball" Redding for the Poincianas. Many who saw both Williams and Satchel Paige considered Williams the peer of (if not a bit better than) Satchel. Redding, no slouch himself and

6. Riots and the Noble Experiment

the Giants' ace in 1917, is credited with 30 no-hitters during his career. Williams prevailed 1–0.[33]

As the weather warmed so did the Giants' performance. Foster informed the *Defender* that, far from being dethroned, the Giants won the series by a margin of four games. The team again entrained for exhibition games throughout the South and returned to Chicago, having won 15 and losing but 1.[34]

7

The Spanish Flu

1918

Nineteen eighteen would prove to be a volatile year. World War I was in full swing. American troops had been fighting and dying in Europe since April 1917. The Spanish flu was killing millions around the world. Women, Black and White, were stepping up their fight for a woman's right to vote with marches and demonstrations in cities across the country. Race relations continued heating up. The American Giants were re-grouping.

By Opening Day in early April 1918, six players had received draft notices. None had yet to report, but that day was soon coming. Foster knew he would have to revamp his roster before long. One new addition to the team, 23-year-old Bobby Williams, a New Orleans native, short of stature but a skilled infielder and excellent bunter with speed to burn on the bases, had outplayed Lloyd in Florida and replaced him as the team's starting shortstop. Lloyd subsequently jumped to the Brooklyn Royal Giants. A major point of stability, as always, was Hill. He had captained the team for nine years and was playing the best baseball of his career.[1]

The Giants and Major Leaguers

How the top Black talent stacked up against major league talent was always a question on many people's minds, even in the midst of social turmoil. In May, the Giants were anticipating once again finding out. They were scheduled to meet what the *Defender* heralded as "their hardest and most crucial series in their career." On a Saturday—May 18, 1918—they were to face an all-White team "of all major league talent": the Army's 86th Division team based at Camp Grant, named for Union General Ulysses S. Grant, located in Rockford, Illinois. A few did have major league experience. Most, however, had played in the high minors. Unfortunately, the game was canceled by the commander of Camp Grant, who said only, "All I can say is that orders from the highest camp authorities prevented our coming." Thousands who had bought tickets to the game were disappointed.²

On Sunday the Giants did face the all-white Beloit, Wisconsin, team reported to be reinforced with two major leaguers. The first, Oscar "Happy" Felsch, slugging outfielder for the Chicago White Sox, had just resigned from the pennant-contending team in favor of a job with a Milwaukee, Wisconsin, gas company and playing semi-pro ball on the weekends. Felsch was a Milwaukee native and was described by writer Eliot Asinof as "easy going and badly educated." He would return to the White Sox for the 1919 and 1920 seasons.

Felsch is best known for joining seven other Sox who, angry at White Sox owner Charles Comiskey's refusal to pay them what they thought they were worth, agreed to throw the 1919 World Series to the Cincinnati Reds in return for a payoff from gamblers. A lengthy trial exonerated the players from any legal charges, but their major league careers were abruptly ended. Newly appointed major league commissioner Kenesaw Mountain Landis, a Chicago federal judge, banned Felsch and the others from baseball forever in 1920.

In later life Felsch was a primary source for Asinof's book *Eight Men Out,* which documented what has become known as the Black Sox Scandal.³ Bunny Hearn, a journeyman pitcher for five major league teams, who had recently resigned from the Boston Braves also citing dissatisfaction with his salary, was the second major leaguer mentioned.⁴ Neither Felsch nor Hill played. Hearn did, however, and shut the Giants out, 1–0, in the first game. The Wisconsin crew eked out a 2–1 win in game two.⁵ The games' outcomes demonstrated that the Giants, even without Hill, could stay with a major league pitcher.

The Flu

Baseball, the country, and the world would soon be confronted by the deadly and well-publicized Spanish Flu of 1918. A lesser-known variant of it had broken out two years earlier. Surgeon General Rupert Blue, known more for his bureaucratic infatuations and skills than for his public health expertise, received reports from state and county health officials in January 1916 from all parts of the country. They raised alarms about "the most serious epidemic of influenza ever known to exist in this country." Cases in the nation's capital were said to be large. The city's health department had yet to take official notice of the outbreak. They would before the year was out.

Causing many deaths and spreading rapidly, the 1916 influenza was most virulent in large cities, including Chicago. Topping the list of the hardest-hit cities were Cleveland and Detroit which had each suffered more than 100,000 cases. Blue, saying federal authorities were "practically helpless," put the responsibility for stemming the spread on local authorities, who in turn turned to the public to take "the proper precautions."[6]

Chicago's African American public health expert was Dr. A. Wilberforce Williams, a prominent African American physician. He worked at Provident Hospital with Daniel Hale Williams, the renowned physician and surgeon who in 1893 performed the first successful operation on the human heart. Williams served as the *Defender*'s health expert from 1911 to 1929. He advised readers in his weekly column on internal medical problems that included respiratory diseases, syphilis, gonorrhea, and chancroid (a bacterial infection causing open sores on the genitals). Much of his advice on coping with influenza rings true today; some not so much.

Many deaths from influenza and the grippe could be avoided, Williams wrote, if people: avoided whiskey; did not fill up on rock candy, linseed oil, glycerin, or gin or rum or cod liver oil; avoided crowds and gatherings; did not sneeze, hack or spit in the home cuspidor; avoided kissing, did not sneeze or cough in others' faces; and avoided patent medicines which are, he said, sold only to make money for the producer. He also counseled people to keep windows open to invite in as much fresh air as possible, practice good personal hygiene, consult a doctor as soon as possible, and follow the doctor's instructions. "Old people," Wilberforce cautioned, "should be especially careful as their resistance is lower, and death can overtake them in just a matter of days."[7]

Such outbreaks of influenza at that time were, according to John M. Barry, author of the best-selling book *The Great Influenza: The Story of the Deadliest Pandemic in History*, not unusual, but paled in impact and scope to the 1918 influenza pandemic that two years later would sweep the world as the result of a new and more virulent virus.[8]

Like many viruses, the 1918 version came in waves. The first started in the spring, surfacing probably in the Midwest, first at army bases, such as Camp Grant, then spreading to cities, many of them near military bases, and overseas to Europe and Asia. By the fall the disease was in its second and far more lethal wave reaching epidemic proportions. Chicago was particularly hard hit. On a single day, October 5, 1918, Chicago's Health Department reported 1,053 new cases and 101 deaths.[9]

Once the flu's potency came to be appreciated, attempts to contain it escalated rapidly, some more successfully than others. On October 2, Chicago police were authorized to arrest any Chicagoan who coughed or sneezed without using a handkerchief or who violated the city's spitting ordinance—whether on the streets or in movie theaters, courts or any place of public gathering. Calls went out to nearby states and Canada for doctors and nurses to help treat Chicago's exploding number of cases. The Red Cross distributed gauze masks. Chicago Public Health Commissioner John Dill Robertson closed 10 schools in District 99. He assured students none would be punished if they chose not to attend the schools that remained open. Chicago's open schools made the city only one of two school systems; New Haven, Connecticut, was the other, where classroom education continued.[10]

Robertson, however, adamantly opposed shuttering businesses. Dr. C. St. Claire Drake, the Illinois superintendent of public health, had proposed the move in a private meeting of state health officials and Chicago politicians. To do so, Robertson argued, in his official report on the epidemic, would undermine community morale. "It is our duty," he pleaded, "to keep our people from fear. Worry'" he asserted, "kills more people than the epidemic."[11]

Robertson was not alone in touting the preventive power of calm. "DON'T GET SCARED," appeared in large letters in newspapers throughout the country. *Literary Digest*, which enjoyed a wide circulation, advised its readers, "Fear is our worst enemy."[12] Such advice was not always calming. How could people not become fearful seeing friends and family members dying around them? A young nurse at the Great Lakes Naval Training Station suffered nightmares for years remembering "bodies stacked in the morgue from floor to ceiling like cordwood." Other advice issued by the Public Health Service included such suggestions as "Remember the 3 C's, clean mouth, clean skins, and clean clothes; keep the bowels open; Food will win the war. Help by choosing and chewing your food well."[13]

The American Medical Association (AMA) attacked such advice as useless and dangerous. The association offered in its periodical, *Journal of the American Medical Association* (*JAMA*), two primary measures for controlling the flu's spread; "the most complete isolation as the best course of action," and the use by everyone of gauze masks.[14] William Henry Welch, one of the nation's leading physicians and an advisor to the military at the time of the war, endorsed *JAMA*'s conclusions after a tour of army bases in June 1918. He proposed the use of masks by everyone at all bases and that new arrivals at camps be quarantined together to avoid cross infections with soldiers already at the base. More specific "social distancing" measures included "putting more space between beds, stretching tent flags between beds, and suspending a curtain down the center of a mess tent.

Today we know that to be effective advice, but not everyone realized the value of masks and social distancing in 1918. A major contributing factor to the flu's wildfire-like spread was the drafting of millions of young

Many facilities enforced the use of masks as their effectiveness became known. Here a Seattle, Washington, streetcar conductor allows a masked rider to board while denying boarding to an unmasked man (Library of Congress).

7. The Spanish Flu

Camp Grant as it appeared during the height of the flu (Library of Congress).

men for World War I. Once drafted or had volunteered, they reported to a cantonment (army base or navy base). The six Giants' draftees went to Camp Grant.

The virus had yet to arrive at Camp Grant, but it was lurking nearby at the Great Lakes Naval Training Station, a scant 100 miles away. There the virus had "ripped through the barracks very much like an explosion."[15]

The appointment of a new commander at Camp Grant, Col. Charles Hagadorn, on August 8, marked the beginning of a tragic series of events for the recruits stationed there. Most, many farm boys among them, came from Northern Illinois and Wisconsin. They lived in hastily built wooden barracks. Dirt roads contributed to dust-filled air in late summer except when rain turned the roads to mud. A short, brooding West Point graduate and a bachelor at age 51 for whom the army was his family, Hagadorn was confident in his decisions. As a line officer he drew plaudits for his service in the Spanish-American War and chasing Pancho Villa in Mexico. He had a reputation for issuing orders which many considered to be impulsive and inexplicable but which most agreed were on target. Based on his experiences in the Canal Zone, where he had seen tropical diseases controlled and having faith in Camp Grant's medical staff, he was convinced that the influenza could be controlled. He saw no need for masks or social distancing but did instigate a "virtual quarantine," meaning soldiers could not leave the base without his permission and only for "the most urgent reasons."[16]

So confident was Hagadorn that on September 20 he issued an order stating, "There must as a military necessity be a crowding of troops. The Camp Surgeon under the circumstances authorizes a crowding in the barracks ... beyond the authorized capacity.... This will be carried out at once as buildings are newly occupied."[17] The first cases appeared the next day. Their number escalated quickly. A week later the camp's hospital held 4,102 cases, far beyond the 610 cases the week before. Two soldiers had died. The supply of gauze masks, while not issued to the general population but which had covered the faces of the early cases, came to a halt due to a lack of material and people to make them.

By October 4, more than 100 men at Camp Grant had died. Five thousand were ill. Two thousand of the 3,108 soldiers, mostly young men 18–21 years old, who traveled in a cramped, unventilated train from Camp Grant to Camp Hancock near Augusta, Georgia, were hospitalized on arrival.[18] Caring for the sick and dying now took precedence over training for war.

Hagadorn no longer called the shots. Now he did everything the medical staff asked of him, but the virus marched on. On October 8, after hearing the latest daily Camp death toll, which had risen to over 500, Hagadorn ordered everyone to leave the building and stand outside for inspection. An odd order, but everyone obeyed it. Half an hour later, soldiers on the parade ground heard the loud report of a single pistol shot: Hagadorn had taken his own life. The situation at Camp Grant was not unique. Twenty-eight hundred troops reported ill in a single day at Camp Custer, outside Battle Creek Michigan.[19]

Dr. A. Wilberforce Williams continued to advise Chicago's civilians. He opened his October 12 weekly column by saying, "We are in the throes of a fearful epidemic of what is commonly known as Spanish influenza." His report included a lengthy discussion of the nature of influenza and complications that those affected might experience, followed by advice on how to prevent it. His recommendations remained largely unchanged from those he had put forth two years earlier, but came with a heightened emphasis on the value of sunlight and fresh air. "If you have a dear," Williams wrote, "and want to kill him or her in the most frightful way, just … close all the windows, put on more coal—heat the room hotter … do not give cold drinks of any kind, and in a few days you will get Master Death. You will help the undertaker along in his business." He touched on but did not give the wearing of masks and what we know today as social distancing the priority that the AMA did. At the end of his column he did advise people to "put your handkerchief over your nose and mouth whenever you cough or sneeze … and keep out of crowds, especially theaters and crowded street cars, as much as possible."[20]

The situation at army bases began to improve by mid-October. The *New York Times* reported a decrease in new cases. On October 16 the *Times* reported 5,688 new cases, down from 6,498 the day before. There were 170 recorded deaths for the day, down from 710 the day before. While the spread at army installations was declining, the influenza continued to spread among the civilian population with alarming speed. In Washington, D.C., for instance, it continued "unabated" even though government clerks wore gauze masks, recently distributed by the Red Cross, on crowded streets and in offices, all of which remained open. Some in D.C. wore masks in barber shops "and to a limited extent elsewhere." The *Times* cited Illinois as a state showing a "steady increase on the whole."[21]

7. The Spanish Flu

A striking example of the spread among civilians occurred in Philadelphia. What we know today as "a community spread event," was in the offing. The Liberty Loan campaign had planned a massive parade for September 29 to raise money for the war effort. Mayor Thomas B. Smith appointed Dr. Wilmer Krusen, a gynecologist, to be Director of the Philadelphia Department of Public Health and Charities. Krusen, while aware of many cases and deaths at the Philadelphia Navy Yard, insisted the parade posed little threat to the civilian population. He refused all pleas, and there were many, from the city's medical and public health officials to cancel the parade. On September 29, the largest parade in the city's history stretched for two miles while several hundred thousand people stood shoulder to shoulder to watch it. More than 1,000 people died within ten days, causing the closing of theaters, churches, schools, and other Liberty Loan events.[22]

Prior to the Philadelphia parade, cities across the country had organized parades to promote patriotism, salute nurses, and raise money for the war. The Red Cross organized many. In mid–May the organization put on the largest nation-wide series of parades ever held on one day. Five million marchers participated in a drive to raise $100,000 for the war effort. Nurses at military installations led the way, followed by public health service nurses, mothers with sons in service, and civic and volunteer organizations.[23] Before the month was out parades had been held in cities and towns such as Hagerstown and Annapolis, Maryland; Cambridge, Massachusetts; Waynesboro, Pennsylvania; and Fairmont, West Virginia.[24] President Wilson unexpectedly strode to the front of a parade in New York City on May 18. He walked two miles, leading hundreds of nurses marching 16 abreast down Fifth Avenue. Similar parades were held at the same time in the city's other four boroughs.[25]

Parades continued even as the influenza tightened its grip on the country, but Americans began to take the invader more seriously. By October inductions had been halted, cases increased across the country, and Congress had allocated one million dollars to fight the flu. Democratic Senator J. Hamilton Lewis of Illinois introduced a bill in Congress calling for ten million more, the Supreme Court extended its recess by a month, and the U.S. Public Health Service was finally leading the fight against the flu.[26]

Chicago, nevertheless, held its own large parade two weeks before Philadelphia's. On September 14, 1918, 12,000 Red Cross nurses gathered for a parade. Dressed in the white and gray uniforms of the Red Cross, they paraded through Chicago's Loop as 100,000 people lined the streets to view the parade as a "token of honor to Red Cross Day." A ban on large gatherings was in the works but not yet issued.[27]

Red Cross nurses, observed by thousands, march in Chicago in July 1918 (Library of Congress).

Many lives could have been saved in Chicago had such a ban been in effect. The flu took the lives of 8,510 Chicagoans in just the first three months of its full-blown power, September to November 1918. The flu gradually subsided but did not vanish. In the first two months of 1920, deaths from the flu totaled 11,000 in New York and Chicago. John Dill Robertson, who had promoted staying calm as a defense against the flu in 1918, now organized 3,000 professional nurses into regional squads to cover the entire city of Chicago. Every individual who contacted the flu had his or her residence tagged. The flu finally faded away in the next several years, but not before killing somewhere between 20 and 40 million people worldwide.[28]

The Games Go On

No reports of a Giants player contracting the flu could be found. The flu, in all probability, struck down three players of other teams, all while in the Army. Pearl Franklin "Specks" Webster, a glasses-wearing catcher for the New York Lincoln Giants, survived the outbreak but died in France of "lobar pneumonia." Arthurs Kimbro, an infielder, also playing for the

Lincoln Giants, succumbed at New Jersey's Fort Dix before receiving his discharge papers. A third player, Norman Triplett, a reserve outfielder with the Hilldale Club, died in France of "measles and pneumonia."[29] All things considered, the flu apparently had a relatively small impact on the health of Black baseball players.

Black baseball games continued through the summer and early fall of 1918. On June 9, 14,000 fans streamed into Schorling's Park to see the Giants tame the ABCs 5–2. Rube's Giants roamed the East in their Pullman car for four weeks in July and August playing games in Cincinnati, New York City, Pittsburgh, Washington, D.C., Atlantic City, and Darby, Pennsylvania, five miles southwest of Philly, for a three-game series in early August. The Giants took the rubber match by the comfortable margin of 12–4 before 3,000 spectators. Hill contributed a double and two singles.[30] Two weeks earlier the Bacharach Giants had edged Hill and company 5–4 in Atlantic City.[31] Back in Chicago, the Giants faced the Cuban Stars in a doubleheader. The game notice in the *Englewood Times* noted, "The big park ... should give the Cubans a good send-off."[32]

One game of note more for its social significance than the play on the field was a Friday afternoon game against the Indianapolis ABCs in August in the nation's capital. The games were played in American League Park, home to the major league Washington Senators managed, by but not yet owned, by Clark Griffith. The game attracted the who's who of the city's Black population; army and navy officers, judges, physicians, newspaper editors, and high-ranking civil servants. About 8,000 in all—the men in formal attire and ladies in bright costumes—filled the stadium. A Harvard graduate and the first African American judge in the city's Municipal Court, Robert H. Terrell, threw out the ceremonial first pitch to a standing ovation. Foster and ABC's manager C.I. Taylor received sustained applause when they emerged from their respective dugouts. The Giants built a 6–1 lead in the seventh inning, prompting Taylor to call Oscar Charleston in from centerfield as a relief pitcher. In a rare appearance on the mound, the man considered the best player in Black baseball and the Negro Leagues, held Foster's nine scoreless for the remaining two innings. Charleston was not as surprising a choice as a reliever as might appear. His initial tryout with Taylor's ABCs in 1915 was as a pitcher. The Giants won, but few, other than those with bets laid down, cared much about the score.[33]

Bobby Williams, the first Giant to enter the service, missed the eastern trip entirely. Three other players, Jude Gans, Frank Wickware, and Leroy Grant, started on the trip but had to report for duty by August 5.[34]

In July the flu was building to its full strength, but its severity went unappreciated in the world of Black baseball as was the case in other segments of society. Team owners strove to increase the size of crowds at games. Several changed the start times of weekday games from mid-afternoon to twilight. The new time benefited those able-bodied men who chose to work rather than fight—a choice mandated by the Selective Service Division as long as the work was in "a necessary civilian occupation." Many who had chosen a government job didn't get off until 4:30 or 5:30, by which times most games would have ended. Rube agreed to the change "as long as attendance held up." Though they lost their first twilight game, 3–1, to the ABCs, a fairly good crowd turned out for the next game. Foster was convinced.[35] Ten thousand watched as a dispute between Umpire Ed Goeckel and Rube went on for thirty minutes during a late September game in Beloit, Wisconsin. Other Black teams initiated a similar schedule.[36]

Some Restraints on Games Enacted

Lacking any direction from the federal government, state and local governments were responsible to make their own decisions on how to confront the flu. Not all made the same decision. In Baltimore, for instance, the health commissioner prohibited the playing of all baseball games in the city by October 15.[37] The games continued in Chicago until an order from the city's health directors banned large group gatherings in the Windy City at the end of October.[38]

An acknowledgment of how the flu was impacting baseball attendance in Chicago surfaced on October 13, when the American Giants faced another team of "All-Star Big Leaguers." The game was notable for two reasons. First, it was played in the midst of the influenza's second wave, which caught the attention of the *Defender*'s reporter, Dave Wyatt, a former player for Frank Leland and teammate of Rube. "Jack Frost and his hellish cohorts, influenza, pneumonia, colds, and chills," Wyatt noted, "kept the crowd down to just a few thousand." Secondly, the *Defender*'s headline "Big Leaguers" was misleading, a not infrequent occurrence. Of the nine players in the All-Stars' box score, several had seen "a cup of coffee" in "the bigs." The rest had not. The Giants won easily 7–0. "Hill," Wyatt wrote, "as always, showed good form."[39]

Not all public gatherings were subject to restraints. Some funerals continued to be held indoors, such as the one for Bruce Petway's brother, Howard, who died as the result of an operation. Howard's funeral was held at his residence in St. Paul, Minnesota, in late October and attended by many people.[40]

In spite of the loss of Lloyd, six players taken by the draft, the sudden addition of six new players, and the flu epidemic, Rube managed to lead the Giants to a first-place finish among western independent clubs—a cluster of topflight Black teams including, in addition to the Giants, the ABC's, Cuban Stars West, Dayton Marcos, and the Homestead Grays.[41] The raging flu finally shut down baseball during the 1918–1919 winter. The Giants did not travel to Cuba, Florida, or anywhere.

Indiscriminate Segregation at Royal Poinciana

One who did travel to Florida, however, was J.H. Murphy, editor and owner of the *Baltimore Afro-American*, a Black weekly newspaper. Murphy was in Palm Beach in March 1919, to attend a conference conducted by the Rev. John Hurst, the 36th bishop of the African-Methodist Church. Following the conference the two men, joined by Robert J. Young, a Baltimore resident and conductor of an orchestra which would provide the music for the Royal Poinciana's evening dance, and the Rev. George E. Carter, a minister in Palm Beach, had lunch at the hotel. The Black foursome encountered the same form of segregation as had the players. The group's lunch was not in the main dining room because, Murphy said, "we cannot eat in the main dining room." Blacks were not alone in being subject to discrimination. Murphy also noted that Jews, "no matter who they are or how wealthy ... are seated in a portion of the dining room closest to the kitchen and are not allowed to sit elsewhere. So, after all, the American white man's prejudice is not all directed at the Negro." Commenting on segregation generally, Murphy said of his impending trip back to Baltimore, "Much to our regret we will have to JIM CROW it again. But, well, we are down in the South and some day we hope things will be better." Murphy added "we had no invitations to the dance, so we contented ourselves looking at the decorations...." "The way the white folks danced," Murphy said, "reminded us very much of the Community Dances (in Baltimore) on Saturday and Wednesday evenings."[42]

Ball Parks Reopen

Baseball was back in business for the 1919 season. Fans turned out in record numbers as the flu was beginning to abate. On Opening Day, 8,000 saw the Giants shutout the White team, Rogers Park. Hundreds of Whites rooted for the Rogers Park nine. Games between the Giants and the Cubans proved especially popular. Twenty thousand filled Schorling's Park on Decoration Day (now Memorial Day) to see their favorites fall to the Cuban Stars.[43]

By the fall of 1919, the virus was on the wane, allowing people to congregate more safely.⁴⁴ The 25,000 spectators who saw the Giants lose a late August doubleheader to the Cubans in New York City's Dyckman Oval were in considerably less danger than they would have been a year earlier. The same went for the 15,000 who welcomed the team back from an Eastern trip to see them split a double header with their island brethren in early September.⁴⁵

8

President Wilson and the Suffragists

As the flu was thankfully on its way out, the fight in Congress to pass the 19th amendment to the U.S. Constitution assuring women of the right to vote was coming to a head. It had been a long time in the making. In nineteenth century America many, men and women alike, believed the realm of politics and governance belonged to men. Elizabeth Cady Stanton and Lucretia Mott, both social activists and abolitionists, challenged that belief in an August 1848 meeting of women supporters in Seneca Falls, New York.

Using the Declaration of Independence as her model, Stanton authored the Declaration of Sentiments. The document called for women-friendly reforms in education, employment, property rights, religion, and, most important of all, Stanton felt, in laws enabling all women to vote. Mott objected to the latter provision, saying, "Thou will make us ridiculous. We must go slowly." Stanton's husband, Henry, an aspiring lawyer, left town to avoid the appearance of supporting "a ridiculous idea." Stanton held firm. Without the right to vote, she insisted, women would lack the power to change anything.[1]

There were many things the women of Seneca Falls wanted to change. Among them were issues related to alcohol. Many had experienced the debilitating effects on their lives and those of their children brought on by a husband's overindulgence. They wanted the right to own property, to divorce a habitual drunken husband, to have husbands arrested for wife beating, and to protect the family's children from physical as well as psychological abuse. Many wanted the ubiquitous saloon shut down or, at least, somehow regulated. To accomplish these changes would require laws to be changed. To change laws they needed the vote, which was decades away.[2]

For the next 70 years the differences apparent at the Seneca Falls gathering grew in scope and intensity. By the turn of the century many women, known as "Antis," largely educated, married, White, and wealthy, opposed the idea of women voting. Women with interests outside the home were considered by some Antis to be "manly" or "unsexed." The Antis were as committed to their cause as the suffragists were to theirs. In 1903 both groups had opened headquarters in the nation's capital within a block of each other. Both brought large quantities of brochures, pamphlets, and banners destined for congressmen, senators, their staff, the White House, and anyone else they could find. The Antis, fearing the suffragists might take exception to the caustic nature of their literature and engage in violence, hired "the biggest watchman they could find." Seeing the private watchman guarding the Antis' headquarters, the suffragists responded in kind by "engaging the services of another physical giant."[3]

Years before ground zero migrated to the nation's capital, groups of "antis" organized groups at the local level (as had the suffragists). In Baltimore, for instance, women, and some men who agreed with them, formed the Association Opposed to Woman Suffrage in 1911; a more dignified title they thought than would be "an anti-suffrage" label. Members coalesced around the belief that the vote would not bring happiness and well-being to women. The business of women was to raise a family. There were enough men, after all, who could tend to the affairs of state and carry out any needed reforms to make for a better life for all. Working class women, the club's members assumed, would shun the ballot, fearing that if they voted marriage would elude them.[4]

The Antis weren't the only group who didn't want women to vote. Opponents included those whose financial success was insured by the saloon culture. The United States Brewers Association in 1909 adopted a resolution warning, "When the woman has the ballot, she will vote solid for prohibition." The president of the National Retail Liquor Dealers (several years later) in 1912 exhorted his members to realize that "Gentlemen, we need fear the Woman's Christian Temperance Union and the ballot in the hands of women; therefore gentlemen, fight woman suffrage!"[5]

The intense passion each group brought to their position was becoming well known around the country and had the effect of making some wary of engaging with them. The noted Captain Roald Amundsen was in Detroit in late February 1913 to attend ceremonies celebrating his recent discovery of the South Pole. When told that ten suffragists had bivouacked themselves on the hotel's parlor floor wanting an interview with him, the rugged explorer sent a polite note expressing his strong support for the women's vote but stating he preferred ten weeks at the South Pole rather than facing ten suffragists.[6]

President Wilson failed to give a full-throated endorsement of suffrage during his first term (1913–1916). Perhaps he had been put off by the massive suffragist parade down Pennsylvania Avenue in the nation's capital on March 3, 1913, the day before his first inauguration. Arriving at Washington's Union Station expecting to be greeted by cheering crowds, he and his aides were surprised to see only a few people on the platform to greet him. When someone asked, "Where are the people?" the answer was "They're at the parade." An estimated 500,000 spectators lined Pennsylvania Avenue. Many in the crowd showed their disagreement by pelting the largely women marchers, some six to ten thousand strong, with stones and cigar stubs while spitting at and tripping them. Many considered the publicity generated by the parade a major positive turning point in the struggle for women's suffrage.[7]

Encouraged by the publicity, a group of 550 suffragists embarked on a parade down Pennsylvania Avenue five weeks later, this time, as headlines blared, to "Invade the Halls of Congress," or "To Storm the Capitol." There was no violence. Both President Wilson and John Blackof, head of the Civil Service Commission, sent letters to organizers saying they had no objection to the march. Police promised much improved protection over what little had been available five weeks earlier. Each woman was to deliver a petition to a congressman or senator. Each petition bore the signatures of constituents from the legislator's district or state.[8]

Thousands cram sidewalks as suffragists march down Pennsylvania Avenue in Washington, D.C., on March 3, 1913, leaving President-elect Wilson to wonder why so few people greeted him on his arrival at Washington's Union Station (Library of Congress).

The petitions brought about no significant improvement in the suffragists' cause. The Antis kept up their opposition. At the beginning of America's involvement in World War I in 1917, the Antis argued that the push for suffrage detracted from the war effort. The Antis, however, were losing the day as women had won the right to vote in a dozen states. Almost two million had voted in the 1916 elections.[9]

Women, who had gained the right to vote flexed their political muscle, as many feared they would, by giving Prohibition a boost. Among the states where women had gained the right to vote in the 1910s were seven western states that had adopted Prohibition. Michigan's embrace of Prohibition was helped along by revelations that the anti-suffragist movement in the state had benefited from the generous financial support of the Macomb County Liquor Dealers Association. Given the right to vote in Texas' 1918 Democratic primary, women overwhelmingly supported the "dry" candidate, incumbent William Pettus Hobby, over ex-two term governor James E. "Pa" Ferguson, who was anything but "dry," by a margin of 10–1. Stung by his defeat, Ferguson retaliated with a claim that the women's votes were illegal. The votes were indeed legal, of course, and Ferguson remained defeated.[10]

Ferguson wasn't the only man frustrated and befuddled by the idea of women gaining the vote. Opposition to the mere idea of women voting alongside men found frequent expression in newspaper editorials such as this one in the *Philadelphia Tribune*, a Black weekly. The paper declared in 1915 that it "is heartily in favor of giving women all the legal protection they need as women." The writer did, however, draw the line "at giving them the equality in the home and the State which they are in no way physically or mentally capable of living up to." Such equality, the editorial concluded, "would lead to the destruction of the Christian home."[11]

Many women continued to voice their conviction that alcohol was a major contributor to the disintegration of the American family caused by men deserting their families, squandering the rent money on booze leading to evictions and poverty, beating wives in a drunken rage, and terrorizing children.[12] Ax-wielding Carry Nation was a well-publicized example of their antipathy to the tavern. Once they had access to the ballot box, they became a force for change, validating Stanton's belief that the vote was the most important reform discussed at the Seneca Falls meeting.

By 1916, editorials, marches, and protests, both for and against expanding women's suffrage, were commonplace. An example of both types of protest occurred when President Woodrow Wilson, campaigning for a second term, came to Chicago in October 1916. He spoke to 5,000 women supporters at the Auditorium Building, one of the Windy City's

8. President Wilson and the Suffragists

Suffrage supporters holding anti-Wilson signs on a Chicago street. Taken October 30, 1916 (Library of Congress).

largest. Outside the building anti–Wilson women suffragists yelled "Wilson is Against Women."

Suffragists attempted to hand out literature and banners supporting Wilson's Republican opponent, Charles Evan Hughes. Another group, including both men and women, yelling "get the banners" and wielding umbrellas and canes, destroyed as many banners as they could. After all the banners had been seized, police arrived to guard the suffragists, many with torn clothing and disheveled hair, as they marched back to their headquarters. Adding to the day's excitement was the city's Press Club's "colored waiters" demanding a fifty percent increase in pay before they would serve lunch to the chief executive and his party. They got their increase.[13]

The White House became an ever-popular site for protests. A memorable one occurred on July 4, 1917. Police arrested 13 women and four men on charges of unlawful assemblage. Ranging in age from 24 to 54, members of the National Women's Party, formed earlier in the year, came from as far away as Amarillo, Texas. Carrying banners and handing out pamphlets, they marched toward the White House gates followed by hundreds of cheering and jeering onlookers and the police. Officers ripped two banners away from the women. Lucy Burns, who had earned her protest spurs with an arrest in London in 1909 and had advocated for suffrage ever since, fought back and finally gained control of one of the banners. Another suffragist, Miss Kitty Marion, a German born actress with a keen interest in politics, landed several well thrown punches to the face of Charles Morgan, one of four men arrested, who tried to grab the leaflets she was handing out. A.L. Simpson, a D.C. resident opposed to suffrage, tore down another banner. Some of the crowd applauded him. Others booed. Shouts of they "have no sense," they are "idiots" could be heard. Those arrested spent the night in the detention center, the women without benefit of night clothes or toiletries. A local restaurant provided meals to all. Wilson was yachting on the Potomac River at the time. Eleven of the 13 women chose to spend three days in jail in lieu of paying a $25 fine assessed them at their trial on July 6. The remaining two were given separate trials. The men paid and were released.[14]

Finally, after more protests, marches, and arrests, Wilson, in a speech to Congress, declared his support for the Susan B. Anthony Amendment on January 9, 1918.[15] The president's endorsement stood in stark contrast to his anti-suffrage sentiments while president of his alma mater, Princeton University, expressed in a September 5, 1908, letter to Frederic Yates, an English painter who would paint a portrait of Wilson in 1914. In the letter Wilson stated that women could not render judgments on public affairs because they lacked the experience that men had gained, and that "married women could never get the necessary experience unless the present division of duties between husband and wife is to be absolutely altered."[16]

It was all coming to a head. On January 10, 1918, the House of Representatives passed the Amendment 274 to 136, exactly the two-thirds margin required. The Senate refused to vote for eight months, finally doing so on October 1, three months after Wilson had again expressed his support. In a June 7, 1918, letter to Carrie Chapman Catt, president of the International Woman Suffrage Alliance, Wilson completed coming full circle. He wrote "that the full and democratic reconstruction of the world for which we are striving [a reference to the nation's involvement in what Wilson had declared 'The war to end all wars'] … will not have been completely or adequately attained until women are admitted to the suffrage." He ended with his hope that the Senate would pass the amendment at its next session. The Amendment fell two votes short. More marches, protests and arrests around the White House and elsewhere followed. The Senate again took up the Amendment on February 10, 1919. Another vote in the Senate failed again but only by one vote.

The third time proved to be the charm. On June 4, by a vote of 56 to 25, the U.S. Senate passed the Amendment with two votes to spare. Moving with uncommon speed, the suffragists had ratifications in hand by

35 states by early August 1920. One more state was needed. On August 13, the Tennessee Senate voted for ratification by a resounding vote of 25 to 4. The House debated the issue for five days with the Speaker, Seth M. Walker, adamantly opposing passage. When finally taken, the vote ended in a 48–48 tie necessitating a second vote. Amidst the jawboning, horse trading, and arm twisting in the interim, Harry T. Burn, at 24 the youngest member, re-read the seven-page letter from his mother, Febb Burn. In it she urged her son "to be a good boy and vote aye." He had voted nay. When the Speaker Walker called his name a second time he voted "aye," breaking the tie. Then he raced up to the chamber's attic to hide until the protesting crowds dispersed and he could safely return home.[17]

Tennessee's ratification did not dissuade the Antis or the House members who had voted nay. Two weeks later, on August 31, 1920, with 20 members abstaining, the House reversed course to wipe the record clean and disavow the ratification vote. Many of those opposed to the amendment had been in Alabama when the first vote was taken and several pro–Democrats didn't arrive in the chamber in time for the second vote.[18]

The Antis immediately sprang into action, obtaining an injunction forbidding clerks in either Tennessee chamber from certifying the ratification. They also filed injunctions against the governor, the speaker of both Tennessee Houses, and the U.S. Secretary of State, Bainbridge Colby. They planned to get their injunction before the D.C. Court of Appeals and to the U.S. Supreme Court in a last-ditch effort to block the amendment before the upcoming November elections. The Antis knew that Connecticut was on the verge of ratifying the amendment. Of course, if Connecticut did vote for ratification, and the Antis' efforts in Tennessee were successful, the Nutmeg State would be the 36th to ratify the amendment and carry the day. Connecticut's ratification proved not to be necessary. Colby ruled that Tennessee's ratification could not be rescinded. After several formalities, the Susan B. Anthony Amendment became the 19th Amendment to the U.S. Constitution on August 26, 1920.[19] It read, "The rights of citizens of the United States to vote shall not be denied or abridged by the United States or by any State on account of sex."[20]

Even in light of the reality that the 19th amendment was the law of the land, the Antis still continued their fight while the suffragists celebrated. The Antis desperately, and unsuccessfully, argued that ratification had been illegal in five states—Missouri, New Hampshire, Arkansas, West Virginia, and, of course, Tennessee. Hence, they argued that the requisite 36 state ratifications had not taken place. All came to naught.[21]

Many women cast a ballot for the first time on November 2, 1920, joining women from the 20 states that had granted the right when the suffrage movement worked state by state.

As momentous as the 19th Amendment was, its ratification did not clear a path for all women to vote. It would be four years before Native American women were considered citizens with voting rights. It would take even longer for some Asian-American women to achieve the same status. Many Black women were prevented from voting by the same Jim Crow practices as literary tests and poll taxes that had blocked the path to the polls of their husbands, grandfathers, uncles, and sons since the 15th Amendment, giving Black men the right to vote, was ratified in 1870. Not until 1965 were such hindrances declared unconstitutional by the Voting Rights Act of 1965, which barred racially discriminatory practices at the polls.[22]

Dissent Within the Ranks

The suffrage movement itself had been besieged by racial tensions, a striking example of which was the proposal for all Black women to march as a separate unit while White women would march with their state delegations in the first organized suffragist procession in the nation's capital on March 3, 1913. A vocal group of Southern women had refused to march with Black women. Susan B. Anthony, in an effort to avoid alienating them, agreed. One who disagreed, and told Anthony so, was Ida B. Wells-Barnett. A Chicago resident at the time, she had long used her voice and pen to oppose lynching and segregation in all its forms. As a newspaper reporter, owner, and editor she made her views widely known. In Chicago she worked with Jane Addams, a Nobel Prize–winning social activist and reformer well known for her Hull House in an underprivileged area of Chicago.

Barnett insisted on marching with the Illinois delegation. "Either I go with you or not at all," she told the Illinois delegation. "I am not taking this stand because I personally wish for recognition. I am doing it for the future benefit of my whole race." She won her point. All African American women marched with their state delegations in the parade that had so surprised Wilson. In that same year she organized the first suffrage club for African American women, the Alfa Suffrage Club.[23]

Where Foster, Hill and other players stood on the issue of women's suffrage is not known. There is reason to believe Rube's wife, Sarah, supported the cause. As a newly-elected Second Vice President of the City Federation of Women's Club, Sarah may well have been involved in arranging for Barnett to address the group. "Suffrage" was to be the topic of her talk. The Federation scheduled its meeting for March 1, 1913, just two days before the suffrage march in Washington, which made Barnett's participation in the meeting impossible. Another speaker addressed the topic.[24]

9

Pete Hill on His Own

As the 19th Amendment was wending its way through the states in search of ratification, all of the Giants' draftees had returned to the States before the 1919 season ended. All were in good health and with proud records of service. Fortunately, they had a job to return to; not all returning veterans did. Four continued with the Giants. They were Pitcher Tom Johnson, who had served as a lieutenant in the 365th Infantry Division; infielder Jude Gans, a lieutenant with the 59th French Division where he learned the language and wowed the women. Infielder Leroy Grant and shortstop Bobby (Rawhide) Williams, who served with the 803rd Pioneer Infantry in France. Richard (Cannonball) Redding saw combat in France but signed with the Bacharach Giants on his return, and pitcher Frank Wickware saw his career slide downhill after his return. He signed with the newly created Detroit Stars. Hill, at age 35 in 1917, was above the then-maximum draft age (31).[1]

In August of 1918, just three months before the war ended, Congress increased the maximum conscription age to 45, keeping available the choice to work, in an "essential" job, or join the military. In September, Hill, joined by teammates Méndez and Petway, registered for the draft. By that time all three had suddenly acquired a job; Hill and Petway as laborers in the civilian department in the U.S. Army's Quartermasters Corps at 3rd and Iron streets in Chicago, and Méndez as a cigar maker, perhaps a reflection of his Cuban heritage. He listed Rube Foster as his supervisor. Foster, age 38, also registered for the draft in September of 1918. He gave "Ball Player" as his occupation and listed "Mr. Schorling" as his supervisor. How cigar making, or baseball for that matter, were considered essential jobs is not clear. All stayed in the Windy City for the war's duration.[2]

1919 and a New Team

With the war over, spring training for the 1919 season went on as usual. Cold, blustery, spring winds swept over Schorling's Park, where

Foster had assembled 40 players. They would form the rosters of two teams, the Giants, and a new team conceived of by Foster, the Detroit Stars. Rube selected Detroit for a new team because its Black population had grown by 800 percent, 5,000 to 40,000 from 1910 to 1919.[3] Ironically, the same upsurge in black populations in Eastern and Midwest cities that provided Black baseball with an ever-enlarging fan base would also contribute to racial unrest and riots in the years to come.

Rube picked his dependable captain, Pete Hill, to manage the Stars. Rube said of Hill at the time, "He has been captain of the team for twelve years and has at times been as far as 1,000 miles from me and he could always ... bring home the bacon." Wanting to ensure a strong Detroit team that would attract flocks of paying customers, Foster offered no resistance as Hill chose five Giants to accompany him and the remaining players, to the Motor City; Frank Duncan, a consistent hitting outfielder with the same "nervy" antics on the bases as Hill; Bruce Petway, a catcher whose powerful arm kept runners "hugging their bases"; pitcher Frank Wickware, the Giants' ace for most of the 1910–1918 seasons, but whose fondness for booze irritated Foster; power hitter and rookie first baseman Edgar Wesley; and Cuban-born José Méndez, who could pitch and play shortstop with equal and outstanding ability.[4]

Joining Méndez on the mound was John Donaldson, who once pitched three straight no-hitters, and whose prowess at the plate earned him a starting outfield position when not pitching.[5] Hill had a promising roster at his disposal. It should be noted that the departure of 36-year-old Hill from Foster's roster did not hurt the Giants' chances. Replacing him in the outfield was 22-year-old Oscar Charleston for his only year with the Giants.[6] Elwood (Bingo) DeMoss, whom historian Riley considered the greatest Black second baseman in the first quarter of the twentieth century, took over the Giants' captain role, a position he would hold for six years.[7]

Previously a quiet superstar in Foster's shadow, Hill's new role substantially enhanced his visibility. He took to his new challenge with pride and gusto. He promised fans that the Stars "would show the world they are the best."[8] "I am firmly of the belief," the Stars' player/manager added a week before Opening Day, "that I have the best team. Look at my men. They hit, play teamwork, and are fast runners. Listen to me name them: Marcell, third base; Méndez, shortstop; Warfield, second base; Wesley, first base; Hewitt, right field, Hill, center field; Duncan, left field; Petway or Rodriquez, catcher; Wickware, Crawford, or 'Dicta' Johnson, pitchers."[9] With those words Hill ignited a rivalry, which he and Rube hoped would swell attendance in both cities when the two teams met.

9. Pete Hill on His Own

The newly formed Stars entrained for Detroit from Chicago in mid-April amidst a crowd of well-wishers including Foster and "Window Washer Woods," a rabid Giants fan who had circulated and then withdrew a petition asking Rube not to send the new team to the Motor City. Woods, whose nickname was derived from his occupation, was a constant presence at Giants events. At a "peace table" held in the box office of Schorling's Park a week before the Stars left for Detroit, Woods had changed his mind and announced himself "satisfied" with the two teams. Rube responded that if Woods—who, a *Defender* reporter said, "knows more about baseball than Spaulding" (that is Albert Spalding, White, a pitcher, manager, executive, and sports equipment entrepreneur during the early days of professional baseball)—is satisfied then sweet dreams." At the train station, Woods gave a bouquet of roses to Méndez, his favorite player.[10]

Another well-wisher was Hill's Philadelphia Giants manager, Sol White. Upon hearing the news, White wrote, "Bully for Hilly. We are sure Pete will make good as a leader of baseball fellows. He is one of the boys especially fitted for a position of that kind and we wish him well."[11] A local Chicago magazine founded in 1915, *The Half Century,* whose title commemorated the 50th anniversary of the passage of the Thirteenth Amendment outlawing slavery, also wished Hill well. "The city will lose one of its athletic landmarks," the article said. The writer went on to predict, "If he can import his own ability to sense plays, his own foxiness in outguessing pitchers, and coolness under fire, Detroit will be placed on the semi-professional baseball map."[12]

As business manager of the Stars, Rube chose a friend, John T. "Tenny" Blount, to oversee the franchise. Blount managed scheduling, transportation, and lodging arrangements for the players. Rube's new partner owned the Detroit-based Union Card Club, a gambling casino. Before coming to Detroit in 1914 he was famous in Chicago for operating a similar establishment in Chicago's Keystone Hotel. The Stars administrator, born in Montgomery, Alabama, in 1871, was notable for his honesty and light skin. One of his players said, "He was the squarest of men. I never worked for anyone better. If you worked, you got paid." His light complexion allowed him to "pass" when he wanted to.[13]

He had done well for himself. By 1919 a chauffeur-driven, custom-built Marmon Big Eight limousine reportedly worth $10,000 ($148,000 in 2020), was his preferred mode of travel. His chauffeur, Frank Williams, happily drove the machine at the highest possible speeds between Detroit and Chicago for game days. The sportsman entertained lavishly. Following one game he treated Rube and two sportswriters to dinner at Detroit's famous Biltmore Hotel. The Giants had just taken a double header from the Stars, but the twin losses did not embitter Blount. He treated Rube to a five-pound steak, half a watermelon, and a quart of iced tea, and he hosted Rube in his home overnight.[14]

Blount lived just a few blocks from John A. Roesink, a 39-year-old Dutch Jew, the city's foremost promoter of athletic events, and owner of a successful men's clothing store. The Stars' white uniforms, trimmed in blue, with a large red star sewn over the left breast were designed by Roesink. The uniforms had no number or name on the back. A man with a megaphone announced starting lineups and substitutions as was the custom at the time. Roesink was also a baseball buff. He had built Mack Park, the Star's home field, in 1914 as an arena for the "Roesink S & S Team" and industrial teams throughout the city. The park sat at Mack and Fairview Avenues in a White working-class neighborhood about four miles east of Black Bottom—a neighborhood of 60 square blocks and home to most of Detroit's Blacks. A single deck wooden structure with bleachers and theater-style seating, Mack Park could accommodate 6,000. Three thousand more could be placed in roped-off outfield areas and inside the foul lines. The field's short right field fence, 325 feet from home plate, appealed to Hill and other left-handed swatters. Blount's lease of the park allowed the Stars to play there whenever they wanted.[15]

Opening Day

Detroit eagerly awaited the Stars' arrival and their Opening Day game on Easter Sunday, April 20, 1919. Long home to the major leagues' Detroit Tigers, the Stars would be the city's first Black team of significance. "On every corner," the *Defender* reported, "one can hear the fans talking about Capt. Pete Hill and his 'Prairie Devils.'" A delegation from Chicago, including Rube and the *Defender*'s sports editor, as well as fans from numerous Michigan towns including Madison, Flint, and Mount Clemens, attended the inaugural festivities in the newly refurbished Mack Park.[16]

On the eve of Opening Day, Hill announced, "There is one thing sure, we are going to give them [fans] a rattling good time ... and they [the players] will be ready to bring home the bacon."[17] The Stars got off to a fast start, winning their opener by beating the Maxwell Internationals, Detroit's White city champions, in front of 3,500 cheering spectators.[18]

After the opener, the pride of Buena, Virginia, now 37 and starting as usual in centerfield, had quickly gotten the Stars off to an eye-popping start by winning 11 games through the month of May and into early June. One of his contributions came in the second game in the form of a blast over the centerfield fence of Mack's Park; a feat equaled only once before in the Park's history. The White players of Norway Motors, from Norway,

Michigan, lost that game 3–2. The Stars' next opponent, the Knights of Columbus, fared no better.[19]

Throughout the winning streak, anticipation was building among players and fans alike in advance of a seven-game series to start on June 15 at Schorling's Park between the Stars and the Giants. The games were to be a showdown between Rube and Pete. The *Defender* promised a rivalry "such as never been seen before" that will draw more people "than had ever seen two Colored teams meet."[20] Writing in the third person to the paper a week before the start of the games, Hill declared "Old man Pete is as spry as ever and hitting in old time form to date. Pete has hit four home runs, two off the Cubans in one game. Pete says a man is as old as he feels, hence he will never get old." Blount promised, Hill said, "that his men are going to make Uncle Rube bite the dust." Pete closed by saying he missed "old 39th and Wentworth Avenue … but a change of climate sometimes does a fellow good."[21]

The attendance was as predicted for game one, 15,000, but it was the Stars who bit the dust. Whitworth shut them out 3–0, throwing a two hitter. Hill collected both, a double and a single.[22] The Stars bounced back as the series continued with the games alternating between the two cities. The seventh and final game took place in Detroit on August 8. Hill's Stars took the measure of Rube's Giants 10–6, giving the Stars their fifth straight win over the Giants to capture the series, five games to two. Hill committed a rare error in that game but also crushed a pitch from Tom Johnson for one of the Stars' two four-baggers.[23]

Chicago Riots

In the midst of the series which Pete was enjoying enormously, a race riot exploded in Chicago. Tensions between Whites and Blacks on Chicago's south Side had been bubbling for years with the occasional bomb explosion and fistfight. The Black population had nearly tripled from 44,000 in 1910 to 110,000 in 1919. Most lived in or near the Black Belt which sat next to warehouses and the industrial district and included the stockyards. Segregation remained rigidly intact. Attitudes of some Whites toward Blacks were on full display at the ballparks. Shouts from the grandstands of "Nigger!" "Gimmie a shine, coon!" and "Go back to the cotton fields, monkey!" were not uncommon.[24]

Chicago was not the only site of violence. Towns, counties and cities from Nebraska to Texas and Connecticut to California saw mobs of Whites attacking Blacks. At least 52 Blacks died by lynching. Some were burned to death. In total, 1919 saw 25 major riots in which hundreds of people, mostly Black, were killed. Thousands were injured. Tens of thousands fled their homes. Businesses lost millions to looting and forced closures. Perpetrators in Chicago tended to be sailors on leave, slaughterhouse workers, and Southern White farmers.[25]

In Chicago, tensions between Whites and Blacks burst into a full-blown race riot on July 27. The trigger was a crudely made raft of wood planks tied together with rope by five Black teenagers. They stored it at a little-known inlet they called "hot and cold." The Michael Keely Brewery shot hot water into the inlet while the nearby Consumers Ice Company injected tons of cold water. The boys hopped on their raft, drifted into Lake Michigan, and slowly and unknowingly floated towards a Whites only beach. Moments before, a Black group had tried to swim in the White area but were driven off by a fuselage of rocks. One of the Whites, George Stauber, spotted the raft approaching and started throwing rocks at the boys. One of his rocks struck one of the boys, Eugene Williams, on his forehead. Williams fell into the water and drowned.[26]

Pleas to arrest Stauber fell on the deaf ears of Chicago patrolmen who arrived on the scene, Daniel Callahan, Dennis S. Keating, Dominick Feency, and Richard Sinnott. Two detectives, however, did arrest Stauber as a free-for-all broke out between Blacks and Whites on the beach. The melee soon mushroomed into a three-day riot that started in the Black Belt, on the city's south side and spread to the north side and the Loop. Mobs of Whites overturned cars, smashed windows, and started fires. Shots fired by both police and citizens injured hundreds; 23 Blacks and 15 Whites died.

Emily Frankenstein, a 20-year-old student at the University of Chicago and daughter of physician Victor Frankenstein, recorded her impressions and opinions about the riots in her journal. Adding to the racial tensions a week before the riots, Frankenstein noted, was the strangulation of six-year-old Janet Wilkinson, a White grocer's daughter, in the basement of the apartment building where Emily and her parents lived. The perpetrator, Thomas Fitzgerald, Black, a custodian at the nearby Virginia Hotel and a resident of the Frankenstein's apartment building, hid her body under a pile of coal in the apartment's basement. The "entire Chicago police force and thousands of volunteers," according to the *Baltimore Sun*, had searched days for Janet before finding her body. An Associated Press article in *The Washington Post* said, "Seldom has the populace been so aroused over a criminal case here." One Chicago newspaper put up a $2,500 dollar reward. Janet's father offered $500.[27] Emily's prediction that "His trial will be speedy," proved true. On September 22 Judge Robert Crowe sentenced Fitzgerald to be hanged at the Cook County Jail on October 27. Federal Judge Kenesaw Mountain Landis, soon to be appointed commissioner of major league baseball in the wake of Chicago White Sox players throwing the recently completed World Series, denied Fitzgerald's wife's request for a stay of execution. He went before the largest crowd to ever witness an execution in Chicago.[28]

Emily's father saw some of the rioting up close. He reported hearing gunshots and seeing people scurrying down alleys on his way home from making a call at the Vincennes Hotel. Emily laid out who she perceived to be the cause of the riot. "The rioters," Emilie wrote, "were mostly the unruly element of the employees of the stockyards; the colored people who have been brought up north recently and overstepped their freedom and privileges and thought they were better than white folks. And some of the rowdy white toughs, etc. took it on themselves to seek revenge on the innocent colored. Especially so was an athletic club of tough white fellows. [No doubt Ragen's Colts described below.] Four of their numbers were killed and they declared to kill 100 negroes for every one of their 4 killed." She described a fire "back of the [stock] yards. Hundreds of the little homes of the white people, poor and hard-working were burned out. It could not be determined whether it was started by colored men or white men disguised as colored men.... Many innocent black families were escorted under police protection to railroad stations to go back south."[29] Whether any did could not be determined.

Police and more than 2,000 national guardsmen finally established order in the city. They patrolled the Black Belt for more than a week before withdrawing. People returned to jobs at the stockyards and elsewhere.[30]

A Chicago commission charged with determining the cause of the riots singled out the Ragen's Colts as chief instigators. Formed in the early 1900s as an independent White baseball club named after one of its pitchers, Frank Ragen, the group had become a 2,000-member street gang by 1918. Largely Irish but also including Italian, Jewish, and Polish youths, the gang came to dominate the Chicago underworld by the late 1920s, working closely with Al Capone. In 1917, however, Ragen's Colts still fielded a baseball team. The Giants faced them twice that year in October. The Colts' star pitcher Ed Corey, whose 1918 cup of coffee with the White Sox amounted to one, two-inning appearance, held Rube's men to five hits, winning the first encounter 2–1. Two weeks later the tables turned with an 11-hit 12–4 Giants win. Hill went hitless in both games.[31]

The Colts' baseball activities subsided as they turned their attention to crime. In 1926 a *Chicago Defender* editorial would describe their role in the 1919 riots as one of "waylaying women in the streets, abusing then, torturing children ... and keeping white people fired with a desire to kill." The same editorial described them at that time as "an organization of cut-throats, thugs, gunmen, and general outlaws operating under the name of an athletic club." The paper decried the impunity with which they operated and concluded "They should be disbanded."[32]

A grand jury handed down indictments against 51 individuals (31 Blacks and 20 Whites). Charges included murder, assault with intent to kill, conspiracy to riot, and carrying concealed weapons. The Civil Service Commission tried the patrolmen in October. Eight rioters faced trials in Criminal Court.[33]

In addition to negligence of duty, Patrolman Callahan was charged with firing his pistol at random and leading a group down a railroad track yelling "Let's get the dirty niggers." Sinnott was charged with deliberately firing his gun at a Black boy at the suggestion of a White bystander and wounding him twice in his legs. Two White officers and two White civilians testified in support of the patrolmen. One of the civilians, J.D. Baker, used the term "nigger" repeatedly in his testimony until Major R.R. Jackson, sitting in the courtroom, complained. The Commission acquitted the four patrolmen of all charges. A jury in Criminal Court acquitted Stauber of murder charges.[34] Of the eight Blacks tried in Cook County on riot-related charges, three received a life sentence, one was sentenced to 20 years, and four won their freedom.[35]

Riots and the Giants

The Giants were in Detroit when the riots started. They had outplayed the Stars 7–1 in Navin Field, home to the Detroit Tigers, while the Tigers were on the road. A record of the players' reactions to the riots could not be found, but they were certainly aware of them—if not through phone calls from friends and family then from the headline in the *Detroit Free Press* the following day, "Race Riots Spread Over Negro Belt." The lead story told of a "Negro" found fatally wounded only a few blocks west of Schorling's Park, and of three Blacks dragged off street cars and beaten to the point where their skulls had been fractured. Many of the Giants lived in or near the Black Belt, including Bruce Petway, Jose Méndez, and Hill.

The riots had seemingly little impact on the players. The dinner that Tenny Blount hosted for Foster and two *Defender* sportswriters took place during the riots. The games continued until the seven-game series had been completed on August 3. Two of the *Detroit Press*'s headlines that week read, "Negroes Fleeing Chicago As Fury of Battle Increases" and "Troops Lent to Stop Chicago War as Mobs Kill Seven." The Giants could not return home to face the Bacharach Giants as scheduled because the militia was camped out in Schorling's Park, located in the Black Belt. The troops took good care of the Park, which suffered only minor damage. The Atlantic

City Bacharachs canceled their western trip. Some of the American Giants may have returned home for several days before returning to Detroit for a two-game series July 10–11. Foster had scheduled a month-long series of games in the East starting on July 13. They went on as planned. The Giants visited Pittsburgh, Philadelphia, New York, Cincinnati, and Dayton. Before leaving Detroit, Rube took custody of a new car presented to him by the Maxwell Automobile Company, which sponsored a White semi-pro team that played against many of the best Black teams. The accompanying plaque saluted Rube's "character as a ball player and a businessman." The Giants would not return home until August 31.[36]

Riots Elsewhere

Chicago was not the only city beset by race riots in 1919. A similar four-day disorder had occurred in Washington, D.C., a week earlier from July 19–23. At President Woodrow Wilson's command, an army and a Marine battalion took to the streets to restore order. Three tanks and loaded machine guns were held in reserve. Six people were killed, 50 men and women severely injured, and hundreds suffered lesser injuries. Other riots occurred that summer in more than three dozen cities, including Knoxville, Tennessee; Longview, Texas; Norfolk, Virginia; Philadelphia; Charleston; and Bishop, Arizona.[37]

Red Summer

The time during which most of the riots occurred, late summer to the fall of 1919, is known as Red Summer, a term coined by NAACP activist and author James Weldon Johnson. Feelings were running high between Whites and Blacks. Working class Whites felt increasingly resentful of Blacks as competition for jobs increased. To replace White workers drafted into the service, many Northern companies recruited Black workers from the South, starting the Great Migration which lasted until 1940. The country was in an economic slump following World War I. The demobilization of veterans, both Black and White, was done quickly and without any planning for absorbing veterans into jobs.[38]

Black Voices and New Fears

Blacks were taking a more assertive stance demanding equality and racial justice. Among the leading Black voices in Chicago was that of Major Jackson, who years earlier had managed a team for Leland and helped him establish the "Chateau de la Plaisance." Now Jackson was a member of Chicago's City Council and president of the Colored Knights of Pythias, a national organization fostering peace and harmony among men brought into being by the White Knights refusal to allow Blacks to join their organization. In a September 1919 speech to the organization's annual convention in Atlantic City, Jackson gave voice to the feelings of many in attendance. He said, "Let me say to the world that twelve million people of our race kept the fires of America burning. Let us keep them burning until we burn up every Jim Crow sign and every Jim Crow car in this country."[39]

Blended with racial tensions was the fear on the part of a growing number of Whites that Blacks were turning to communism following the 1917 Bolshevik revolution in Russia.[40] President Wilson fanned the flames with his assertion "that the American Negro returning from abroad would be our greatest medium in conveying Bolshevism to America."[41] Times were tense.

The Games Continue

The tensions sweeping the country were reflected at the ballpark in the racial slurs voiced by some White spectators, but the games continued. As the season entered late September, Hill, now touted by *The Defender* as "the slugging demon of the Stars," led his players to a sweep of a doubleheader over the Cubans, with two triples in game one and two round-trippers in the second. The Stars team, the *Defender* announced, "Was playing better and faster ball than most semi-pro teams in the country."[42]

A Scandal

As Hill's first season in Detroit wound down and the 1918 flu was losing its deadly impact, Game One of the 1919 World Series between the Chicago White Sox and the Cincinnati Reds was played at Redland Field in the Queen City, so named by early-nineteenth-century settlers to connote Cincinnati's rapid economic and cultural growth.[43] The Reds prevailed in the Series, 5 games to 3. The games became known as the Black Sox Scandal of 1919. Rumored to be the case but not known for sure at the time, eight Chicago White Sox players took money from gamblers to throw the Series. The rumors did nothing to dampen the public's interest in the Series. A total of 236,928 people attended the games in person while crowds of upwards of 15,000 jammed New York City's Time Square to follow the games on the Square's scoreboard.[44]

The rumors were proven true a year later. The newly-appointed Commissioner of Baseball, Kenesaw Mountain Landis, formerly a federal judge in Chicago, who, until his death in 1944 kept the majors segregated, banned all eight from major league baseball forever.

Hill's Second Season as Manager

Hill's first season as a club pilot was a resounding success. The Stars reportedly won 62 games while losing 18 for a .775 mark.[45] The team from the Motor City faced all the strongest eastern and Midwest teams: the American Giants, the Hilldale Club of Darby, Pennsylvania, the Bacharach Giants of Atlantic City, the Cuban Stars, Chicago Giants, and Dayton Marcos. The Stars lost only one series, that to Rube's Giants, and had the best won-loss record of any of them.[46]

Writing again in the third person to *The Defender*, the Stars' manager waxed enthusiastic over the upcoming 1920 campaign. He noted, referring to the season just past, "It was Hill's first year ... and even greater things are expected of him the coming season for he is a pretty wise old bird having played under the old master, Rube Foster." Two newly-discovered Texans, a pitcher, whose name Hill did not disclose, but who surely was Andy Cooper, who would eventually join Hill in Cooperstown, and a third baseman further buoyed his optimism. The new man at the hot corner shared the manager's last name. "It is said," wrote Hill in his letter to the *Defender*, "that all Hills can play ball." While no doubt true, the Texas infielder, Johnson Hill, wouldn't play for the Stars until 1921 and would show up again playing for Hill with the Milwaukee Bears in 1923. Pete Hill said he was wintering in Detroit and would make the city his new home. He promised he would again try to break Babe Ruth's home run record, having fallen just one short in 1919.[47]

There was no one better than the Bambino to compare oneself to when it came to home runs. Both hit from the left side of the plate. Pitchers feared both. Ruth had set a new major league home run record in 1919, his last year with the Red Sox, with 29 in 130 games. Noted Black baseball historian Gary Ashwill credits Hill with 28 homers in 80 games. Sixteen of Hill's home runs were against good Black teams. Twelve were against lesser competition. Fourteen were hit in 27 home games at Mark Park, whose short right field fence Hill had mastered.

That Hill was an exceptional hitter and would have starred in the majors had it not been for the color barrier is beyond question. At age 37 he still had plenty of pop in his bat. While with Detroit he hit two of the longest home runs over the centerfield fence ever seen at Mack Park and the longest homer ever seen at Atlantic Park, home of the Bacharach Giants in Atlantic City, New Jersey.[48] What remains in doubt, as is often the case when comparing Black baseball performances with those of major leaguers, is the accuracy of the comparison. Could Hill have stroked 27 homers in 80 games against major league pitching in 1919? How many homers could Ruth have swatted against Black baseball pitching in 1919? We will never know.

Racial Tensions Remain High

Though the rioting in 1919 had been quelled, tensions remained high in Chicago. A March 25, 1920, telegram from John R. Shillay, secretary of the NAACP in New York City, to Illinois Governor Frank Orren Lowden and Chicago Mayor William "Big Bill" Hale Thompson urged the two to "avert threatened race friction" in the city. The bombing of Black residences that created bitterness among Blacks determined to defend their families prompted the telegram. The message had no effect.[49]

Two Chicago race riots flared up in 1920. One in June started after a group of Blacks on their way to a meeting to discuss returning to Africa blocked a street with a bonfire and burned an American flag. The second in September began after a group of three Blacks slit the throat of a White man sitting on his porch. In each case bands of Whites roamed the Black Belt overturning trolley cars and pummeling Black riders. Fights between Blacks and Whites involving fists and sticks broke out everywhere. Police restored order repeatedly.[50]

10

Finally: A League for Black Baseball

Amidst the rioting, Foster was putting the final touches on his plans for an organized league of the best Midwestern Black teams.

Ten years earlier in New Orleans in late December 1910, Felix S. Payne, Black politician, gambler, night club owner, newspaper publisher, bon vivant, and one-time owner of the Kansas City (Kansas) Giants, had been elected as the temporary secretary of the proposed Negro National Baseball League and Beauregard F. Moseley as temporary president. To be headquartered in Chicago, the eight-team league would consist of one club in eight different cities: Chicago; Louisville; New Orleans; Mobile; St. Louis; Kansas City, Missouri; Kansas City, Kansas; and Columbus, Ohio. Each owner would contribute $300 to fund a treasury. A pool of players to populate the teams would be agreed upon by the owners.

The group also resolved that one-half of the umpires would be Black and would be paid $5 a game. While Foster did not include this resolution in his proposal, he was an active supporter of Black umpires. Representatives from the eight cities elected Moseley, Payne, and Frank Walker, the New Orleans representative, to an executive committee to work out the details. The league never came to fruition, perhaps because, as historian Larry Lester has suggested, transportation costs of getting teams to league cities would be too expensive.[1]

Rube, who had developed a relationship with Payne, wanted a league that would be owned and operated by "Race men." Such a circuit, he argued, would bring stability to scheduling, stem the constant jumping of players from one team to another, and eliminate the stranglehold exercised by middlemen who allowed access to parks they controlled only for a sizeable fee. Nat Strong, a White, Jewish New Yorker was, for instance, thought to have controlled 150 parks in the East. In a typical arrangement 10 percent of the gate went to the middleman, 65 percent to the team owners or $500 to each team, whichever was less, and never more that 25 percent to the players.² Hill's success in Detroit in a park not controlled by a middleman was the most recent sign that Black baseball could stand on its own financially. *Defender* sportswriter Cary B. Lewis reported seeing crowds of 10,000 spectators paying "professional baseball prices" for tickets to Stars games in July of 1919.³

Team Owners Meet

On February 13, 1920, at the Paseo YMCA in Kansas City, Missouri, the Father of Negro League Baseball convened a meeting of selected team owners, sportswriters Dave Wyatt and Cary B. Lewis from Chicago, Elwood C. Knox from Indianapolis, and attorney Elisha Scott from Topeka, Kansas. Scott was nationally known for his wit and dramatization in the courtroom. He was the winning attorney in school desegregation cases in Coffeyville and Weir City, Kansas, and was instrumental in the federal government's granting the first ever charter to a Black corporation for a national bank.⁴

The red-brick building was not only spacious but one of the few facilities catering to Blacks. The Y was the only place in Kansas City where Black clubs, Boy Scouts, Bible and other study groups could meet, and where Blacks could play basketball and swim. Blacks also found lodging, a dining hall, a cafeteria, and meeting rooms at the Y. The building opened in 1914. Julius Rosenwald, a Sears and Roebuck executive, made a generous start-up donation. Funds raised by both Blacks, including Payne, and Whites made up the difference. Payne hosted Rube and his wife Sarah during their stay in the city.⁵

Foster led the Kansas City deliberations. He charged the sportswriters and Scott to fashion the new circuit's constitution, referred to as "the baseball bill of rights." The foursome also agreed to serve as arbitrators of any disputes. Charter members of the league, in addition to Foster, were C.I. Taylor, Indianapolis ABCs; John "Tenny" Blount, Detroit Stars; Lorenza Cobb, St. Louis Giants; John Matthews, Dayton Marcos, who sent a note saying he was ill but would abide by the group's decisions; J.L. Wilkerson (White), Kansas City Monarchs; and Joe Green, Chicago Giants. Leland died in 1914. Control of the team went to former Chicago Giants player Green. Though initially wanting a group of all "Race men" owners, Foster made an exception for Wilkinson based on his successful experience with the multi-ethnic All-Nations Club and his strong Kansas City Monarchs club, which could be expected to draw large crowds throughout the circuit. Foster represented the Cuban Giants, who associated themselves with the league as an independent team. Other associate teams included

10. Finally: A League for Black Baseball

the Hilldale Club from Darby, Pennsylvania, the Atlantic City Bacharach Giants, and the Cuban Stars of the East. Owners of the associated clubs ponied up $1,000 each.

Each charter member signed the constitution and contributed $500 ($6,500 in 2021 dollars) to create the league's treasury. The group elected Foster as league president, a position for which he felt himself uniquely qualified.[6] In a letter to the *Defender* two months in advance of the meeting, Foster laid out his experiences as a successful team owner. He took those who promoted games to task for their naïveté and lack of understanding of the game's finances. "They forget," he wrote immodestly but probably correctly, "that I have been a player, whose intellect and brains of the game have drawn more comment from all the leading baseball critics than all the Colored players combined.... They do not know, as I do, that there are not five players nor three owners among the clubs who know the playing rules.... If we are to advance, we must do so under leadership that has been tried and proved able."[7] His letter left no doubt who Rube thought had the requisite leadership skills to take charge of the newly-created Negro National League. The other executives were C.I. Taylor, treasurer; and J. Leslie Wilkinson, secretary.[8]

Rube served as an unsalaried president, but he did not go uncompensated. He collected five percent of all league game receipts.[9] He distributed the monies in ways that benefited both the league and himself. Some of the funds provided financial stability to the teams, the lack of which had caused some to go under. Rube also used the money to support players' salaries to prevent them from "jumping"; for transportation costs and hotel bills for teams stranded on the road due to canceled games; and for ballpark rentals. He established a schedule of games among the league's teams with an eye to maximizing revenues. As Negro League historian Leslie Heaphy has said of Rube's strategy, "You're not going to bring the Detroit Wolves (a lower-tier Black team) to Chicago on the weekend; you're going to bring the Kansas City Monarchs to get the best crowd and then your team is going to make the most money."[10]

In another financial move, Rube bought bats, baseballs, and other equipment at wholesale prices and mandated that owners buy the items from him at retail, the difference going to the league treasury. Other executives initially balked at Foster's financial initiatives but eventually realized joining forces held out more of a promise of success than did going it alone. The newly-elected league president conducted the league's business out of a refurbished automobile garage on Chicago's Indiana Avenue between 33rd and 34th streets which he renamed the American Giants Garage.[11]

To prevent one or two teams from dominating the NNL, which Rube thought would cause fans to lose interest and teams, thereby, to lose money, Foster directed the sportswriters to assign players to each team with an eye to spreading the talent evenly among them.[12] The writers presumably did as Rube asked, but it should be noted his Giants won the 1920–1923 league championships, perhaps another testament to the abilities of the man as a manager.

In the process of bringing a measure of order to the leading Midwest Black teams, the NNL was the first league to survive more than a year, Foster made out well himself. Rube reportedly earned $11,200 (over $142,000 in 2021 dollars) in 1920[13] and admitted to clearing $22,000 in 1922.[14] His earnings allowed him to purchase what he considered to be "one of the finest homes in Chicago (3242 Vernon Avenue)," a Chrysler "runabout" and an Apperson Jack Rabbit sedan, both of which he enjoyed driving on Illinois' highways and byways at upwards of 70 miles an hour.[15] He also enjoyed the feel of cash. In his earlier days he carried substantial sums in his wallet until 1914 when a pickpocket relieved him of $600 ($15,000 in 2020 dollars) while he and 25 ball players were on a Chicago streetcar.[16]

Sarah Foster

Rube's constant travel put the child-rearing and household duties on Sarah, his "Smoochie." She supported Rube's baseball endeavors and was pleased by his financial success. Their home sat on the edge of Hyde Park about seven miles south of downtown Chicago and a few blocks from Lake Michigan. Sarah maintained an active social life. By 1913 she had been elected second vice president of the City Federation of Women's Clubs, consisting of women's clubs in and near the city. She was an active member of the Young Matron's Club whose members gave lectures on prominent Black Americans, entertained at meetings with vocal solos, engaged in games of whist, a card game, and often enjoyed a "dainty three-course luncheon." At a June 1915 meeting of the club Sarah gave a paper entitled "History of the American Giants."[17]

Rube was not the only member of the Foster family to travel. In August 1917, Sarah gathered up 11-year-old Earl Mack and his sister, 5-year old Sarah Watts, for a month-long trip to explore the Rocky Mountains. Also active in charitable activities, she joined with a group of women to collect "free will contributions" from spectators at a September Sunday Giants' game in 1918. The funds bought coal for The Amanda Smith Orphanage and Industrial Home for Abandoned and Destitute Colored Children. An orphanage for African American girls, the organization was founded by Amanda Smith, a former slave and Methodist missionary, and opened in Harvey, Illinois, a Chicago Suburb, in 1899. Tragically, the buildings burned to the ground in 1918 shortly after the benefit game, but with no loss of life.[18]

Getting Back to Business

At a subsequent NNL meeting in December 1920 in Indianapolis the executives, now more comfortable with Rube as their leader, re-elected him as president and added the secretary title for the coming year, ratified a new constitution spelling out expectations in greater detail, transferred the Dayton franchise to Columbus, Ohio, and admitted the Hilldale club as a full member in a prelude to the forming of a second league, the Eastern Colored League (ECL).[19]

Even though an occasional player on a NNL team would "jump" to another, and teams were known to skip a league game here and there if a more profitable exhibition game was available, Foster's genius provided a measure of stability for the eight NNL teams and a working model for the Black baseball leagues that would follow.

Prohibition: A "Noble Experiment"

Four weeks before Foster convened the Kansas City meeting, everything had been put in place for Prohibition to settle over the nation. The Eighteenth Amendment had passed both houses of Congress in 1918 and was ratified by the requisite 36 of the 48 states on January 16, 1919. The accompanying Volstead Act, passed over President Wilson's veto, went into effect on October 28, 1919. The Act took its name from its sponsor, Minnesotan Andrew John Volstead, son of Norwegian immigrants, a Republican, one of the few members of Congress who supported an anti-lynching law, almost an abstainer himself, and chairman of the House Judiciary Committee.[20] The Act spelled out enforcement activities to enforce the Amendment's provisions. Both the Amendment and the Act would prove so ineffectual that, in the words of historian, Daniel Okrent, "The drys had their law, and the wets would have their liquor."[21] The intensity of some peoples' feelings against Prohibition is attested to by the seven boxes of hate mail addressed to Volstead preserved in his papers at the University of Minnesota.[22]

Not everyone opposed enforcement of the Volstead act. Notable was Republican Presidential candidate Herbert Hoover. In his acceptance speech at the 1928 Convention in Kansas City, nine years into Prohibition, he declared Prohibition "was a great social and economic experiment, noble in motive and far-reaching in purpose." His statement gave rise to the movement's nickname, "the noble experiment."[23]

Noble or not, it did not take long for the money-making potential of the now illegal manufacturing and transporting of beer, wine, and spirits, some of it of highly questionable quality, to spur many into illegal businesses. Others had already been in the business. Three men in Wilmington, Delaware, for instance, lost their race in August 1918 to escape lawmen in hot pursuit of the men's "auto truck," owned by one of the men's employers, who used the truck to transport milk. At issue were milk cans in the truck that held 31 quarts of whiskey to be sold in Hampton, Delaware, a "dry" jurisdiction. The three were charged with transporting liquor from "wet" to "dry" territory.[24]

Chicago and Detroit became the primary Midwest centers of action for both "drys" and "wets." On October 18, 1920, Chicago's Mayor, Major A.V. Dalrymple, promised residents "a booze lid that will stop even a drop of real whiskey from trickling into Chicago." The mayor's pledge was contingent on the cooperation of the railroads and shipping express companies. Some railroads had agreed, but not the express companies. "The matter of transportation by motor trucks will be," the mayor said, "addressed later." All that would remain to secure the lid, His Honor said, would be stopping the moonshiners, estimated to be operating more than a thousand or more stills in Chicago.[25] The lid never appeared thanks in large part to the murderous Genna Brothers (Mike, Angelo, Peter, Tony, Sam, and James), who operated from 1920 to 1925 by which time three had been killed. They paid fifteen dollars a month to hundreds of mom-and-pop still operators in apartments in the Near West Side for their products. The brothers grossed $350,000 a month (roughly five and a half million in 2021 dollars). The stills were so numerous that the neighborhood smelled of alcohol day and night.[26]

On November 29, 1920, government officials followed up Dalrymple's promise with another one; to make Chicago "the most unhealthy place for crooks and the driest city in the United States by Christmas." They based their optimism on 31 recent indictments, including police officers, railroad officials, and N.D. Nebelcamp, a distillery official and president of the Louisville, Kentucky, baseball club, for violating the Volstead Act. Members of the ring obtained blank permits—issued by the government to distilleries to supply alcohol to legitimate businesses such as the perfume industry—forged the required signatures, and took delivery. In addition to issuing promises, Chicago's city government had filed suits to close hundreds of bars. Such efforts would continue, in the words of Illinois' Attorney General Edward J. Brundage, "until there was not a drop of intoxicating liquor in any of Chicago's 3,000 'dry saloons.'"[27]

10. Finally: A League for Black Baseball

Example of a homemade still used in Chicago's apartments.

In spite of Brundage's good intentions, a syndicate, extending from Chicago to New York to Louisville, was exposed in Chicago on February 21, 1921, by the Internal Revenue Department for smuggling millions of dollars of whiskey. Police, government officials, politicians and businessmen were implicated.[28]

Assurances aside, the illegal libations continued to flow. The manufacture and transportation of booze was not illegal everywhere. In addition to thousands of illegal stills in backwoods and in the basements and apartments of America that made bathtub gin and assorted other beverages, distilleries in countries where manufacturing booze was legal, such as the Bahamas and Canada, manufactured prodigious quantities. Delivery took a variety of paths.

Bahamian rum was loaded onto ships which sat in the Atlantic Ocean just beyond the three-mile limit. Smaller gray and camouflage painted vessels took on a load and, reminiscent of Confederate ships breaching the Union blockade during the Civil War, attempted to evade capture by the Coast Guard. Once on shore, further distribution took place, most often via railcar (not all railroads banned shipments) or truck. Trucks were often waylaid by armed men who off-loaded the hootch and left wounded guards and battered vehicles in their wake. Similar escapades took place along the banks of "that well-known sieve," the Detroit River which separated the city from Canada, where production was quite legal.[29]

Not all purveyors of illegal spirits were successful. Here is a shipment of rum successfully interdicted by the Coast Guard (Library of Congress).

Other purveyors of spirits sold their wares directly to customers who could make their way to boats in international waters. The *Standard Times* of New Bedford, Massachusetts, reported that a schooner lying 20 miles offshore was "dispensing refreshments in a truly hospitable manner to all drought-ridden individuals who could sail, row, or swim out to the trim-looking fisherman." Readers were invited by said fisherman, Bill McCoy, to "Come out any time you want to; the law can't touch us here, and we'll be very glad to see you."[30] Others, such as Robert Wood Johnson, II, of Johnson & Johnson, Inc., would approach an ocean-based rumrunner and buy a bottle or two for evening cocktails.[31]

Secrecy and disguise were of the essence. The arrival of a rail car full of "soap" in Chicago was not unusual.[32] Just as the Coast Guard patrolled the Atlantic shores for rumrunners, so did Federal prohibition agents patrol the banks of Lake Michigan seeking to intercept small boats and their crew headed for Michigan from Canada. On one patrol, Major Dalrymple, the now prohibition enforcement officer for Illinois, Wisconsin, Indiana, and Michigan, intercepted not a boat, but a torpedo. "The torpedo leaves the Canadian border," he explained to a *Baltimore Sun* reporter, "at a moderate rate of speed about three feet under water. And when nearly spent is picked up by one of the many small boats that infest the lake." The false bottom of one boat, whose shotgun-toting owner said he was duck hunting off the northwest coast of Florida where ducks were rare, yielded 200 quarts of liquor.[33]

By January 1922 Chicago had earned the distinction of being "the wettest spot in the entire country." Fueled in part by returning soldiers' love of the uninhibited lifestyle in war-torn Europe, decorum took a back seat to fast living among those Chicagoans who could afford it. Author Eliot Asinof described scenes in Chicago of "people riding around recklessly in cars that became houses of prostitution on wheels; people dancing a wild new dance, the shimmy and cootie crawl. The city" he concluded, "was a three-ring circus of sport, crime, and sex."[34] Popular movies included Charlie Chaplin in *Shoulder Arms*, Douglas Fairbanks in *His Majesty the American*, Will Rogers in *Almost a Husband*, and Mary Pickford in *The Hoodlum*.

Detroit, where Hill had been installed as manager in 1919 of the Motor City's Detroit Stars, was a close second. By one account Detroit hosted between 15,000 and 25,000 speakeasies. One set up shop in plain view of the city's main police station. Brothels were on the rise. By the mid–1920s the Detroit booze industry was second only to mushrooming automotive enterprises in terms of revenue and jobs.[35] Though Prohibition had been introduced at the state level in 1917, the city had spent, in the words of historian Larry Engleman, "ten years as the City on a Still."

The city also served as a way station for the transfer of booze from Canada to the U.S. It was not unusual for 1,500 to 2,000 cases of liquor to cross the Detroit River daily and make their way into Detroit and Chicago.[36] Sealed railroad cars carrying forged documents as well as spirits left the rail yards in Windsor for the short trip to Detroit. Another delivery system involved a motorized cable pulling sled-mounted containers from an uninhabited island to a waterside house in Grosse Point, a Detroit suburb. Much of the hootch was transported by the Mosquito Fleet, a flotilla of small craft more dangerous than its name may suggest. Many boats were manned by armed men willing to shoot it out with authorities.[37]

Americans' declining inhibitions and rising thirst combined to thwart law enforcement efforts partially because many officials were themselves complicit either as active participants or by turning the proverbial blind eye. In a 1923 bootlegging case brought before Detroit's Judge Edward J. Jeffries, the prosecutor told His Honor that the evidence, a large cache of liquor, had disappeared from the police station where it was being held, presumably for safe keeping. "That's a poor place to bring liquor," Judge Jeffries declared as he dismissed the case. Two years later, attorney Clarence Darrow, in town to defend a man accused of murder, regularly lunched with judges and other officials at Cohen's Speakeasy. On the day of the verdict the group adjourned to a vacant courtroom where a supply of Scotch awaited them.[38] In September 1921 Charles Fitzmorris, Chicago's police chief, expressed his belief that "half of the city's policemen were bootleggers." "In Chicago," he continued, "there is more drunkenness than there ever was, more deaths from liquor.... Prohibition enforcement in Chicago," he declared, "is a joke."[39]

A joke of another kind, mixing irony with hypocrisy, was perpetrated by George L. Cassiday, an unemployed World War I veteran. As President Warren G. Harding's administration took office in 1921 in Washington, D.C., George set up a bootlegging operation in the basement of a U.S. House of Representatives office building. Stylishly dressed, including an emerald-colored hat, and perpetually in possession of two large leather briefcases, he cheerfully obliged his congressmen clients. He strolled the halls of the House with impunity. Some members gave him a key to a desk drawer for regular and discrete re-stocking, many did business in person, and a few placed orders through a staff member. Cassidy regularly attended caucuses and hung out in the House gallery to watch some of his customers "give rattling good speeches about how well Prohibition was being enforced." The job entailed long hours when the House was in session, usually from 9:00 a.m. to late into the evening. He went about his business unhindered until 1925 when a Capitol Police Officer arrested him for carrying liquor in a briefcase. Banned from the House Office Building,

10. Finally: A League for Black Baseball 131

he set up shop in the basement of what is now the Russell Senate Office Building. There he found missing the "general spirit of good fellowship and conviviality" that he so enjoyed in the House. Few senators would do business in person. Most ordered through aides and staff members. One kept his "stuff" on the top shelf of a private office bookcase where bound volumes of the *Congressional Record* resided. Cassiday found room among the volumes. The senator referred to him as "my librarian." Known as "The Man in the Green Hat," Cassiday was again arrested in 1930. He eventually drew an eighteen-month prison term.[40]

In another instance of political officials skirting Prohibition, 200 Massachusetts delegates to the 1920 Republican convention arrived by train in Chicago in June of 1920. As the train was leaving Canada and entering the U.S. at Niagara Falls, a customs inspector asked passengers in the first car to put all liquor containers on the floor. Twelve bottles appeared but were quickly retrieved as the inspector went about patting down passengers in other cars. Containers from those searches were destroyed.[41]

Prohibition continued as a joke, though not a funny one, in Chicago and elsewhere, through the violence-prone years where the likes of Al "Scarface" Capone and the Saint Valentine's Day Massacre made headlines until 1933 when the 21st Amendment mercifully repealed the 18th Amendment—the only amendment to the U.S. Constitution to suffer such a fate.

Did It Work?

The short answer is "No." Historian Michael Lerner points out that even with the "notoriously unreliability" of statistics surrounding Prohibition "it is very clear that in many parts of the nation more people were drinking and people were drinking more." But in addition to failing in its intended purpose, to reduce, if not eliminate, the flow of alcohol, Prohibition had a number of other unintended negative consequences.

Restaurants struggled without liquor licenses. Thousands lost jobs due to the closing of breweries, distilleries, and saloons. The need for barrel makers, truckers, waiters and those in related trades fell off dramatically. The federal government lost nearly 11 billion dollars in taxes while forking over 300 million dollars to fund largely ineffectual enforcement efforts. Loopholes abounded. Pharmacies, as we have seen, could buy alcohol for a variety of "medical" reasons. The number of pharmacies owned by bootleggers rose substantially. Wine was allowed for religious services, stimulating a big increase in the number of self-professed rabbis. Equipment needed to build a still could be bought at hardware stores. Pamphlets issued by the U.S. Department of Agriculture contained operating instructions. The grape industry sold juice concentrate with "warnings" to buyers not to let it sit too long lest it start fermenting. Black-market booze of ever declining quality took the lives of thousands.[42]

How did women fare once Prohibition was the law of the land? The role of women changed for the better during the 1920s. Their support for the 18th Amendment, coupled with winning the right to vote nationally, demonstrated women could be effective in the political arena. While many chose to remain in the traditional homemaker role, women had a greater range of choices. Some had gained experience in the workplace prior to 1920 when many took jobs that had been held by men during World War I, found they enjoyed the working life and wanted to continue in it. For many it was the first time they had made money of their own. More women left the rural countryside for the city in search of opportunities in industry and government. As Prohibition continued, women joined men at the bar drinking freely with them at speakeasies and wherever else drinks were being poured. Though still discriminated against in pay and promotions, women had gained considerable social, economic, and political independence and were no longer viewed as beholding to their husbands and other males.[43]

11

Year Two in Detroit

With Prohibition a year old and the fledging NNL starting to take shape, Hill invited 25 players to Mack Park in late March 1920 for spring training. Several new faces made his Detroit Stars roster. Hill had particularly high expectations for his Texas pitching recruit, 24-year-old Andy "Lefty" Cooper. An imposing presence on the mound at 220 pounds and 6 feet, 2 inches tall, Cooper was blessed with superb speed and control. Hill held out similar hopes for right-handed 19-year-old Bill Holland from Indianapolis. Smaller in stature than Cooper at 5 feet, 9 inches and weighing 180 pounds, Holland baffled hitters with an array of five pitches. Hill, now 38 and again the Stars' player/manager, was generously described by the *Defender* as "scampering like a youth just breaking in."[1]

The arrival of wife Gertrude and 11-year-old son Kenneth in Detroit boosted his spirits. After living apart for most of 1919, the threesome settled in Detroit in early April 1920. Kenneth served as the Stars' mascot and bat boy until July when he traveled to Pittsburgh for a summer-time stay with his grandmother and uncles. Gertrude spent the month of August in New York and Atlantic City where she had relatives.[2]

The Stars tuned up for their first game of the 1920 season with games against independent White clubs. They slaughtered the Jackson (Michigan) Independents, 23–0; put away the Derby Truck Company nine, 12–0; and got by the Chicago-based Cowpers, 6–3.[3]

More serious opposition, in the form of the Cuban Giants, arrived at Mack Park from Havana. The Opening Day game, May 15, 1920, marked the beginning of a scheduled five-game series.[4] The Royal Rooters Club, preceded by a 20-piece band, escorted the teams to the field in "machines" (automobiles) followed by anyone with a "machine" who cared to join in. Box seats had long been sold out. Some still needing to buy tickets skipped the long lines and clambered over fences to gain free admittance. Many, finding no seats, parked themselves in the outfield and along the foul lines. Those remaining outside the park were so boisterous someone called the police. Once they restored order and the game was about to start, club

The 1920 Detroit Stars. Standing, back row (L to R): Bill Holland, Edgar Wesley, Bruce Petway, Fred Long, Bill Gatewood, Webster McDonald (?), unknown. Seated, middle row (L to R): Joe Hewitt, Pete Hill, Tenny Blount, Jimmie Lyons, Andy Cooper. Seated, front row (L to R): unknown, unknown, Frank Warfield, unknown (courtesy Gary Ashwill).

officials and players from both teams gathered at home plate where a floral arrangement in the shape of a baseball diamond was displayed. Mayor James J. Couzens, who made a fortune as an early backer of Henry Ford, threw out the first ball. To the delight of the 15,000 fans crammed into every nook and cranny of Mack Park (designed to hold 6,000), Hill's team won decisively, 7–2.[5]

The Stars repeated their winning ways in the next game. Maybe the men from the land of sugarcane needed a few days to get acclimated to the States. They roared back in games three and four, walloping the Stars, 11–3 and 12–6, to even the series.[6] The Cubans had played the Stars "level."[7] The fifth game was not played.

The NNL Opens for Business

May also saw the first NNL game—a contest between Joe Greene's Chicago Giants and Taylor's ABCs in Indianapolis on May 2. Sportswriter

Dave Wyatt opened his account of the game with the following heartfelt words: "One of the largest and most enthusiastic gatherings ... who ever assembled to do homage to the grand old national game witnessed the initial contests that ushered into being what is purported to be the most important and far-reaching step ever negotiated by the baseball promoters of our Race since the birth of the game more than forty years ago."

The ABCs won the inaugural game, 4–2.[8] A long-held dream by Rube and others in Black baseball had come to fruition.

The Stars Struggle

The Stars continued feasting on independent teams and hosted a number of league games. They mastered the Kansas City Monarchs in game one of a mid–July doubleheader, 8–3. Hill, along with first baseman Edgar Wesley, both left-handed hitters, connected for homers over Mack Field's welcoming right field fence. The Monarchs took the second game. By the end of July, after downing the Cubans two games to one, the Stars were in second place behind Hill's former team and hoped to be on their way to a pennant.[9]

Cooper was now in the Stars' regular rotation but having a rough time of it. He started two league games. The Stars lost both. The Monarchs rode over the Stars in a 5–1 win on August 20 at home behind the four-hit pitching of John Donaldson, who had hurled the previously year for the Stars. A month later, Rube's Giants entertained the Detroit crowd with an 8–3 victory at Cooper's expense.[10] Even so, crowds at Mack Park remained supportive of the team. In an early August game, 11,000 of the faithful filled Mack Park to see the Bacharachs go down to a 4–3 defeat. Hill's homer supplied the winning margin.[11]

Hill and Blount did not manufacture enough wins to grab the pennant. The Stars finished the NNL season in a disappointing second place behind the American Giants. On a more positive note, the Stars won the Michigan Semi-Pro Championship Tournament for the second consecutive year.[12] Previous to the Stars' two wins in the tournament, Roesink's S & S nine had won the state championship 14 times in 15 years.[13] Winter found Hill and Blount re-vamping the Stars' roster with an eye toward besting Rube's nine for the 1921 NNL championship campaign.[14]

Separation, Divorce?

After the 1920 season ended, Hill's father-in-law, John Lawson, arrived in Chicago "for an extended visit" with his daughter, Pete's wife,

Gertrude. Lawson said he would like to have his friends call on him at Gertrude's residence, 5225 Indiana Avenue, Apartment 2. Pete stayed in Detroit. While no record of a divorce between Pete and Gertrude could be found, Lawson's arrival may have been prompted by their divorce or separation. Gertrude's mother had died several years earlier.[15]

1921

The Stars opened 1921 with a tilt against the Detroit Creamery nine (White) on Saturday, May 7. Hill stole the show with a triple and a one-handed, over-the-shoulder snag of a ball destined to be a three-bagger. His catch brought the raucous crowd to its feet. His throw to second doubled up the hapless runner for a double play. The Stars won 8–6. Two weeks later Hill's nine handed another independent White team, the Brisco Motors, a 3–1 defeat.[16]

The opening 1921 NNL home stand began on Saturday, May 14, with a two-game series against the Bacharachs. Blount invited the *Defender*'s sporting editor and reporter, Dave Wyatt, to Detroit for the games and lent him his Marmon car. A downpour forced the Opening Day parade to be postponed a day until game two on Sunday. Police motorcycles, with lights flashing and sirens blaring led a brass band and cars filled with players from both teams from the Hotel Biltmore to Mack Park. Fans again followed in their automobiles. Chilly weather kept the crowd down to a more manageable 9,000, but some still watched from the field. Pre-game activities included a short speech at home plate by Michigan physician Dr. J.R. Ames. On behalf of the team, Tenny Blount received a large floral arrangement, again with a baseball diamond in the middle. John Roesink presented each Detroit player with a new "sunbonnet."

The game was less to the crowds' liking than the preliminaries. The Stars, who had prevailed the day before 9–8 in a slugfest featuring five homers and six doubles, fell victim to their eastern opponents whose Sunday onslaught against both Holland and Cooper resulted in a 7–2 loss for the Stars.[17]

By Independence Day, Blount and Hill had reason to believe, after a slow start, that their winter work was bearing fruit. The team was in first place "by a comfortable margin," thanks to timely hitting with 39-year-old Pete leading the way and the steady improvement of pitchers Holland and Cooper. *Defender* sportswriter Roy Jackson practically ceded the pennant to the Stars with half the season remaining. "The way they are hustling," enthused Jackson, "it seems as though Manager Pete Hill has purchased through tickets to 'Pennantville.'" Blount and Hill, Jackson reported, were more circumspect "because they realize the season has a long way to run."[18]

Detroit's Racial Tensions

As the Stars maintained their grip on first place, the NAACP was holding its twelfth annual conference in Detroit from June 26 to July 1, 1921. A month earlier, one of the country's most deadly race riots had occurred in Tulsa, Oklahoma. A booming oil town where many, including Blacks, made piles of money, Tulsa's lack of law enforcement did little to curb robberies, prostitution, gambling, sale of home brews that rendered one temporarily insane, and lynchings. From May 31 to June 1, White mobs went on an unrestrained 18-hour rampage against Blacks. Thousands were left homeless. Over 150 people died. Property damage ran into the millions.[19]

While no race riot on the scale of the ones the previous year in Chicago and Washington, and the recent Tulsa conflagration, had struck Detroit, they were twenty years off; the city was not without its racial tension. Most of the increasing number of Blacks arriving in the Motor City found themselves in the lowest paying jobs, many in the auto industry, when they could find jobs at all; poor, disorganized, and living in substandard housing. The Klan had stoked racial prejudices for years. Thousands of members, including a fair number of policemen, had swelled its membership in recent years. Cross burnings in front of City Hall and the Wayne County Building would reach their peak in 1923. The Klan offered to pay the train fare for any Black willing to return to the South. Few accepted. The hooded night riders fought every relief program the city proposed for Blacks.[20]

Over a thousand people from around the country, both Black and White, attended the NAACP conference. Michigan Republican Governor Alex J. Groesbeck welcomed the delegates as did the city's Republican mayor, James J. Couzens.[21] An impassioned article on July 6 in the *Philadelphia Tribune*, a Black weekly, expressed the concerns of many people at the conference. The writer cited lynching and mob violence as "our most indefensible national crime." The article attributed the cause of racial conflict "to an increased lack of sympathy and lack of justice on the part of the Whites." Barriers to progress by Blacks included a lack of education for children; segregation in the armed services, federal departments, and public transportation; unjust treatment in the courts, and a "honeycomb of secret societies like the Ku Klux Klan who stir up race hatred by innuendo and appeal to the lowest brute instincts."[22] Conferees put passage of a federal anti-lynching measure at the top of their list of action items. Representative Leonidas C. Dyer, an 11-term White Republican congressman from Missouri and civil rights activist, had recently introduced such a bill.[23] Congressional efforts to enact an anti-lynching law have failed repeatedly over the past 100 years. That changed on March 29, 2022, when President Biden signed the Emmett Till Anti-lynching Act of 2022 into law. The act is named after a 14-year-old Black boy who died at the hands of a group of White men in Mississippi. The problem? Allegedly whistling at a White woman in 1955. Till's brutal murder sparked national outrage and was a catalyst for the emerging civil rights movement.

The issue hit close to home when two months later a riot and lynching had been avoided in the nearby suburb of Hamtramck. Sam Griggs, Black, shot two White boys, wounding both. A White crowd beat Griggs with fists and baseball bats. They tied a rope around his neck with the intention to lynch him. Police rescued Griggs, who admitted the shooting but said he was fired on first.[24]

Hill's Stars on Top for a Bit

Two weeks after the NAACP conference ended, sportswriter Roy Jackson's upbeat prophecy seemed well-founded. On the strength of Hill's home run in game 1 in a July doubleheader and a run-scoring double in Game 2, the Stars swept both contests from the Columbus Buckeyes, an NNL team, on their home grounds, Neil Park.[25] By late August, however, the Stars had fallen to fourth place. Tenny promised "we will not stay there for long," as they arrived in Gary, Indiana, for game one of a five-game series against Rube's Giants. Still in possession of his Marmon and his friendship with Foster, Tenny offered to chauffer the Giants' owner if he promised to lay off his corncob pipe while in the limo.[26]

While it is not known if Rube agreed to Tenny's stipulation, it is known the Stars, behind the four-hit, shutout pitching of Andy Cooper, won game one, 3–0.[27] A later game in Detroit did little to move the Stars above fourth place as they lost to the Giants, 8–3. The Stars' fortunes faded further as Hill's charges lost more than they won through the end of August and early September. The Hilldale Club delivered the coup de grace by taking five of six games from their Motor City visitors in mid–September, eliminating any chance of a championship flag being hoisted at Mack Park.[28] Spectators, nevertheless, continued to pay 55 cents for a pavilion seat and 35 cents for a bleacher post.[29] Tenny, disappointed in the Stars' performance, decided a change in managers would improve their fortunes.

Philadelphia Re-Visited

Casting about for new opportunities, Hill found one with an old friend, George "Chappie" Johnson, a teammate on the 1903 Cuban X-Giants, 1904 and 1906 Philadelphia Giants, several "Coconut League" teams, and the 1909 Leland Giants. His playing career lasted from 1896 to 1921 with 14 teams as a well-respected catcher and first basemen. One of the few NNL players to enjoy an extended managerial career following his playing days, Chappie skippered a variety of teams thru 1937. A flashy dresser sporting spats, carrying a walking cane, and employing a valet to carry his bags to the ballpark, Johnson insisted on being addressed as "Mr. Johnson." In 1922 his team was the Philadelphia Royal Stars Baseball Club, formerly known as Norfolk All-Stars of Philadelphia. Both iterations rated a notch or two below the NNL teams. In a frequently overlooked stop in Hill's career, he served as the 1922 Royal Stars' captain.[30]

The Royals belonged to the independent Philadelphia Baseball Association, consisting of three classes of teams; Class A—White teams within the city; Class B—White teams beyond Philadelphia; and Class C—all "colored" teams. Not all of the latter were based in Philadelphia. The Baltimore Black Sox and Bill Pettus's Richmond Giants were also Class C members. The Royals played their home games in Shetzline Park at Broad and Bigler streets in South Philly. The park had recently been upgraded with a new grandstand and bleachers added to increase the park's seating capacity to 12,000 people.

Johnson planned on three games a week while at home on Mondays, Wednesdays (Ladies Day), and Fridays. Games throughout New England and the South, and away games, most in nearby venues, completed the schedule.[31]

At some games south of the Mason-Dixon Line separate seating for White and Black spectators was the norm. A flyer promoting a three-game series between "Pete Hill's Philadelphia Royals" and "Pettus's Richmond Giants" in Norfolk, Virginia, in late September, announced in bold print "Part of Grandstand for White Patrons."[32]

Johnson promised fans several well-known players would make this year's team even better than his Norfolk Stars of 1921. Nine of the 19 Royals' players had experience with such top-notch NNL teams as the New York Lincoln Giants, Bacharach Giants, and the Indianapolis ABC's, but, with one exception, none had stellar careers. The exception was a tall, southpaw pitcher, Jess (Nip) Winters. The hard-throwing lefty had posted a 3–2 record against top NNL teams the year before and was, in the eyes of historian James Riley, the best pitcher in the Eastern Colored League's history. An aging Pete Hill was by far the best known, but his skills had diminished notably. When it came time for an all-star game "between the pick of the white and colored players of the Philadelphia Baseball Association," in mid–August, Hill was not among them, though he did have his moments.[33]

In a blow-out win, 18–0, over the Tate's Stars of Cleveland in August, Hill, playing right field, added a double and two singles to the Royals' total of 18 hits. The Cleveland team took its name from owner George Tate, a Black Cleveland business man and secretary of the NNL in 1922, the only year the Tate's Stars played in Rube's league. In August, Johnson assured the *Evening Public Ledger* in Philadelphia he was confident his Royals would be in the mix for the Philadelphia Baseball Association championship. He was disappointed. Not only were his Royals not in the mix—the Richmond Giants won the Black division—but according to Gary Ashwill, baseball historian and director of the Seamheads Negro Leagues Database, a championship series against the White teams never took place. Seamheads credits the Royals with a 10th-place finish among 11 non-league-affiliated independent Black teams, going 3-8-1 in games against major Black opposition. The Royals folded at the end of the year.[34]

Milwaukee

After a disappointing turn with the Philadelphia Royals, Pete, at Rube's invitation, took the reins of another new NNL team, The Milwaukee Bears, fashioned, like the Detroit Stars, from players assembled by Foster. Four members of the New Orleans Crescent Stars, who had impressed Foster on a recent barnstorming tour, joined others for chilly spring training at Schorling's Park in early April 1923. Hill was on hand to direct the workouts. The *Defender*, once again, and this time a bit generously, said at age 41 he "looked like a three-year-old colt." The *Pittsburgh Courier* welcomed Pete back. "So Pete Hill will step back into the big time," the paper said. "The entire baseball world rejoices in his good fortune. They are hoping he makes good. Hill is a former Pittsburgh lad and has contributed greatly to the perpetuity of Negro baseball."[35] Athletic Field (later named Borchert Field), home to the American Association's minor league team, the Milwaukee Brewers, was the Bears' home field when the Brewers were on the road.

Milwaukee tuned up for the 1923 season with exhibition games against Chicago-based White teams, the Logan Squares and the Cermacks. The NNL season began in earnest with the arrival of the Cuban Stars in Cream City, so named for Milwaukee's many cream-colored buildings. To the pleasant surprise of Foster and Hill, the Bears downed the men from the Island 8–5 on April 28. Less fortunate the following day, the Bears were edged by the Cuban Stars, 4–3. The games marked early appearances of "colored" umpires in an NNL game in the persons of Lucien Snaer and Leon Augustine, a development applauded, and no doubt spawned, by Foster.[36]

In advance of a two-game series between the Bears and Rube's Giants in May, a *Defender*'s sportswriter, Rube Foster, sketched out the strong points of both teams, gilding the lily a bit in regard to the Bears so as to make the upcoming game seem competitive to readers. He concluded his article by saying "brown-skin" umpires Caesar Jamison and William (Cap) Embry would work the games. After noting that everyone makes an error and asking fans to give them a warm welcome, he wrote, "It is something that we have all looked forward to and something that is here to stay, according to the president of the league, A.R. Foster."[37]

A Long Season for the Bears

Neither the umpires' skin color nor the fact that two umpires instead of one now worked the games provided much solace to the Bears. Perry Hall, who appeared in just one game as a pitcher for the Bears but extended his career to 1945 as an infielder with other teams, recalled, "Most of it [the Bears] was rookies. All of them were young fellows. They didn't have too good a ball club."[38]

They did well with independent teams, posting, for instance, two wins over a town team in Angola, Indiana, and beating the Tipton Legion (Indiana) team.[39] It was another story against NNL teams. Their opening season split with the Cuban Stars was one of the rare times the team's won-loss record stood at .500. By the end of May the Indianapolis ABCs led the league. The Bears did break the ABC's ten-game win streak with a 7–1 romp over the Hoosiers on May 20 but only after having lost three straight to Taylor's nine. By early June, Milwaukee was in seventh place in the eight-team NNL with a 5–15 record.[40] The rest of the Bears' season was highlighted by a double-header loss to Detroit in late June; a tie, one win, and two losses against the Birmingham Black Barons in July, and losses in August to Rube's team.

Hill played irregularly but hit well on those occasions when he did patrol the outfield. In one July non-league game, against the Chicago-based Heights, the 41-year-old demonstrated he could still swing the bat. He swatted five singles. An article in the *Chicago Heights Star* just the week before cited only two Bears, both relatively unknown, first baseman Andrew Wilson and second baseman Andrew Pryor, as "high class players. Hill, the article stated, "was once considered a great outfielder." Hill's five bungles may have given the writer cause to reconsider his assessment of Hill's current abilities. In any event, when their season came to a merciful end, Hill's roster finished dead last with a record of 14–32.[41] The Bears' franchise dissolved. Pete was again in search of new opportunities.

12

On to Baltimore

At 42, Hill was in the twilight of his spectacular career. He had been a durable and dependable team player who was always among the leaders, if not the leader, in batting averages and game-winning clutch hits. Fans had raved about his circus catches in the outfield, rifle-like throws to bases that doubled up runners, and speed around the bases. Though he might have made more money by jumping from the American Giants at some point to another team, he never did—a rare occurrence for a player of his caliber. He thrived playing for Rube Foster. Foster, in turn, recognized Hill's leadership and loyalty as evidenced by naming him the Giants' captain for many years and choosing him to manage the start-up Detroit Stars and Milwaukee Bears. Foster, however, would not play a role in Hill's career after that.

1924

As 1924 began, Hill was without portfolio. Several clubs made offers to him to manage their team. George Rossiter and Charles Spedden, both White and hell-bent to bring a championship to their Baltimore Black Sox, saw Hill as the man who could get it done. The two outbid the other clubs for Hill's services. Hill was delighted. "I'll be glad when the bell rings," referring to Opening Day, he wrote in his acceptance letter to Spedden from his home in Detroit.[1] The two men gave Hill complete authority over the team as well as the responsibility for the Sox becoming a winner. Hill's official duties were only to manage.

The Sox began play as an independent team in 1916 and gradually improved to the point where it became a charter member of the ECL in 1923. The League, founded in 1923 by Ed Bolden, an employee of the Philadelphia post office and owner of the Hilldale Club based in Darby, Pennsylvania, was created to do for the leading Black teams in the East what Foster's NNL was designed to do for teams in the Midwest.[2]

Spedden, an executive with the Baltimore & Ohio Railroad, was the Sox's original owner. He sold the team to Rossiter and stayed on as the team's business manager.[3] Rossiter, a native Baltimorean of Irish descent, owned a restaurant—some accounts refer to it as a speakeasy. He was famous for his generosity to the players and politicians who frequented his eatery, "George Rossiter's Sea Food House." Known as a "near-beer saloon," near-beer wasn't the only beverage available. Prohibition agents seized a "small quantity of alleged liquor" from Rossiter's establishment at 1001 South Hanover Street. The bartender tried to dump it into a rinsing tank when the agents arrived unannounced in October of 1922.[4]

Rossiter enjoyed playing the game as well as owning a team. As a young man at age 21 he played several years with the Relay Athletic Club of Baltimore between 1900 and 1910. By 1923, at age 29, he was selected by Baltimore promoter Nick Maddox as the first sacker for the Baltimore All-Stars. Rossiter's interest in sports also included boxing. On August 27, 1923, for instance, he staged a series of outdoor boxing matches, "an all colored offering," at Maryland Park, the Sox's home field.[5]

Hill's new job pleased W. Rollo Wilson, sportswriter for the *Pittsburgh Courier*. "Pete Hill," he wrote, "deserves a good team and if the owners spend the money and get the players the ancient Pittsburgher will give them a run for their roll and their confidence."[6] The owners did as Wilson hoped.

Spedden promised to "junk" the present club. He released all but four from the last-place 1923 club. Among those he kept was Jud "Boojum" Wilson, who compiled a reported .325 batting average in the course of his 24-year career that earned him a plaque in Cooperstown. The Sox's executives enticed several players to jump to the Sox with generous offers, paid the expenses of eight others to travel to Baltimore from California where they'd been playing in the CWL, and doubled their salaries.[7]

The two made no secret of their willingness to spend. "It costs money to get the best players," Rossiter said to a reporter for the *Sun* in August 1923. "But we," he continued, "are willing to spend and hope to give Baltimoreans a championship colored team next season. Spedden and myself are going West next month to make a roundup. We expect to sign a number of stars and will offer them flattering inducements to wear our uniforms."[8]

The two constantly kept an eye out for promising players and took an active role in recruiting them as the 1924 season progressed. In May 1924, Hill thought he had signed third baseman Henry Blackman, formerly of the Indianapolis ABCs. When Blackman, known for his snappy throws, ability to drop a bunt on a dime, and a respectable batting average, failed to appear, Spedden caught a train to Indianapolis and personally escorted him to Baltimore. Sadly, his time with the Sox lasted only two months. A liver ailment killed Blackman in August.[9]

In late June 1924 Spedden learned that the Pittsburgh-based Homestead Grays manager Cum Posey had dropped John Beckwith, an exceptionally talented if temperamental infielder, from the team. Posey offered little detail, saying only, "Beckwith was unable to fit into our organization." Before other clubs interested in the 5'11½", 226-pound slugging shortstop, notably the Lincoln Giants and the Bacharachs, could put a contract in front of the ex-Gray, Spedden hopped on the next train to Pittsburgh only to learn Beckwith was headed home to Chicago. An overnight train ride put Spedden in Chicago. The next day Spedden wired the *Pittsburgh Courier*, "On my way east with Beckwith." "Beckwith's acquisition," the *Courier* proclaimed, "has made Baltimore one of the strongest teams in the East."[10]

As generous as the owners had been with players' salaries, they reduced the club's 1924 travel expenses by purchasing "a big white bus." "Last year," Spedden said, "we spent several thousand dollars in railroad fares. This year, we'll burn gasoline and get better service at less cost."[11] Infielder Connie Day offered to drive the bus. Spedden nixed Day's offer saying, "The ball players have enough to do during a double header.... I'm afraid it would be too hard on Connie."[12]

Maryland Park

The Sox played their games at Maryland Park, which baseball historian Jules Tygiel described as being at one time a "sewer ... which featured broken seats, holes in the roof, non-working toilets, and weeds on the field."[13] By the time Hill arrived, however, the team's Board of Directors had vastly improved the park. A new coat of green and white paint had been applied to the repaired grandstand and bleachers. Steam rollers smoothed the outfield grass which soccer players churned up every fall. The infield was refilled with soil and rolled down. Grandstand seating had been upgraded and the bleachers had been covered. "The diamond," in their words, "presents a beautiful appearance."[14]

Hill Builds His Team with Raids

In another move to fashion a pennant winning team, Rossiter and Spedden invited Hill to join in the player procurement effort. Hill responded by raiding NNL teams including his former Detroit Stars, the

Indianapolis ABCs, and the Birmingham Black Barons. These moves did not sit well with *Defender* sportswriter Fay Young. "Hill shows his appreciation for what Foster and Blount have done for him by raiding ... clubs in the Western leagues," Young exclaimed. "Are baseball players human beings or are they ingrates?" he fumed.[15] Hill's raids were but one example of escalating tensions between the two leagues, which strained the peaceful relationships among teams that Foster had hoped to promote.

Another *Chicago Defender* castigated him in an article titled "Pete Hill Through as a Player and Manager." It drew a sharp response from Pete. Writing in the *Pittsburgh Courier,* he fired back, "I do not take exception to this (slowing up as a player) but I never heard of a man my age being too old to manage.... The old saying is every knock is a boost, so knock on Mr. Knocker.... I like to make friends, but a man does not know who his friends are today.... I will be the only bench manager in colored baseball with the possible exception of Rube Foster."[16] Given limited team rosters, managers usually played as well as managed.

To make sure the players Hill had selected from NNL teams made it to Baltimore, he met them in Detroit and Indianapolis during the last week in March and escorted them to Baltimore for spring training.[17] One of them, Christopher (Crush) Holloway carried the nickname "the frog" because of his proclivity to "jump" from team to team.[18] Holloway was pleased to join forces with Hill. In an interview with Negro League historian John Holway, Holloway credited Hill with being "a great manager. He also played left field (as did Holloway). He was a left-handed hitter and hit to left field. He's the man who taught me how to hit to left field."[19]

Hill could teach a man to hit to any field. Ben Taylor, who would succeed Hill as the Sox manager in 1926 and put together a 30-year Hall of Fame career as player and manager from 1910 to 1940, told historian James Riley, "He will probably never have an equal as a hitter. I think he is the most dangerous man in a pinch in baseball."[20]

Another who jumped his signed contract was Kansas City Monarchs' outfielder Wade "Heavy" Johnson whom the NNL immediately blacklisted. The *Defender* noted his actions "will do him lots of harm." Johnson fled the Monarchs after signing a contract and ordering several specially made bats. Both leagues often blacklisted jumpers, but rarely did it matter. In Johnson's case, he jumped back to the Monarchs in 1925 after one year with the Sox. Johnson played in the NNL for several more seasons before retiring in 1933.[21] The *Defender* hinted that Hill had suffered a similar fate, reporting that the NNL directors had banned him from further participation in any league club. The same article, with the same lack of detail, noted that "his troubles that led to his discharge as manager of the Detroit club ... may be aired, much to the Baltimore manager's detriment."[22]

Raids Continue

Hill was not the only ECL manager plucking players away from Midwest teams. The Lincoln Giants, Hilldale Club, and the Harrisburg Stars, who landed the biggest catch of all, Oscar Charleston, grabbed a total of 14 NNL players. By one account, Foster's refusal to return pitcher Richard Whitworth to the Hilldale Club, which Whitworth had "left" the year before to play for the American Giants, ignited what *Pittsburgh Courier* sportswriter Chester L. Washington, Jr., called "one of the most sensational diamond raids in history." The wheels were coming off Foster's efforts to bring harmony to Black baseball. The NNL wobbled along until 1931 when the combined effects of the Great Depression and player raids reduced the League to a shell of itself. Bolden's nervous breakdown and dissension over player salaries put an end to the ECL in the spring of 1928.[23]

1924 Gets Underway

Both leagues, however, were alive and well in 1924. Two days before Opening Day in Baltimore, Rossiter, eager to build a fan base for his new roster, held a Friday night dance at the New Albert Auditorium, located on Pennsylvania Avenue in the heart of Baltimore's Black entertainment district, to introduce the new team.[24] On Sunday, April 13, before 5,000 spectators, the Sox opened their 1924 season. They whipped two independent White teams: the Irvingtons, 11–1 and, later in the day, the Newarks, 5–3.[25]

The Chase for the Pennant Begins

With two games under their belt, Hill's charges started league play against the Bacharachs in a three-game series during the last weekend in April. A thousand well-wishers saw them drop the first contest 7–2. Six thousand turned out the next day for a Sunday double header at Maryland Park. They filled the grandstand and the bleachers. Late comers climbed up on the roof. After both teams marched to home plate from centerfield to the strains of "Glory," and Rossiter, Spedden, and Pete each received a bouquet of flowers, the Bacharachs dashed any hopes for a fast Black Sox start: 6–4 and 10–7. "Colored" umpires oversaw the action for the first time at Maryland Park. In a twin bill the following Sunday against the Washington Potomacs, Hill, having voided his pledge to not play and wanting to show he still could, held down centerfield for both games. He doubled

The 1924 Baltimore Black Sox. (Incorrect date on photo.) Standing, L to R: Unknown, O'Neal Pullen, Crush Holloway, Pete Hill, Connie Day, Jud Wilson, Joe Strong, Wayne Carr. Kneeling/Seated, L to R: Wade Johnston, Bill Force, mascot, George Britt [Britton], unknown (courtesy Gary Ashwill).

in the winning runs in game one for a squeaker of a win, 10–9. He singled and scored a run in game two as the Sox romped over the D.C.ers, 15–2.[26]

The winning and Pete's hitting continued. In the second game of a double header in early July against the Carnegie Elks of Pittsburgh, a White semi-pro team managed by Honus Wagner, the retired Hall of Fame shortstop for the Pittsburgh Pirates and subject of the most expensive baseball card ever printed, Hill's ninth-inning pinch-hit triple propelled the Sox, who had taken game one 8–1, to a 6–5 victory. An *Afro-American* reporter captured Hill's game-two heroics in these words: "Hill was called on to save the day. The old veteran ball player marched to the plate amid the cheers of thousands, slid the wad of tobacco to the left cheek and bided his time.... The third pitch seemed to satisfy Pete. He took a mighty swing, sending the sphere up against the left field wall good for a triple."[27]

As feared and dangerous as Hill was at the plate, he had his disappointing moments. A memorable one came in a game against the Bacharachs in June at Maryland Park. By the bottom of the eighth inning the Sox had tied the visitors 1–1. With two out and the bases loaded, Hill, sensing an opportunity to blow the game wide open, inserted himself as a pinch hitter for the Sox's right-handed pitcher Robert "Big Boy" McClure. Hill faced Arthur "Rats" Henderson, a side-arm throwing right-hander who had a fast-breaking curve that looked just like his fast ball until the bottom fell out at the last moment. Hill swung at three of Henderson's offerings missing each one. Back on the bench Hill watched with interest as his Sox shut out the Bacharachs for the next four innings, squeaking by the Atlantic City team with a 2–1 win in the twelfth inning.[28]

Baltimoreans liked what they were seeing. Eight thousand streamed into Maryland Park on July 19 to see the Sox split a double header with Bolden's Hilldale Club. This time Hill managed both games from the bench. Even after the split, the Sox still held down second place in the ECL standings. There, however, the team stayed.[29] Critics took note of a decline in the Sox's play, none more colorfully than *Pittsburgh Courier* sportswriter W. Rollo Wilson. "The defense," he wrote, "is a sieve…. Pitchers have developed sore arms…. Batters are troubled with astigmatic myopia and myopic astigmatism…. Fielders are as afraid of catching a ball as they are of catching smallpox. If Pete Hill does not bring his charges up," Wilson concluded, "they will be in a sub-cellar."[30]

Hill managed to avoid the sub-cellar, but the Hilldale nine outplayed the rest of the league for the remainder of the season to claim the pennant. The Sox's second-place finish disappointed Spedden and Rossiter. Not only did the ECL pennant escape them, but their generosity at the season's start came back to bite them in the form of a big deficit. Rumors flew that Rossiter would cut players' salaries significantly, sell the team, or sell several of the high-priced stars. Changes would be made, but none of the rumored actions took place, to the relief of fans and players alike.[31]

The Sox Challenge White Teams

While Rossiter contemplated his options at the end of the season, Spedden for the fifth time in five years challenged Jake Dunn, owner of the White International League Baltimore Orioles, to a five-game series. Once again Dunn declined.[32] Spedden issued no more challenges to Dunn.[33]

Spedden fared better with the Philadelphia Athletics. The Sox split a post-season doubleheader against the Athletics' starters at Maryland Park in front of 8,000 fans on October 12, 1924. The Athletics, under manager Connie Mack, who was more amenable than most major league managers to play Black teams, were a bonafide major league team if not a powerhouse that year. The A's had placed fifth in the eight-team American League with a 71–81 record. The Soxs lost the first contest 4–2, even though Beckwith's fourth-inning homer drove Baltimore native Eddie Rommel, four years into his 13 seasons with the A's and known as "the father of the knuckleball," from the mound. The second game was called after 6½ innings due to darkness—which may have been a blessing for the Sox. They prevailed

8–7, but the A's were coming on strong, scoring four tallies in the bottom of the sixth inning. *Sun* sportswriter Herbert Wilkinson said, "The games gave the fans a fair comparison of the strength of the Sox and the Athletics."[34] That they did, as the Sox offered the major leaguers' stiff competition that afternoon. Hill did not play, presumably managing from the bench.

Hill as Sportswriter

Hill did more in Baltimore than manage and win an occasional game with his bat. The Baltimore-based *Afro-American*, a Black weekly, put him on as a sportswriter with a regular column entitled "Kinky Questions" and an occasional article. How the column got its title is not known. In it he answered questions submitted by readers. An example: "Dear Pete—Can the pitcher start the game and be taken out at any time? G.M. Richmond." Pete's answer: "No. In our first game this year with the Washington club, the same question came up. The pitcher who starts the game has to pitch to the first batter. The said batter has to either reach first base or be put out."[35]

He also offered his opinion in print. The first "Colored World Series," played in the fall of 1924 pitted the winner of the NNL, the Kansas City Monarchs, against the winner of the ECL, the Hilldale Club, in a best of nine games contest. All games were played in neutral ballparks. Stating in the *Afro-American* that "hundreds of fans throughout the East have asked my opinion on the relative strengths of both teams," the newly hired sportswriter wrote a detailed comparison of the starting players for each position for each team. He came down on the side of Kansas City. In another article for the *Afro,* penned when the Monarchs trailed two games to one, Hill stuck by his prediction. The Monarchs narrowly won the series 5 games to 4. "Hill," the *Afro* reported after the series ended, "wears a big smile these days." Pete told his *Afro* readers, "I told you so."[36]

A Change in Status

Shortly thereafter, Rossiter denied rumors that Hill would be supplanted as manager by the Sox's shortstop and power hitter, the moody John Beckwith. Feeling assured of a job for 1925, Hill again visited his mother and brothers in Pittsburgh before driving on to Chicago where he spent the winter.

Two weeks before Christmas, however, Hill learned the rumor had been true after all. A change in managers, Rossiter thought, would improve the Sox's pennant chances. Not willing to lose Hill, Rossiter appointed

12. On to Baltimore

The 1925 Baltimore Black Sox. Standing, L to R: Bob McClure, unknown, Connie Day, Heavy Johnson, John Beckwith, Jud Wilson, unknown, Crush Holloway. Seated, L to R: Bill Force, Harry Jeffries, George Britt [Britton], Pete Hill, Joe Strong, Jim Jeffries. Seated in front, L to R: Julio Rojo, mascot, Robert Clarke (courtesy Gary Ashwill).

him the team's business manager and press attaché, explaining that his knowledge of the game will be a big asset. Not incidentally, the most consistent hitter in the game would still be available to pinch hit. Pete took the change in stride, proudly stating to the *Pittsburgh Courier,* "Watch the Sox!" just before Opening Day.[37]

What Hill contributed to the Sox's business fortunes is unclear, but he continued to swing a decisive bat. A pinch-hit triple by "old man Pete Hill" off the right field wall against the Lit Brothers, a Philadelphia-based team sponsored by two brothers, Samuel and Jacob Lit, owners of a department store bearing their name, won the second game of a July double header. In another July twin bill, this one against the Carnegie Elks, "The old man socked one in the fifth inning driving in two runs."[38]

While achieving success against independent clubs, things were not going as well for the Sox in league games. Beckwith's managing was creating unrest and dissension among the players, several of whom failed to obey their manager's orders. The tipping point came in early August, when Beckwith slugged an umpire in Harrisburg, Pennsylvania, during a game with the Harrisburg Giants. Spedden managed to get the suspension issued by the ECL against Beckwith lifted, but the slugger's managing days were over. "Beckwith is just an ordinary ball player from now on. Pete Hill will handle the reins," Spedden told the *Afro*.[39] That he did, but the dissension had taken its toll on the team. The Sox, their pennant-winning dreams dashed, finished third in 1925. Beckwith was not there at the end. He simply left the team later in August with not so much as a fare-thee-well. By so doing he avoided being arrested for his Harrisburg outburst. Rumors circulated the Foster would give three players in a trade for Beckwith, who wanted to play in Chicago where he lived and ran a pool hall. Not wanting to have to face him, the Sox refused to release him. He re-emerged as the Sox third baseman for the first part of 1926 but was traded to Harrisburg in mid-season.[40]

Thinking again that a change in managers would improve the Sox's chance for a pennant, Rossiter and Spedden gave Hill his walking papers at the end of the 1925 campaign. They gave the manager's post to Ben Taylor, a member of the famous Taylor family, which sent four brothers, C.I. Taylor among them, to the highest echelons of Black baseball and Ben to Cooperstown in 2006. The new Sox manager, according to Riley, "was considered the best first baseman in black baseball until Buck Leonard came along and ... is well deserving of his niche among the greats in Black baseball history."[41]

Along with the announcement of Taylor's appointment came the statement that Hill was rumored to manage the Birmingham Black Barons. The *Pittsburgh Courier* was more definitive on the subject. The paper ran an article on August 22 stating "that Pete Hill has been scheduled to take over the management of the

The only known picture of Pete Hill in civilian dress (courtesy of Ron Hill).

12. On to Baltimore

Birmingham Black Barons."⁴² Neither the rumor nor the article turned out to be true. Hill hoped the Sox would retain him. In a December 1925 letter to the *Afro*, Pete wrote that he was in Buffalo, New York "with my old time friend 'Home Run' Johnson.... He is very anxious for me to remain here and help him put a club together. I have given him no answer as Mr. Rossiter has been very fair with me.... I would like to return, but the club would have to be run far differently than last season.... My regards to the fans."⁴³ With that, Hill retired from the Negro Leagues.

Rossiter and Spedden never were able to field a pennant winner. After the ECL closed its doors in 1928 a new league, the Negro American League, appeared in 1929 with essentially the same cluster of teams as the comprised the ECL. The Black Sox, now under the leadership of just Rossiter, finally raised its one and only pennant-winning banner at Maryland Park that year.⁴⁴

13

Pete's Final Moves

No pensions, endorsement deals or broadcasting spots existed for ex–Negro League players with a 7th grade education[1] in the mid-1920s, no matter their achievements on the diamond. Some former Black players, such as Chappie Johnson, attained positions as managers or coaches of independent or Negro League teams, or as coaches or scouts for minor league and, in a few cases, major league teams. A few turned to umpiring in the Negro Leagues. Others found jobs in the post office. Lloyd was a school custodian in Atlantic City after his retirement. Pete found a role in baseball.

He stayed in Buffalo and remained friends with Johnson, often sharing living quarters with him. Johnson in 1916, after a 13-year career in Black baseball, moved to Buffalo where he became active in semi-pro ball as both player and manager for several Black teams. His teams included the Pittsburgh Colored Stars of Buffalo, the Buffalo Giants, and the Buffalo Steel Giants.[2] In 1920 he managed the Stars, a member of the eight-team Buffalo Semi-Pro League, for owner Oscar Bright, a clerk in the city's Water Works Administration. The Stars had built a reputation for playing clean, sportsman-like baseball and started the 1920 season with the best wishes of the *Buffalo American*.[3]

Black baseball had preceded Johnson to Buffalo. Bud Fowler was managing an independent, traveling team, the Black Tourists, in the early 1900s. Fowler's nine met the Black Rocks, a Buffalo-based White team named after the city's Black Rock district, at the Roots grounds in May 1909. Henry Endres, a self-employed coal dealer, managed Buffalo's Black Rocks and solicited other teams for games. Among the prominent Black teams that answered Endres' calls were the Cuban Giants, Cuban Stars, and Brooklyn Royal Giants, who had entertained fans on Buffalo's Pine Hill grounds in 1908. There is no evidence that the Leland or American Giants ever made it to Buffalo.[4]

Before the 1920 season started Johnson joined the Bacharach Giants' three-week tour of the South. When he returned to Buffalo he had the

Bacharach's leading pitcher and one of Black baseball's most feared hurlers, "Cannonball" Dick Redding, in tow. Redding agreed to pitch the Stars' Opening Day game.[5] So enamored was Johnson of his Southern tour with the Bacharachs, that he organized a similar trip for his Stars the following spring. On the team's return to Buffalo in the spring of 1921, Redding had again signed a contract to pitch the Stars' opening-day game.[6] The results of Redding's games could not be found, but it is a sure bet his presence boosted attendance considerably.

As a player at age 42 for the Stars, Johnson still had a lot of gas in the tank. In a slugfest against the Pine Ridges, a Buffalo-based White team that the Stars beat, 15–13, Johnson, playing shortstop, went three for three at the plate contributing a homer, two singles, and a stolen base. Two years later as the Stars' captain, Johnson led the Stars to the Buffalo semi-pro team pennant. In a key July game Johnson left his sick bed, where he had been for three days, to lead the Stars to a 15–2 rout over Neuman's Fighting Phoenix team in front of a record crowd of 3,700 spectators in Doll's, pronounced "Dole," Park to take first place. Described in the *Buffalo Enquirer,* for reasons not clear as "the whitest man in baseball," the captain managed with a heavy hand, giving directions to every batter about what to do before each went to the plate, much as Foster had done. The Stars' winning ways generated offers of games from teams in Chicago and Ohio and an agreement that the Stars would face off against every team in the newly established Michigan-Ontario League. Stars owner Oscar Bright fulfilled the offers. He took his team on the road during the week, but made sure his team was home on weekends to play before the loyal and larger Buffalo crowds.[7]

After leaving the Stars and managing the Buffalo Giants for the 1923 season, Johnson, at age 50, signed in 1924 with a newly organized team, the Steel City Giants, owned by C.W. Estill, president of the Colored Citizens Civic League of Lackawanna, New York, six miles south of Buffalo. He continued to play with lesser teams before finally retiring from baseball in 1932.[8]

Hill Gets Involved in Buffalo Baseball

Hill did not wait long to step into Buffalo baseball. He connected with a variety of teams, the names of which often changed from time to time. Whether the names really changed or the writers were misinformed, is not known. Hill's teams played games where they could be found, primarily in Western New York State.

By July of 1926 the 44-year-old Hill, now called Petey Hill in the Buffalo papers, was managing and playing for Petey Hill's Colored All Stars.

In the same month a notice in the *Afro-American* said Hill "has a fast club of ball tossers," playing in the Rochester, New York, area and throughout New England. The article noted that he would like to play a game against his old Baltimore mates. A record of such a game could not be found.[9]

At times, Hill's team was part of the day's entertainment at town picnics and celebrations. In late July 1926, the W & D Diners of Silver Creek, named for a nearby village on the shore of Lake Erie, provided the opposition. The game was played in nearby Sheridan, New York. Hill played right field. Other entertainment included speeches by local dignitaries, a 100-yard race for men, one for the ladies, a Fatman's race, and one for girls under the age of 15. The W and D Band of Silver Creek played throughout the day.[10]

Shortly after that game, Hill took his Petey Hill's Colored All-Stars to the village of Lewiston, New York, located on the Niagara River seven miles north of Niagara Falls and 20 miles north of Buffalo. There Hill's players manhandled a White aggregation of local players, 10–1. Highlights of the game included heavy hitting by the Stars and a leaping catch by their centerfielder Taczack in deep left-centerfield. He landed on a car's radiator and lost consciousness for five minutes but was not seriously hurt. Cars often parked at the edge of ball fields, sometimes to provide lights for an evening game.[11]

In July of 1927 Hill returned to Sheridan to again be part of the day's entertainment. The *Jamestown Evening Journal* cited his team as "the Colored Elks of Dunkirk formerly Petey Hill's Colored All Stars."[12] A month earlier in June the *Niagara Falls Gazette* previewed a game between Hill's team, referred to as Pete Hill's Elite Colored Elks, and the Niagara Cardinals. By this time Johnson and Hill had joined forces, at least for this game. Johnson was listed in the box score as the Elk's second baseman.[13] A month later Hill's team garnered another moniker after a clash with the local White lads in Ellicottville, New York, 45 miles south of Buffalo. The town's paper reported that "the fast travelling Petey Hill's Colored Elks of Buffalo dropped a game to the local lads, 7–5."[14] A year earlier, in August 1926, Hill's All-Stars had been a featured part of the town's Old Home Week facing off against a team of locals. The Red House Collegians and the Rexalls of Franklinville played the second game. The winners and losers of those games played each other the next day. Other attractions included free pavement dancing, acrobats, tumblers, trapeze performers, and high ladder dives into a tub of water.

Jamestown, New York, 70 miles south of Buffalo, was a frequent stop for Hill in 1926. There his All-Stars clashed with Billy Webb's Spiders. Webb had played for and managed independent White teams throughout New York and Pennsylvania before organizing the Spiders in 1915. From

1915 until Webb's death in 1935 he took on numerous barnstorming teams, including White major leaguers such as The Babe Ruth All Stars, the Boston Braves, and two well-known Negro League teams, the Homestead Grays and the Pittsburgh Crawfords.[15]

On an August 1926 foray to Jamestown, Hill took along a friend, Sam Langford, known as the "Boston Tar Baby," one of the leading contenders for the world's heavyweight boxing crown during the 1910s. Langford, described as "a close friend" of Hill, was in Buffalo, and Pete invited the recently retired Canadian-born boxer, a veteran of 300 fights but none against the premier White pugilists of the day and no heavyweight title bout, to make the trip with him.[16] Petey's nine took two of three games from the Jamestown Spiders as Langford cheered them on.[17]

A year later the same paper identified Hill's team as "Petey Hill's Colored Stars of Buffalo formerly the Pullman Colored Giants." Whatever the team's name, the writer clearly knew who Hill was, extolling him as "the famous, sensational outfielder, Petey Hill himself whose color alone kept him out of the big leagues."[18]

In May of 1928, the *Warren Tribune*, in Warren, Pennsylvania, introduced yet another team name. "Locals," the paper reported, "open the 1928 season Monday evening opposing the Black Mohawks, formerly Petey Hill's Colored Stars."[19] In 1932, at age 50, Hill was still skippering a team. The *Lockport (N.Y) Union Sun and Journal* alerted its readers on July 19, 1932, that "a fast colored team, Petey Hill's Colored Stars of Buffalo," would be coming to town two days hence.[20] In a return engagement two weeks later, the same paper named Hill's team "as the Colored Sanders of Buffalo formerly heralded as Petey Hill's Stars."[21]

Red Caps

At some point Hill organized the Buffalo Red Caps, possibly with Johnson.[22] Little could be found about the team. Two references to a team by that name in 1930 were found, but neither mentioned Hill or Johnson.[23] The team's name came from the players' jobs as railroad porters who identified themselves to travelers in depots by sporting a red chapeau. Looking for a steady income stream, Hill and Johnson had both taken jobs as porters themselves in Buffalo. Hill looked after the luggage of those patrons riding the Delaware Lackawanna and Western Railroad, connecting Buffalo with New York City. Johnson did the same for New York Central riders whose lines went north from Manhattan to Boston and west through Buffalo, Chicago, and St. Louis. Johnson may have introduced Hill to the ranks of the red cap porters as Johnson had been Chief Red Cap for the Delavan and Ohio Railroad in 1925 during the off season.[24] Hill did well for himself as a red cap. From 1937 to 1951 he earned a total salary of $21,900, about $220,000 in 2021 dollars, plus an unspecified amount from tips.[25]

Red Cap teams were not unique to Buffalo. The first red chapeau-topped players first took the field in the summer of 1912. The Grand Central Redcaps consisted of 13 Black teenagers from Williamsbridge, New York, an upper-class Black community six miles north of Harlem. Members were the sons of porters at Grand Central. Notable among them was Wesley Williams, the 16-year-old son of James H. Williams. Known to one and all as "Chief," James, the son of slaves, in his role as head of New York City's Grand Central porters, aka Red Caps, served as the terminal's first high-ranking Black officer for nearly 50 years. The likes of writer and civil right activist James Weldon Johnson, Eleanor Roosevelt, and Joe Louis asked for him by name to escort themselves and their luggage to and from the trains. From his ranks of red caps came such notables as singer and activist Paul Robeson, congressman and minister Adam Clayton Powell, Jr., the city's first Black fireman, Samuel "Jesse" Battle, and New York's first Black police officer, James' son Wesley.

Always looking for ways to promote camaraderie among his charges, serve the community, and perhaps inspired by his son's 1912 team, James, in 1916, organized a team of Red Caps to play in the New York area. Two years later Williams improved his roster with several Black stars whose best years with the Lincoln and Royal Giants were behind them. The *Defender* touted the signing of James' highest profile player, catcher Pearl Franklin "Specks" Webster in March of 1918 as a sign "the Red Caps will have one of the fastest teams in the East." Unfortunately for James, Specks soon jumped to the Hilldale Club before being drafted into the army. A frequent opponent, the Pennsylvania Red Caps, consisted of porters at New York City's nearby Penn Station.[26]

A Red Cap team had appeared in the City of Brotherly Love in 1916. George M. Victory, a porter at Philadelphia's then-named Broad Street Station 30th Street and an artist whose one-man oil paintings show in 1949 was attended by the heads of the Pennsylvania RR Company and Gimbel's Department Store, organized the Pennsylvania Red Caps. Before World War I draft calls siphoned off players, the team played such first-class Black teams as the Hilldale Club and the Atlantic City Bacharach Giants. Twenty years later, Victory organized a short-lived league of Red Cap teams with entrants from Grand Central Station in New York City, Washington, D.C.'s Union Station, and terminals serving the Norfolk and Western Railroad. Similar teams were formed in Wilmington, Delaware, and Jacksonville, Florida.[27] The latter team's reputation attracted some of the best Black players looking for a good paying job in addition to a baseball contract.[28]

Still Remembered

A heart attack took Pete Hill's life as he was driving to Buffalo's railroad depot on December 19, 1951. He pulled his car to the curb, where a passerby called firemen, who pronounced him dead. The Buffalo newspapers made brief notice of his death, mentioning only his name age, and cause of death. Sadly, nothing was said about his illustrious baseball career. Pete died practically invisible to the Buffalo community but not without resources. He left "real property" to Dolletha Steep Walker, his landlady, and his remaining estate, valued at $6,000 (about $66,000 in 2021), to his son, Kenneth, then living in Gary, Indiana.[29]

Baseball had not forgotten Pete since his retirement from the Negro Leagues. His name, as one of the best Black players of his day, regularly appeared in the columns of leading African American sportswriters in the 1930s, 40s and 50s. *Chicago Defender* sportswriter Al Monroe sought out Hill for an interview in October 1935. Asked by Monroe who was the greatest pitcher he had ever seen, Hill answered, not surprisingly, "Rube Foster." His answer to the question who was the greatest hitter stunned Monroe. Perhaps Monroe was expecting Hill to name himself or another Black batter. Instead, Hill replied, "That fellow on the Cubs," Hill replied. "I cannot remember his name, who hit one over the fence on Rube Foster when the National leaguers needed just one run to win the ball game."[30] Hill could have been referring to game two of the three-game series in 1909 between the Cubs and the Leland Giants. Rube did pitch in that game, but there were no homers.[31]

Sam Lacy, civil rights advocate and influential sports columnist for the *Afro-American*, included Hill as one of five, including Josh Gibson and Satchel Paige, "big leaguers who couldn't be big leaguers because of their color," in his May 17, 1951, column, just seven months before Hill's death.[32] A year earlier the *Defender*'s Russ J. Cowans included Hill as one of 20 players who starred from 1919 to 1928.[33] Hill led the list of outfielders nominated by Wendell Smith of the *Pittsburgh Courier* in 1948, as players "who could have strengthened any big league club."[34] Even his occasional visit to Chicago, such as the one in February 1948, merited a mention in the *Defender*.[35] A week after Hill's death, Frank A. Young (Fay) took readers on a trip down memory lane of his prowess.[36]

As late as 1968, Lacy brought Hill's name to the attention of his readers once more. As a member of the Baseball Writers Association beginning in 1948 and the Association's first African American member,[37] Lacy voted each year on major league players nominated for election to the Hall. He did so, however, without enthusiasm, feeling that voting was an obligation. He saw the Hall as a shrine only for White players, which it was at the time with the singular exception of Jackie Robinson's 1962 induction. To make his point that there were Black players deserving of induction, Lacy stated that Willie Mays and Mickey Mantle, both deserving of a plaque in Cooperstown when their careers ended, "may have had trouble breaking into an outfield comprised of Oscar Charleston, Pete Hill, and Jud Wilson."[38] The three are in the Hall as is Lacy himself—inducted into the writers' wing of the Hall in 1998, five years before his death in 2003.[39] In 1987 Lacy, still beating the drums loudly for Negro Leaguers in the Hall, noted that Rube Foster, inducted in 1981, 50 years after his death, had described Hill as "probably the finest all-round baseball man I've encountered."[40]

Hill and Johnson were among the 50-plus former Black players invited as special guests by the Negro National League to attend the second 1939 East-West game, Black baseball's all-star game, in Yankee Stadium August 27, 1939; the first year a second East-West game was played.[41] More than 50,000 attended the socially resplendent East-West games, first held in Comiskey Park in 1933, to see Black baseball's finest players in action.

Nor did Pete forget baseball. During a Chicago visit with his son Kenneth, serving with the United States Army Service Corps, in mid–December 1942, Hill, at age 60, told the *Defender* he'd "like to be in the game now." He said he could "murder this new fast ball. The old ball had to be really hit to get extra bases. You had to put the wood on it, sure enough," he said.[42]

Son Kenneth Takes a Stand

Hill's visit with his son might have been part of a family reunion. Gertrude was now living in the house the three shared while Pete was with the American Giants, 5141 South Wabash Avenue in Chicago. Kenneth spent Christmas at his mother's around the same time as his visit with his father, but it is not known if the three of them met. Kenneth went on to complete his service at Fort Huachuca, located outside the town of Sierra Vista, Arizona, fifteen miles north of the Mexican border. He returned to Chicago in the summer of 1945 after the war, hoping to further his education, only to face rank discrimination.

Administrators at Coyne Electrical School (now Coyne College) told him "pointblank" that he would not be accepted "because of my being

13. Pete's Final Moves

colored." He fired off a letter to the *Defender*. "If we are good enough to give our lives on the battlefield," he wrote, "then we are good enough to seek an education which is rightfully ours. I hope you will ... denounce this undemocratic institution."[43] The *Defender* did as Kenneth asked by publishing a September 1, 1946, letter to the editor, by Molly Leiber, a member of the Illinois American Youth for Democracy. She pointedly noted, "We tell the world that we are the greatest democracy. Isn't it about time we took that a little more seriously?" She implored readers to write S.C. Narlan, of the school and General Omar Bradley, head of the Veterans Administration.[44] At the time of her writing, the Chicago *Star* had been conducting a campaign to integrate the school. Two weeks after Leiber's letter was published, the school's Board voted to admit "negroes who meet our requirements."[45]

Kenneth spent the rest of his life in Gary, Indiana, where at some point his mother joined him. Gertrude passed away of influenza in 1976 at Gary's West Side Nursing Home at the ripe old age of 99.[46]

14

Hall of Fame

By 1976 the Negro Leagues had been out of business for 16 years as the increasingly integrated major leagues signed the best of the Black players, starting with Jackie Robinson in 1947. Black fans followed them to major league ballparks. The White baseball establishment, notably the Hall of Fame, moved with glacial speed in honoring the best of the Black players.

Hill's induction into the Hall in 2006 capped 36 years of controversy and compromise over inducting Black players. None had been admitted for their play on Black teams when Ted Williams said during his induction speech in 1966, "I hope someday Satchel Paige and Josh Gibson will be voted into the Hall of Fame as symbols of the great Negro players who are not here only because they weren't given the chance."[1] Newspapers, including the *Chicago Defender, Chicago Tribune,* and *New York Times,* carried columns similar in message to Shirley Povich's in the *Washington Post.*

"Williams," Povich wrote, "was no less than magnificent when he bethought himself of the great Negro League players ... and with a sweep of his hands towards the Hall of Fame building in the background, called for their belated recognition."[2] At the time, only one African American, Jackie Robinson, had a plaque in Cooperstown. Though he played one year in the Negro Leagues, 1945 with the Kansas City Monarchs, he went into the Hall in 1962 for his major league segregation shattering play with the Brooklyn Dodgers.

Prospective Black baseball players and Negro Leaguers faced two obstacles to induction: the Hall's requirement that members had played ten years in the major leagues; and inconsistent record-keeping that was making comparisons among players statistically challenging. Of course, no Negro League player could meet the ten-year mandate. Ford Frick, considered by many the father of the Hall of Fame for spearheading its development in 1936, and Paul Kerr, the Hall's president at the time, nevertheless insisted on it.[3] In replying to a letter from James McAlister of the *Sporting News* inquiring about inducting Satchel Paige, Kerr replied it was unfortunate that Paige was not eligible, adding it was not Paige's fault, "but just the circumstances of the times."⁴ The Hall's chairman of the board from 1977 to 2000, Ed Stack, voiced a similar concern in 1978. "Traditionalists worry that admitting Black veterans to Cooperstown will cheapen the Hall. The important thing is to restrict the Hall of Fame. Keep it a quality election. I think that's very important."⁵

Clifford Kachline, the Hall's historian from 1969 to 1982, did not think racial bias was at play. In an interview with the author, he emphasized the ingrained traditions of baseball that work against change, citing as an example the difficulties overcome in introducing the designated-hitter rule in the American League. He noted further that two Blacks, Robinson and Roy Campanella, the latter inducted in 1969, were in the Hall, and that other Blacks, Bob Gibson, Fergie Jenkins, Willie Mays, and Reggie Jackson, were on their way to the Hall. He made no comments about other Black players.⁶

Monte Irvin, who played in the Negro Leagues with the Newark Eagles and in the majors with the New York Giants and Chicago Cubs, had a different take. In a 2006 interview with the author, he said, "You know how it is. Given the history of our country, there's always something like that behind the scenes.... Something could have been done earlier."⁷

Baseball commissioner Bowie Kuhn made no public comments about people's motivations but, after heated arguments with sportswriter Dick Young, a New York sportswriter known for his abrasive style, and conversations with Roy Campanella, a first-rate catcher for the Negro League Baltimore Elite Giants who followed Robinson to Brooklyn and to Cooperstown, concluded the ten-year requirement and sketchy record keeping were, in his words, "too technical. Had they not been barred," the commissioner continued, "they would have been great major league players and certainly Hall of Famers among them.... This is precisely the kind of situation that required the bending of rules."⁸ Campanella agreed. When asked by reporters how Campy could, given the Negro Leagues' uneven record keeping, support catcher Josh Gibson, often called the Black Babe Ruth, for the Hall, he replied, "All I know is that when I was on the Negro all-stars with Gibson, he caught, and they put me on third base."⁹

Kerr remained unmoved. Knowing this and realizing he would need Kerr's support and that of other Hall of Fame directors, Kuhn did what all good bureaucrats do in tense situations: he appointed the Committee on Negro Leagues in 1970. He selected his assistant, Monte Irvin, to chair it. In addition to Irvin, Negro Leaguers on the committee consisted of Judy Johnson, who played for 20 years and was a scout for the Philadelphia Phillies; Campanella; Bill Yancey, Negro League shortstop for twenty years and a scout for the Yankees and Phillies; and Frank Forbes, a senior judge with the New York Boxing Commission and former Negro League player and scout for the New York Giants. Two veteran sportswriters who had long advocated for the inclusion of Negro Leaguers in the Hall, Sam Lacy from the *Afro-American* and Wendell Smith from the *Pittsburgh Courier*, represented the press. Negro League team owners were represented by Alex Pompez of the New York Cubans and Cuban Stars and a scout for the New York Giants, and Ed Gottlieb of the Philadelphia Stars. Everett D. "Eppie" Barnes, Colgate University's athletic director and former president of the National Collegiate Athletic Association, was the committee's only White voting member. Joe Reichler, public relations director for former Commissioner Spike Eckert and Dick Young, served as non-voting members.

The committee selected 30 players of Hall of Fame caliber after establishing four rules to guide the selections:

    1. Those selected must receive at least 75 percent of committee members' votes.

    2. Selection would be based on playing ability, integrity, sportsmanship, and character.

    3. Only one player would be inducted annually unless more than one received 75 percent of members' votes.

    4. Players must have performed prior to 1947 and have played in the Negro Leagues for at least ten years.

The committee unanimously selected Satchel Paige in February 1971. The committee chose Paige as the one to break the ice, Irvin said, "Because he was pretty well known to the American people." Kerr, impressed with the thoroughness of the committee's work, now agreed that some Negro Leaguers could be inducted but insisted their tablets not be hung among those of the existing members. They should be, Kerr insisted, displayed in a separate wing. Kuhn publicly agreed with Kerr but privately banked on a public outcry to void Kerr's requirement.[10]

Jackie Robinson was among the first to weigh in. "It's the same goddamned thing all over again. If it were me," he said with feeling, "under those conditions, I'd prefer not to be in it."[11] *Newsweek's* Stan Isaac wondered "if a new wing will be built. Or whether a Black architect will design it. Or whether Black guides will direct the tourists."[12]

Kuhn's strategy worked. The *New York Times* reported in July 1971 "that due to severe criticism of this separate but equal treatment," Kerr's proposal, had been dropped.[13] Even so, Paige's induction met with less than universal acclaim. Many of his supporters protested that induction by a special committee, instead of by the established process by which major league players were inducted, tainted Paige's induction. Among them was Frank H. Saunders, Black sportswriter for the *Michigan Chronicle*. The special committee, Saunders wrote, "follows too closely the established

14. Hall of Fame

pattern of a society in which the Black man becomes a first-class citizen when it comes to fighting wars, paying taxes ... but when it comes to equal opportunity, well that's the other side of the barn." Even Kuhn acknowledged, "Technically, he's not in the Hall of Fame, but realistically the Hall of Fame is a state of mind." Paige, for his part, said simply, "I guess they finally found out I was really worthy." Believing the technical to be as important as a state of mind, Paige's supporters continued to press their concerns. They met with some success. The *Baltimore Sun* in August announced that Kuhn and Kerr agreed future inductions of Negro Leaguers would follow the established process.[14] That, however, did not happen.

The special committee continued. Over the next six years the panel inducted eight players in the following order: catcher Josh Gibson, whose titanic homeruns were legendary; first baseman Buck Leonard, considered comparable to Lou Gehrig; Monte Irvin; James "Cool Papa" Bell; Judy Johnson; Oscar Charleston; Martin Dihigo, a Cuban by birth considered by many the most versatile of all Negro League players; and shortstop John Henry "Pop" Lloyd. The committee then disbanded in 1977.

Controversies erupted over how and exactly why the committee chose to shut down. Newly-appointed Board chairman Ed Stack's concern may have been a factor. Disagreements with the committee's selections surfaced. Effa Manley, general manager of the Newark Eagles and a vocal advocate for civil rights, was particularly irate that Rube Foster had been overlooked. "Why in hell," she said, "did the Hall of Fame set that committee up, if they were going to do the lousy job they did."[15] "I am completely disgusted with actions of the old committee." She wrote in a 1977 letter to Negro League historian John Holway, "How that former bunch could have ignored Mackey [Biz], Wells [Willie], Lundy [Dick], Day [Leon]," she fumed.[16] Holway took issue with the committee electing two of its own (Irvin and Johnson). "Blacks," Holway added, "can play the crony game as much as whites do." Holway and Ira Glasser, executive director of the American Civil Liberties Union, considered filing a court suit to force the Hall to admit more Negro Leaguers. Former Black player George Giles, a first baseman known for his superb fielding, speed, and bat control during a career spanning 1927–1939, threatened court action under civil rights laws.[17] No legal action was filed, but the dissidents had a point. Oscar Charleston, John Henry Lloyd, Bullet Joe Rogan, and Turkey Stearns, in addition to those cited by Manley, were at least as deserving, and in many cases, more so, than the nine the committee selected.

The process of inducting Negro Leaguers had not been completely stalled. Amidst the controversies, Negro Leaguers, including Rube Foster in 1981, trickled into the Hall under a variety of processes, which applied equally to all players, set up by the Hall. From 1978 to 2005 nine Negro League players were inducted while 89 major league players, executives, and umpires, had been so honored.[18]

Dale Petroskey and Jane Forbes Clark, who both assumed their positions as Hall president and board chairperson, respectively, in 1999, thought it time for an in-depth assessment of the Negro Leagues and its personnel. Asked why now—when such a study had been sought for 30 years—Petroskey answered, "I thought it was the fair thing to do. Before, we knew maybe 20% of the available information. Now we know 90%."[19] Petoskey had a point. Thirty years had passed since Robert Peterson had compared researching Black baseball to coping with a slippery strand of spaghetti. During those three decades the research and literature on the Negro Leagues exploded. With a grant from Major League Baseball, Petroskey convened a committee of Negro League historians led by Larry Hogan of Union County College in New Jersey and independent Negro League scholars Dick Clark and Larry Lester. After five years of research and discussion by over 50 researchers, a group of 12 baseball historians, appointed by the Hall's Board of Directors, elected 17 Negro Leaguers in 2006.

They included

> **Seven Negro League Players**: Pitcher Ray Brown, a mainstay of the Homestead Grays dynasty in the 1930s and 40s; outfielder Willard Brown (no relation to Ray), the league's most prodigious home run hitter during the 1940s; pitcher Andy Cooper, who was noted for excellent control and a wide range of pitches during his 21-year career; catcher Biz Mackey, who was not only unparalleled behind the plate and dangerous with the bat but also versatile, playing every position on the field at one time or another; outfielder and first baseman Mule Suttles, who combined power with a .300-plus average for most of his 26-year career; outfielder Cristóbal Torriente, the sparkplug of Rube Foster's American Giants in the 1920s, who had power at the plate, speed on the bases, and a strong arm; and infielder Jud Wilson, named by Satchel Paige as one of the two best hitters (Gibson being the other) in the Negro Leagues.
> **Four Negro League Executives:** Effa Manley, the general manager of the Newark Eagles, 1937–1948, who strove valiantly to bring some order to a sometimes chaotic enterprise and was the sole woman to be inducted into in the Hall; Alex Pompez, a wealthy Harlem gambler who owned three teams from 1916 to 1950 and promoted the game skillfully; Cum Posey, credited with making the Homestead Grays one of the most successful teams, highlighted

by winning nine consecutive Negro League pennants; and J.L. Wilkinson.

One Pre-Negro Leagues Executive: Sol White, an infielder for many teams, both Black and White, from 1887 to 1912, best known as a manager, sometimes as player/manager, of top Black teams during his career.

Five Pre-Negro Leagues Players: Infielder Frank Grant, considered the best second baseman in Black baseball during his 20-year career, 1886–1905, with the country's top Black teams; Pitcher José Méndez, Cuban-born who combined speed and deception on the mound with the best Black teams in Cuba and the United States; catcher Louis Santop, renowned for a strong arm that could deliver a ball over the centerfield fence as well as delivering a lifetime .406 batting average during a 25 year career; first baseman Ben Taylor, a heavy hitting, slick fielder whose career as player, manager, and coach spanned 31 years with 22 teams. And John Preston "Pete" Hill.

That year the Hall also welcomed Bruce Sutter, a relief pitcher for the Cubs, Cardinals, and Braves, who pioneered the split-finger fastball.[20]

None of the 17 was alive at the time of their induction, but all, apart from Hill, were represented by relatives in Cooperstown, New York, on July 30, 2006, when the largest class in the Hall's history joined the ranks of baseball's immortals.[21] It would take 15 years and another special committee before more Black players who never played a day in the majors would be elected. In the meantime the Hall inducted 55 players.[22] In December 2021 the Early Baseball Era Committee, which considered those who played prior to 1950, elected Bud Fowler and Buck O'Neil from among a slate of 10 candidates. As a player, O'Neil is best-known as a smooth fielding first baseman from 1937 to 1955 with several teams, most notably the Kansas City Monarchs, a team he later managed. He made history in 1962 with the Chicago Cubs by becoming the first Black major league coach. He served as the unofficial ambassador of Negro League baseball as chairman of the board of the Negro Leagues Museum in Kansas City and as a narrator for Ken Burns' documentary on baseball. He narrowly missed election in 2006. The Early Baseball Era Committee will meet again in 2031 to consider candidates for the 2032 Induction year.[23]

Epilogue

The struggle for according Hill his well-deserved recognition did not end with his Hall of Fame induction in 2006. The research done to establish his given name and birthplace resulted in errors. When unveiled, Hill's name on his bronze plaque read *Joseph* Preston Hill, not *John* Preston Hill. The printed materials produced by the Hall gave his birthplace as Pittsburgh, Pennsylvania, not Buena, Virginia. It is not clear how the mistakes were made, but the discrepancies went unnoticed until April 2007. Baseball historian Gary Ashwill in North Carolina and a colleague, Patrick Rock in Kansas, began asking if the information was wrong. They believed his first name was John and that he was born in Culpeper County, Virginia.

Ashwill relayed their findings to Hill's great niece in Los Angeles, who immediately contacted Ron Hill, Pete's great-nephew and a former college football player, Marine, jazz musician, and supervisor of a Pittsburgh jail. He e-mailed members of the selection committee seeking clarification. Hearing nothing back, he contacted the editor of the *Culpeper Star-Exponent* asking for help. The editor forwarded the request to White columnist Zann Nelson, whose weekly columns featured stories of local historical interest. She relished the assignment, telling *Pittsburgh Post-Gazette* reporter Kevin Kirkland, "The injustice is that so many people, our African-American ancestors, have been obscured, obliterated. Anytime I can open somebody's eyes, bring a little more justice through knowledge, it's gratifying." Nelson's research corroborated Gary Ashwill's findings about Pete Hill's true name and birthplace. She and Ron Hill then pressed the case for a correction to the Hall of Fame's initial information.

Though the process took four years, the Hall of Fame, with descendants of John Preston "Pete" Hill from Ohio, Boston, Los Angeles, and Pennsylvania in attendance, unveiled a new bronze plaque at a special ceremony in Cooperstown on October 12, 2010, on what would have been Hill's 128th birthday. Ron Hill exclaimed at the time, "Seeing that plaque put the icing on the cake. We will accept it as a family on behalf of him."[1]

The Hall of Fame–issued postcard stating Hill's name as Joseph, not John Preston "Pete" Hill (courtesy of Ron Hill).

The corrected postcard (courtesy of Ron Hill).

The Hall also issued a new Hall of Fame plaque postcard, which is produced for every inductee, with John Preston "Pete" Hill replacing the Joseph Preston "Pete" Hill.

Finding Hill's Grave

While the Hall was correcting its information about Hill, a search for his grave was underway. Hill's death certificate stated that his body had been shipped to Chicago, but said nothing about a cemetery. Kenneth had shipped his father's body to the Holy Sepulchre Cemetery in Alsip, Illinois, 15 miles south of Chicago, but no one knew about it. Holy Sepulcher is a Roman Catholic cemetery, which may explain his son's choice. While Pete's mother had been a Baptist during her life in Pittsburgh, little is known about Pete's religious beliefs. His son Kenneth had married a Catholic woman and had purchased three burial lots at Holy Sepulchre. The other two remain vacant. Pete was buried in the third one, an unmarked grave.[2]

The location of Hill's grave remained a mystery for years. Some believed, but had no proof, that he had been buried in Burr Oak Cemetery, just outside Chicago, also in Alsip, Illinois. Burr Oak seemed a likely possibility. Until 2009 the Black cemetery had been the burial place for prominent African Americans, including civil rights figure Emmett Till, singer Dinah Washington, boxing champion Ezzard Charles, and, as of 2004, about 60 Black baseball players. Adding to the mystery was the concern that Hill's site might never be found due to the Burr Oak scandal of 2009. Four employees were caught digging up graves, re-selling the plots, and burying the disinterred remains in a large pit. All four served time in prison.[3]

Dr. Jeremy Krock, a pediatric anesthesiologist in Peoria, Illinois, had been on the case since 2006. Caring about graves was a family tradition for Krock. "My grandparents and great aunts and uncles were always attentive to family graves," he told National Public Radio's *Weekend Edition* reporter Greg Echlin. "And it's something we do," Krock continued. "Back then," he said, "it was Decoration Day (now Memorial Day). Every Decoration Day we went out and tended to the graves." Explaining why he devotes so much time to finding unmarked graves of Black ball players, Krock told Echlin, "They played in anonymity, and I just don't feel it's right to spend eternity in anonymity, to be buried in an unmarked grave after they passed away. It's just an injustice."[4]

Krock began his search for unmarked graves of Black ballplayers in 2003 when he discovered outfielder Jimmie Crutchfield, from Krock's hometown of Ardmore, Missouri, a small coal-mining town, was among those Negro Leaguers with an unmarked grave. Krock raised the funds necessary for a gravestone for Crutchfield as well as two others, John Donaldson and "Candy Jim" Taylor. In 2010, with the support of SABR, Negro League historian Larry Lester, and financial contributions from readers of Lester's Negro League newsletter, White Sox owner Jerry Reinsdorf, former commissioner Fay Vincent, and former major league player, manager, and coach Don Zimmer, Krock marked his 19th grave with a 150-pound memorial, that of pitcher Bill Gatewood. The stone read:

NEGRO LEAGUES BASEBALL
PITCHER AND MANAGER
"BIG BILL"
WILLIAM M. GATEWOOD
1881 1982.

A drawing of a baseball in a glove replaced what normally would have been a dash between the years.[5]

From Hill's death certificate Krock knew Hill's body had been shipped to Chicago. Four years of searching public records and newspaper archives and contacting Chicago area Black funeral homes and Black cemeteries such as Restvale, Lincoln, and Mt. Glenwood proved fruitless. While watching the movie *Cadillac Records* in 2010, featuring blues jazz performers such as Muddy Waters, Krock learned one of the musicians, Little Walter, was buried in a Roman Catholic cemetery. "I decided then to refocus our attention on some other less obvious cemeteries," Krock said after viewing the movie. His inquiry to the Catholic Cemetery Database turned up the location of Hill's grave on November 8, 2010. By 2013 a granite marker had been placed on Hill's grave thanks to the fund-raising efforts of Krock, Lester, and Hill's great-nephew, Ron Hill.[6]

Back to Culpeper

More honors were to come Hill's way. Three weeks after Hill's 2010 re-induction into the Hall of Fame, Pennsylvania's Allegheny County Council issued a Proclamation honoring John Preston "Pete" Hill for "his lifelong, inimitable contributions to baseball as an outstanding player and as an exceptional manager."[7]

As the search for Hill's grave was unfolding, Nelson was advocating for memorial markers to be established honoring Hill in the county of his birth. Her findings caught the eye of Kathleen S. Kilpatrick, director of Virginia's Department of Historic Resources. She designed a marker

Virginia Department of Historic Resources' roadside sign honoring Hill, located at 26255 Rapidan Road, Rapidan, Virginia (author's collection).

and Gary Ashwill, in consultation with the department's Randall Jones, wrote the text. Following her Board's approval, the marker was unveiled in October 2010 in the presence of many of Hill's descendants and several baseball historians. Nelson underlined the significance of the occasion, saying, "Certainly, the fact that Culpeper can now claim two Hall of Fame baseball players (the other being Eppa Rixey, White, and a pitcher for the Phillies and Cubs from 1912 to 1933) is fun and a genuine source of pride." "Hill," she continued, "was a real-life superhero rising from the same streets and fields that we walk every day. Times may be different, and many of the hard core obstacles that Pete Hill faced have dissipated. Yet we share similar struggles and desires for opportunity, fairness, security, and success."⁸

Nelson received a letter from Virginia's governor, Robert F. McDonnell, congratulating her "for the superb research you recently completed on one of Culpeper's greatest, and until now, long lost sons, Pete Hill."⁹ SABR's Negro League Committee honored Nelson with the John Coates Next Generation Award, named for a Negro Leagues researcher who died before completing his work. The marker can be seen today on Virginia State Route 615 (Rapidan Road).¹⁰

Another honor soon came Pete's way when on February 4, 2011, the Virginia House of Delegates issued House Joint Resolution No. 810 celebrating his life and accomplishments and noting that, after 400 hours of research, Zann Nelson had confirmed that Pete was born in Virginia.

While the Hall of Fame, Virginia's governor, the state's General Assembly, and the state's Department of Historic Resources found

Plaque erected by the Culpeper County Supervisors located at Culpeper Sports Complex on Competition Drive in Culpeper, Virginia. It includes a rare 1909 photograph of the left-handed hitter as a Leland Giant. He has choked up several inches on the bat making it easier to swing and rap out his famous line drive singles. Note no insignia on jersey or pants. Cuban's catcher Gonzalo Sanchez is behind the plate. White umpire Ed Goeckel calls balls and strikes. Spectators watch from a wooden grandstand (author's collection).

Nelson's research convincing, members of the Culpeper County Board of Supervisors were not so sure. At its July 2011 meeting, Board Chairman Bill Chase decided more research was in order before its members voted on a motion to erect a marker honoring Hill at the county's youth-league sports complex. Chase asked local historian George Bryson to look into the matter.

Reporting back at the Board's September meeting, Bryson said he didn't know if Hill was born in Buena or Culpeper County. "Was Pete Hill born here? Maybe." Bryson said. In a manner similar to those who advised against inducting Negro Leaguers into the Hall of Fame due to incomplete record keeping, Bryson cited being unable to find Hill in official records as the reason for his uncertainty about Hill's birthplace. Rebukes to Bryson's conclusion followed swiftly. Supervisor Roberts pointed out the challenges she had faced in her personal research. She could "find no official government record" of her grandmother's birth in Rappahannock County in 1900. Nelson expressed surprise that Bryson had not included any of the available research in his report. Among other documents unearthed had been Hill's social security application, which Gary Ashwill had turned up two years earlier.[11] The application cited Rapidan, the nearest post office to Buena, as his birthplace.

Appropriateness of the wording came under scrutiny. Supervisor Steve Wallace, in favor of a marker but not 100 percent sure Hill was born in Culpeper, suggested, as Ashwill had earlier, the county's marker should state that Hill "was born near here." The Department of Historic Resources had chosen that wording for its marker.

The September meeting turned more contentious when a member pointed out that the Board at its July meeting had approved a marker and its funding for White Hall of Famer Eppa Rixey. Several of Hill's descendants and others voiced aloud a concern that racial bias may be at play. Ron Hill first gave voice to the heretofore unspoken concern, saying, "Racism is alive and well." Educator Nan Butler Roberts reminded the group that "One of the things we all need to have in check is we all have some biases." "People know I'm not a racist," responded Bryson. Chase, feeling he'd been tagged as such, announced he didn't appreciate the charge and was "personally offended by it." To which Roberts replied, "To hear some say 'I'm not a racist,' or 'I don't have anything against anyone,' it puts up my antenna."

Nelson's request to address the gathering was abruptly turned down by Chase, who said, "We don't have any other speakers. This isn't a public hearing." The Board eventually did approve the Pete Hill marker and its funding by a 5–2 vote. The two members voting "No" said they did so out of concern for the cost of the project. A marker honoring Hill now stands adjacent to the one for Eppa Rixey at the Culpeper Sports Complex on Competition Drive in Culpeper. Both were erected and paid for by the county. Hill's birthplace is listed as "Buena, Culpeper County, Virginia."[12]

The Legacy of Early Black Baseball

Hill, Foster, Johnson, Taylor, Schlichter, Leland, Charleston, Blount, Rossiter and the hundreds if not thousands of others who made Black baseball possible during the first two decades of the twentieth century laid the foundation and pioneered the way for Black teams and players who would follow, who are better known today, and who eventually provided the gateway to the majors for Black players. The great Black teams of the 1930s and 1940s such as the Homestead Grays, Kansas City Monarchs, Pittsburgh Crawfords, Newark Eagles, Baltimore Elite Giants, Memphis Red Sox, and players such as Satchel Paige, Josh Gibson, Buck Leonard, Willie Wells, Roy Campanella, Don Newcombe, Jackie Robinson, Junior Gilliam, Larry Doby, Hank Aaron, Biz Mackey, Mule Suttles, Monte Irvin, Cool Papa Bell, among many others, arose from the early century pioneers who showed that people would pay to see the games, appreciate the respite from segregated life provided by the games, and admire the abilities of accomplished athletes whose skin color just happened to be various shades of Black.

Chapter Notes

Preface

1. "Baseball Hall of Fame Election Year Checklist," Baseball Almanac, https://www.baseball-almanac.com/hof/hofmem3.shtml. Accessed November 9, 2020.

Introduction

1. Robert W. Peterson, "Blacks in Baseball," https://www.britannica.com/sports/baseball/Blacks-in-baseball. Accessed September 16, 2021. Alton Hornsby, Jr., *Chronology of African-American History: Significant Events and People from 1619 to the Present* (Detroit: Gale Research, 1991), 41.
2. Robert W. Peterson, "Blacks in Baseball."
3. "June 21, 1879: The Cameo of William Edward White,"SABR Games Project, https://sabr.org/gamesproj/game/june-21-1879-the-cameo-of-william-edward-white/. Accessed March 27, 2021.
4. "Ball Players Do Not Burn," *Sporting News*, March 23, 1889.
5. Robert W. Peterson, "Blacks in Baseball."
6. "Rube Foster Was a Puzzle to Locals," *Harrisburg Daily Independent*, September 19, 1905.
7. "Countdown to the Last Steam Train," Bloomber, bloomberg.com/news/articles/2012-10-17/countdown-to-the-last-steam-train. Accessed March 10, 2021.
8. Ira Berkow, "17 from Black Baseball Included in Hall at Last," *New York Times*, July 31, 2006. From 1911 to the time of Foster's death in 1930 the team's name was American Giants. "Chicago" was added later. Foster identified himself as "Manager, American Giants Baseball Team" in a letter to Chicago Defender, published as "Rube Foster's Signed Statement of the Giants-A.B.C. Mixup," July 31, 1915. See also Frank A. Young, "When League Was Formed in 1920," *Chicago Defender*, December 17, 1938.
9. Fred Bowen, "The Score," *Washington Post*, October 7, 2021.
10. Robert Peterson, *Only the Ball Was White: A History of Legendary Black Players and All-Black Professional Teams* (New York: Oxford University Press, 1992), 80.
11. John Thorn, e-mail to the author on June 13, 2021.
12. Bill Glauber, "Elite Giants: The Pride of Baltimore Baseball History," *Baltimore Sun*, April 2, 1990.
13. James "Red" Moore, in-person interview, January 19, 2006.
14. George Cantor, "Stars of the Past," *Detroit Free Press*, September 16, 1992.
15. John B. Holway, *Baseball Stars: Negro League Pioneers* (New York: Mecklermedia, 1988), 23.
16. Leslie A. Heaphy, *The Negro Leagues: 1869–1960* (Jefferson, NC: McFarland, 2003), 16.
17. "I'm Holding Out Because Joe DiMaggio Advised Me To." *Pittsburgh Courier*, April 23, 1938.
18. James A. Riley, *The Biographical Encyclopedia of the Negro Baseball Leagues* (New York: Carroll & Graf, 1994), 488.
19. Charles F. Faber, "J.L. Wilkinson," SABR Biography Project, https://sabr.org/bioproj/person/j-l-wilkinson/. Accessed September 15, 2020.
20. "Baseball's First Multiracial Barn-

storming Team Revealed in 105-Year-Old Postcard," https://news.justcollecting.com/all-nations-baseball-team-postcard-auction/. Accessed November 9, 2020; Riley 242, 545.

21. "All Nation Team Doing Great Work," *Chicago Defender*, October 7, 1916.

22. James A. Riley, *Encyclopedia*, 30–31. Janet Bruce, *The Kansas City Monarchs: Champions of Black Baseball* (Lawrence: University Press of Kansas, 1985), 21.

23. Larry Lester, *Rube Foster in His Time: On the Field and in the Papers with Black Baseball's Greatest Visionary* (Jefferson, NC: McFarland, 2012), 105, as cited in "Pete Hill," SABR Biography Project, https://sabr.org/bioproj/person/pete-hill/. Accessed June 29, 2020.

24. Russell J. Cowans, "Through the Sport Mirror," *Detroit Tribune*, August 19, 1933.

25. For the Win (column), *USA Today*, https://ftw.usatoday.com. Accessed June 29, 2020.

26. James A. Riley, *Of Monarchs and Black Barons: Essays on Baseball's Negro Leagues* (Jefferson, NC: McFarland, 2012), 37.

27. Riley, *Encyclopedia*, 381. The dead ball era, according to baseball historian Paul Dickson, is a popularly used misnomer. Instead of a change to a "livelier Ball," most baseball historians, Dickson said, agree that the era ended in 1920 when major league rule changes made the ball easier to hit by outlawing trick pitches and freak deliveries, replacing discolored and worn balls with new ones, beginning the use of better-quality materials, and batters (think Babe Ruth) becoming more willing to swing for the fences.

28. Lester, *Foster in His Time*, 21–22.

29. "Sez Chez," *Pittsburgh Courier*, March 6, 1943.

30. Cum Posey, "Cum Posey Flays Methods of Conducting League," *Afro American*, July 22, 1933; "Meet Cum's All-Time All-Americans," *Pittsburgh Courier*, December 18, 1937.

31. Jeremy Beer, *Oscar Charleston: The Life and Legend of Baseball's Greatest Forgotten Player* (Lincoln: University of Nebraska Press, 2019) 57–58; Riley, *Encyclopedia*, 543; "Melancholy Jones, Dick Redding, Atlantans on All-Time Nine," *Atlanta Daily World*, August 3, 1939.

32. William F. McNeil, *Cool Papas and Double Duties: The All-Time Greats of the Negro Leagues* (Jefferson, NC: McFarland, 2001), 193.

33. "Our Heroes Make It Three in a Row Over the Giants," *Indianapolis Freeman*, May 24, 1915.

Chapter 1

1. Find a Grave, https://www.findagrave.com/memorial/143079875/reuben-w-hill. Accessed June 9, 2020. While records at the Maple Park Cemetery in Bluefield, West Virginia, where Ruben Hill is buried list him as being the father of the three brothers, Pete Hill listed his father as "Ike" on his Social Security application lending an aura of mystery to his parentage. Nothing further could be found about an Ike.

2. Phone conversation with Ron Hill, July 12, 2012.

3. Allison Brophy Champion, *McClatchy-Tribune Business News*, August 1, 2010.

4. Zann Nelson, "Culpeper: More Baseball Connections," *Culpeper Star Exponent*, January 27, 2010; Find a Grave, https://www.findagrave.com/memorial/143079875/reuben-w-hill. Accessed June 10, 2020.

5. "Cedar Mountain Battlefield," Battlefields.org, https://www.battlefields.org/visit/heritage-sites/cedar-mountain-battlefield. Accessed May 6, 2020.

6. "Civil War Robert Shaw Letters and Papers," Paperless Archives, BACM Research Collection Supplement Disc H.

7. James I. Robertson, Jr., *General A. P. Hill: The Story of a Confederate Warrior* (New York: Vintage Illustrated, 1992), 108.

8. Bob Luke and John David Smith, *Soldiering for Freedom: How the Union Army Recruited, Trained, and Deployed the U.S. Colored Troops* (Baltimore: Johns Hopkins University Press, 2014), 31, 32, 51, 92.

9. Zann Nelson, "Pete Hill: Culpeper County's Newly Discovered Hall of Famer Part 3: Hill's Family History," *Culpeper Star-Exponent*, December 31, 2009.

10. "About Homewood," HELP Initiative Pittsburgh, https://helppgh.org/help-communities/about-homewood/. Accessed July 2, 2021.

11. Much of the information about Hill's life in Buena came from the groundbreaking

Notes—Chapter 1

and extensive research done by Gary Ashwill, much of it posted on his blog (Agate Type, at https://agatetype.typepad.com), from historian Zann Nelson's three-part investigative series published in the *Culpeper Star-Exponent* as "Digging Deeper: Culpeper County's Newly Discovered Baseball Hall of Famer" (December 29–31, 2009), and from historian Fred Worth's efforts, which included a trip to Buffalo, New York, to retrieve Hill's death certificate; interview with Ron Hill, April 30, 2020; Kevin Kirkland, "John Preston 'Pete' Hill Had Storied Career in Black Baseball," *Pittsburgh Post-Gazette*, April 8, 2010.

12. 1900 and 1940 United States Census.

13. "Mother of Well Known Citizen Passes Away," *Pittsburgh Courier*, September 26, 1931; "Pete Hill Visits City," *Pittsburgh Courier*, September 26, 1931; "Pioneer Bldg. and Loan Association Declares Dividend," *Pittsburg Courier*, July 28, 1923.

14. Riley, *Of Monarchs and Black Barons*, 38.

15. "Black Sox Players: No. 1 Pete Hill Manager," *Baltimore Afro-American*, January 18, 1924.

16. G.L. Mackey, "Sports Mirror," *Baltimore Afro-American*, April 18, 1925.

17. Gary Ashwill, e-mail to author, October 10, 2020.

18. "Pete Hill," SABR Biography Project, https://sabr.org/bioproj/person/pete-hill/. Accessed October 10, 2020.

19. Riley, *Encyclopedia*, 294–95.

20. *Pittsburgh Daily Post*, April 16, 1901.

21. Jerry Malloy (Ed.), *Sol White's History of Colored Base Ball with Other Documents on the Early Black Game* 1886–1936 (Lincoln: University of Nebraska Press, 1995), 40.

22. "The Seamheads Negro Leagues DB: A Brief Introduction," Seamheads, https://www.seamheads.com/NegroLgs/team.php?yearID=1904&. Accessed March 24, 2021.

23. Sol White, "Sol White Recalls," *New York Age*, January 3, 1931; Chicago Defender in its December 12, 1942, article reporting on Hill's visit with his son, "Pete Hill, Retired Ball Player Visits Soldier Son," also cites the Pittsburgh Keystones as Hill's first team and has him joining the Philadelphia Giants in 1903.

24. Robert Peterson, *Only the Ball Was White*, 244.

25. John B. Holway, *The Complete Book of Baseball's Negro Leagues: The Other Half of Baseball History* (Fern Park, FL: Hastings House, 2001), 43; Jorge S. Figueredo, *Cuban Baseball: A Statistical History 1878–1961* (Jefferson, NC: McFarland, 2011), 69.

26. Neil Lanctot, *Fair Dealing and Clean Playing: The Hilldale Club and the Development of Black Professional Baseball* (Syracuse: Syracuse University Press, 1994), 13–14.

27. *Philadelphia Evening Item*, April 23, 1902, as cited in Lanctot, *Fair Dealing*, 14.

28. "Handball at the P.A.S.C.," *Philadelphia Inquirer*, February 15, 1893; "Aquatic Sports, *Philadelphia Inquirer*, August 19, 1894; "Sport Gossip," *Butte Daily Post* (Butte, Montana), October 31, 1906; "Sidelights on Sporting Stage," *Grand Forks Herald* (Grand Forks, North Dakota), March 30, 1911; "Pushmobile Will Race in Big Meet," *Philadelphia Inquirer*, March 28, 1912; "Big Negro Champion Beat Jim Jeffords," *Harrisburg Courier* (Harrisburg, Pennsylvania), November 9, 1906.

29. Malloy, 31; White, "Sol White Recalls."

30. "Thru the Eyes of W. Rollo Wilson," *Philadelphia Tribune*, June 29, 1944; Riley, *Encyclopedia*, 563, 430, 528, 434.

31. *The Philadelphia Item*, May 12, 1905, as cited in Lester, *Foster in His Time*, 23.

32. Riley, *Encyclopedia*, 625.

33. Ibid., 436.

34. Lester, *Foster in His Time*, 22–24.

35. "Year By Year Leaders for Strikeouts," https://www.baseball-almanac.com/pitching/pistrik4.shtml. Accessed November 10, 2019.

36. Lester, *Foster in His Time*, 230–31.

37. Ibid., 169–70.

38. https://www.ancestrylibrary.com/discoveryui-content/view/40440767:6742. Accessed September 6, 2021.

39. Lester, *Foster in His Time*, 231.

40. "Calvert, TX," https://tshaonline.org/handbook/online/articles/hjc02. Accessed November 1, 2019; *Negro Population 1790–1915*. Washington Government Printing Office, Department of Commerce, Bureau of Census, 791.

41. Layton Revel and Luis Munoz, *Early*

Pioneers of the Negro Leagues: Walter "Slick" Schlichter (Carrollton, TX: Center for Negro League Baseball Research, 2016), 9.
    42. *Indianapolis Freeman*, March 10, 1902, as cited in Lanctot, *Fair Dealing*, 42.
    43. "Dave Wyatt Returns from East," *Chicago Defender*, August 17, 1918; Riley, *Encyclopedia*, 885.
    44. Brian Carroll, *When to Stop Cheering? The Black Press, the Black Community, and the Integration of Professional Baseball* (New York: Routledge, 2007), 22.
    45. "Baseball Pays Last Tribute to Baseball Daddy," *Baltimore Afro-American*, December 20, 1930; Riley, *Biographical Encyclopedia*, 290.
    46. Riley, Encyclopedia, 290–292; Holway, *Complete Book*, 45.
    47. Larry Lester, *Foster in His Time*, 18.
    48. In a corroborating account, Edwin Bancroft Henderson, in his book *The Negro in Sports* (Washington, D.C.: Associated Publishers, 1939), 153, said Foster "served under McGraw as a coach of pitchers for the New York Giants."
    49. Joseph L. Reichler (Ed.). *The Baseball Encyclopedia*, 7th ed. (New York: Macmillan, 1988), 1638, 1983, 1995–96.
    50. "The Underground Railroad in Hancock County," https://www.hmdb.org/m.asp?m=29176. Accessed April 23, 2020.

Chapter 2

    1. Larry Lester, Sammy J. Miller, and Dick Clark, *Black Baseball in Chicago* (Chicago: Arcadia Publishing, 2000), 15; William F. McNeil, *Black Baseball Out of Season: Pay for Play Outside of the Negro Leagues* (Jefferson, NC: McFarland, 2017), 7.
    2. "About the Breakers Palm Beach," thebreakers.com/about-breakers; "About the Royal Poinciana Hotel," pbhistoryonline.org./page/the-grand-hotels-royal-poinciana-hotel; accessed May 17, 2020.
    3. McNeil, *Out of Season*, 6.
    4. *Ibid.*, 23.
    5. "Society at Palm Beach," *New York Times*, January 9, 1910.
    6. "Palm Beach Chips," *Philadelphia Tribune*, February 6, February 23, 1918.
    7. "The Extraordinary Story of Why a 'Cakewalk' Wasn't Always Easy," https://www.npr.org/sections/codeswitch/2013/12/23/256566647/the-extraordinary-story-of-why-a-cakewalk-wasnt-always-easy. Accessed May 20, 2020; "Palm Beach Chips," *Philadelphia Tribune*, February 6, 1918.
    8. *Philadelphia Tribune*, February 23, 1918.
    9. *Ibid.*
    10. Malloy, *Sol White's History,* 8; Riley, *Encyclopedia*, 202–203; J. Gordon Street, "The Cuban Giants," *New York Age*, October 15, 1887. https://www.theclio.com/entry/13391
    11. http://arkbaseball.com/tiki-index.php?page=Charlie+%E2%80%9CTokohama%E2%80%9D+Grant+Conspiracy. Accessed August 6, 2020; Riley, *Encyclopedia*, 330.
    12. Lester, *Foster in His Time*, 168.
    13. "Cuban X-Giants Defy," *Philadelphia Inquirer*, August 23, 1904.
    14. "First of the Series of Three Games ..." *Philadelphia Inquirer*, September 2, 1904; "Cuban X-Giants Land 2nd Game," *Philadelphia Inquirer*, September 3, 1904.
    15. "Phila. Giants Win Championship," *Philadelphia Inquirer*, September 4, 1904; Riley, 847.
    16. "Phila. Giants Win Championship," *Philadelphia Inquirer*, September 4, 1904.
    17. McNeil, *Out of Season*, 9.
    18. "Philadelphia Giants I," https://www.seamheads.com/NegroLgs/organization.php?franchID=PG&tab=seasons&first=1905&last=1905&lgID=All. Accessed March 25, 2021.
    19. The team's record per Phil S. Dixon, *Phil Dixon's American Baseball Chronicles—Great Teams: The 1905 Philadelphia Giants Volume III* (Xlibris, 2010) 33, 46–47, 56–57, 232; Floyd J. Calvin, "Sol White Recalls Baseball's Greatest Days," *Pittsburgh Courier*, March 12, 1927.
    20. Holway, *Complete Book,* 49.
    21. Billy Evans, "Baseball in Cuba Growing Rapidly," *New York Times*, December 4, 1910.
    22. Figueredo, *Cuban Baseball*, 25, 48.
    23. "What Is the Platt Amendment? Definition and Significance." June 1, 2019. blog.prepscholar.com/platt-amendment-definition. Accessed May 3, 2021; "Platt

Amendment." britannica.com/topic/Platt-amendment. Accessed May 3, 2021.

24. "Chronology of U.S.-Cuba Relations," cri.fiu.edu/us-cuba/chronology-of-us-cuba-relations/. Accessed June 30, 2021.

25. Bjarkman, *A History of Cuban Baseball, 1864–2006* (Jefferson, NC: McFarland, 2007), 85–87.

26. "Yanigans Played to a Standstill," *Philadelphia Inquirer*, April 15, 1906. Sometimes spelled Yannigan, the word refers to "a player on the second team in a spring training camp game." (Dickson, 951.)

27. "Baseball Needs Brain and Money," *Baltimore Afro-American*, October 29, 1920; Lanctot, *Fair Dealing*, 14; Holway, *Complete Book*, 52; "Phila. Giants Win Championship Cup," *Philadelphia Inquirer*, September 4, 1906; "International League," *Philadelphia Inquirer*, September 10, 1906.

28. Malloy, *Sol White's History*, 111.

29. "Scranton Defeated," *Scranton Tribune*, April 28, 1906; "Tables Turned on the Giants," *Scranton Truth*, April 30, 1906; "General Sporting Notes," *Burlington Free Press*, December 26, 1905.

30. Malloy, *Sol White's History*, 49.

31. "Athletics Have Close Call," *Philadelphia Inquirer*, October 13, 1906.

32. "Sol White Recalls," *New York Age*, January 3, 1931.

33. Robert Charles Cottrell, *The Best Pitcher in Baseball: The Life of Rube Foster, Negro League Giant* (New York: New York University Press, 2001), 32; Lanctot, *Fair Dealing*, 14.

34. W. Rollo Wilson, "Eastern Snapshot," *Pittsburgh Courier*, January 16, 1926.

35. Lester, *Foster in His Time*, 30; Riley, *Encyclopedia*, 93, 758–59, 363, 610, 883, 563

36. Figueredo, *Cuban Baseball*, 64–65.

37. Ibid., 66–68.

38. "Personals," *Republican-Northwestern* (Belvidere, IL), August 10, 1906.

39. Summary of Hill's trips to Cuba on file at the Buffalo History Museum.

40. Mindy Long, "Lulu Lawson: Traveling Vaudeville Entertainer," *Belvidere Daily Republican*, February 14, 2019; Mindy Long, e-mails to author, May 29–30, 2020.

41. "John Lawson," https://www.seamheads.com/NegroLgs/player.php?playerID=lawso01joh. Accessed March 23, 2021; *Republican-Northwestern* (Belvidere, Illinois) April 10, 1908; *Belvidere Daily Republican*, February 15, 1910.

42. NY Passenger Manifest supplied by the Buffalo History Museum.

43. McNeil, *Out of Season*, 36.

44. Ibid.

45. "Married Last October," *Belvidere Daily Republican*, June 18, 1900; "Mrs. J. Lawson Dead," *Boone County Republican*, May 26, 1903; "Record of a Death in Philadelphia" and "John Lawson Visits Here," *Belvidere Daily Republican*, September 21, 1922; Revel and Munoz, *Schlichter*, 33; Riley, *Encyclopedia*, 387, 434, 528; Bjarkman, *Cuban Baseball*, 145.

Chapter 3

1. Michel Lomax, "Black Entrepreneurship in the National Pastime: The Rise of Semiprofessional Baseball in Black Chicago," in Patrick B. Miller and David K. Wiggians (Eds.), *Sport and the Color Line: Black Athletes and Race Relations in Twentieth Century America* (Philadelphia: Routledge, 2003), 26.

2. Howard W. Rosenberg, *Cap Anson 4: Bigger Than Babe Ruth* (Arlington, VA: Tile, 2006), 436–437.

3. Capanson.com/chapter 4.html. Accessed April 4, 2021; Robert W. Peterson, *Only the Ball Was White: A History of Legendary Black Players and All-Black Professional Teams Before Black Men Played in the Major Leagues* (New York: Prentice Hall, 1970), 30.

4. *Chicago Broad Ax*, August 8, 1908, as cited in Leslie A. Heaphy (Ed.), *Black Baseball and Chicago* (Jefferson, NC: McFarland, 2006), 15.

5. *The Inter-Ocean*, July 13, 1908; Layton Revel and Luis Munoz, *Early Pioneers of the Negro Leagues: Frank C. Leland* (Carrollton, TX: Center for Negro League Baseball Research, 2016), 16.

6. Heaphy, *Black Baseball*, 15.

7. Bjarkman, *Cuban Baseball*, 85–88.

8. "Leland Giants' Trip," *Suburbanite Economist* (Chicago), April 2, 1909; "Special Car for Team," *San Francisco Call*, April 11, 1909.

9. Revel and Munoz, *Leland*, 16.

10. "Cuban X-Giants to Play Here," *Baltimore Sun*, May 13, 1906.
11. "Hill Leads Giants to Win," *Chicago Daily Tribune*, July 6, 1909.
12. "Giants Again Jar Cubans," *Inter-Ocean* (Chicago), July 3, 1909.
13. Revel and Munoz, *Leland*, 18–19; Heaphy, *Black Baseball*, 16.
14. Heaphy, *Black Baseball*, 16; Riley, *Encyclopedia*, 47, 244–5, 309–10, 610–11, 758–59, 486–489; "The St. Paul Colored Gophers Baseball Team is Formed," https://aaregistry.org/story/the-st-paul-colored-gophers-a-special-baseball-team/. Accessed October 26, 2021.
15. Cottrell, *Best Pitcher in Baseball*, 47.
16. Reichler, *Baseball Encyclopedia*,1697.
17. *Chicago Daily Tribune*, October 23, 1909, as quoted in Lester, *Foster in His Time*, 39; Riley, *Encyclopedia*, 515.
18. Cottrell, *Best Pitcher in Baseball*, 47.
19. *Franklin's Paper the Statesman* (Denver, Colorado), September 24, 1910.
20. Riley, *Encyclopedia*, 415; Revel and Munoz, *Leland*, 22; Andrew W. Kahrl, *The Land Was Ours: How Black Beaches Became White Wealth in the Coastal Society* (Chapel Hill: University of North Carolina Press, 2012), 92.
21. Revel and Munoz, *Leland*, 9, 2; "Leland Giants Base-Ball and Amusement Assn. Now Organizing-Capital Stock $1,000,000," *Broad Ax*, March 7, 1908.
22. "Baseball Notes," *Broad Ax*, April 16, 1910.
23. "Great Reception and Smoker," *Chicago Defender*, May 7, 1910.
24. McNeil, 14–15; "Rube Foster Back in Form," *Chicago Defender* (reprinting a January 26, 1910, dispatch from the *Palm Beach Daily News*), February 5, 1910.
25. Larry Lester, *Foster in His Time*, 46; "Leland's Team to Be In Chicago League," *Inter-Ocean* (Chicago), November 7, 1909; Heaphy, *Black Baseball*, 11–12.
26. Major R.R. Jackson, "No Baseball War in Chicago," *Indianapolis Freeman*, December 18, 1909.
27. "Joe Green," https://baseballhistorydaily.com/tag/joe-green/. Accessed June 27, 2021.
28. Riley, *Encyclopedia*, 253, 486, 624.
29. Riley, *Encyclopedia*, 474–475; "Lost Advertisements–The Leland Giants' New Ballpark," https://baseballhistorydaily.com/2015/04/03/lost-advertisements-the-leland-giants-new-ballpark/. Accessed May 10, 2020; "Play Ball," *Chicago Defender*, May 28, 1910.
30. "Baseball," *Suburbanite Economist* (Chicago), August 26, 1910; "Pete Hill," SABR Biography Project, https://sabr.org/bioproj/person/pete-hill/#_edn3. Accessed October 22, 2020; Riley 624, 486, 253; "Baseball," *Englewood Economist* (Chicago), August 6, 1910.
31. "History—Provident Hospital," https://provfound.org/index.php/history/history-provident-hospital. Accessed October 3, 2010.
32. Cary Lewis, "Observe Charitable Day," *Indianapolis Freeman*, August 6, 1910; "Giants Take Benefit Game," *Chicago Defender*, August 27, 1910.
33. Ron Grossman, "How William Lorimer was Expelled from the U.S. Senate," https://www.chicagotribune.com/opinion/commentary/ct-perspec-flash-lorimer-william-senate-roy-moore-1203-20171127-story.html. Accessed October 3, 2020; "Toga for Lorimer," *Washington Post*, May 27, 1909; "Tells of Bribes to Elect Lorimer, *New York Times*, May 1, 1910; "Lorimer Ousted," *Sun*, July 14, 1912.
34. Geoffrey C. Ward, *Unforgiveable Blackness: The Rise and Fall of Jack Johnson* (New York: Alfred A. Knopf, 2005), 98.
35. W. Rollo Wilson, "Eastern Snapshot," *Pittsburgh Courier*, January 16, 1926.
36. "Baseball Scores Over Crap Games," *New York Times*, August 25, 1907.
37. Geoffrey Ward, 148, 312–314; Fay Young, "Café De Champion-Jack Johnson's Wife Ends Life-The Champion Skips Country," *Chicago Defender*, November 13, 1948.
38. "Jack Johnson's Story of His Eight Years in Exile," *Afro-American*, September 3, 1920; "I am not a coward, gentlemen," *Mirror of Life and Boxing World*, July 19, 1913, as cited in Ward, 348; "Jack Johnson: Most Misunderstood World's Champion," *Afro-American*, March 14, 1959.

Chapter 4

1. McNeil, *Out of Season*, 37.
2. "Rube Foster Honored," *Chicago Defender*, November 26, 1910.

Notes—Chapter 4

3. Cottrell, 60; Billy Evans, "Joy in Cuba When Cobb Strikes Out," *New York Times*, December 18, 1910; Bjarkman, *Cuban Baseball*, 146.

4. Figueredo, *Cuban Baseball*, 91.

5. William F. McNeil, *The California Winter League: America's First Integrated Professional Baseball League* (Jefferson, NC: McFarland, 2000), 11–14.

6. "Winter League Magnates Will Hold Forth Today, *Los Angeles Herald*, October 23, 1910.

7. "Giants Revenged for Morning Loss," *Los Angeles Herald*, November 21, 1910.

8. "Winter League Extends Games," *Los Angeles Herald*, December 15, 1910; "Major Leaguers Parade Streets," *Los Angeles Record*, November 19, 1910.

9. "Breezy Baseball Babble," *Fresno Morning Republican*, December 6, 1910.

10. McNeil, *California Winter League*, 35.

11. Riley, *Encyclopedia*, 85. 856.

12. John B. Holway, *Blackball Stars: Negro League Pioneers* (Westport, CT: Meckler, 1988), 65; Riley, *Encyclopedia*, 85.

13. McNeil, *Winter League*, 35–38.

14. L.W. Washington, "Banquet and Reception for Rube Foter and His American Giants at Odd Fellows Hall," *Broad Ax*, May 2, 1914.

15. "Leland's Team to Be in Chicago League," *Inter-Ocean* (Chicago), November 7, 1909; *Suburban Economist*, July 22, 1910; "Old Sox Grounds to Be Remodeled," *Inter-Ocean*, March 11, 1911; "Charles Comiskey," https://www.myheritage.com/names/charles_comiskey. Accessed May 10, 2021.

16. Riley, *Encyclopedia*, 702; "Gets Permit for Ball Park," *Chicago Daily Tribune*, January 17, 1911; Russell J. Cowans, "Thru the Sport Mirror, *Detroit Tribune*, August 19, 1933, as cited in "Pete Hill," SABR Biography Project, https://sabr.org/bioproj/person/pete-hill/. Accessed June 29, 2020; Cary B. Lewis, "Opening of Ball Park," *The Indianapolis Freeman*, May 13, 1912; *Chicago Defender*, August 5, 1911.

17. "New Grandstand for Old Park," *St. Louis Star and Times*, March 21, 1911.

18. "Negro League Provided Blacks with Stability," *Philadelphia Tribune*, January 20, 1989.

19. "John Schorling, Former Ball Park Owner, Dies at 74," *Chicago Defender*, March 30, 1940.

20. "Royal Giants' Fine Showing," *New York Age*, March 30, 1911; Riley, *Encyclopedia*, 111.

21. "Royal Giants Fine Showing," *New York Age*, March 30, 1911; "American Giants Win, 11–1," *Chicago Examiner*, April 6, 1911; "American Giants Beat San Antonio," *Munster Times* (Munster, Indiana), April 25, 1911; "American Giants Win Out," *Chicago Examiner*, April 10, 1911.

22. J.H. Wright, "American or Chicago Giants Which," *Chicago Defender*, July 8, 1911.

23. "Fennimore's Two Big Days," *Fennimore Times* (Fennimore, Wisconsin), July 26, 1911.

24. "Official Program of the Mineral Point Fair," *Mineral Point Tribune*, August 17, 1911.

25. "Rube Foster's Team to Play the Cuban Stars," *Standard Union*, August 23, 1911; "American Giants Are Blanked by Cuban Stars," *Philadelphia Inquirer*, August 30, 1911; "Cuban Stars Lose," *Philadelphia Inquirer*, September 6, 1911; "Stars Tie Up Series," *Philadelphia Inquirer*, September 7, 1911; "American Giants Win Series from Cuban Stars," *Philadelphia Inquirer*, September 10, 1911.

26. "Lincoln Giants Win Doubleheader," *New York Age*, September 7, 1911.

27. Riley, *Encyclopedia*, 483.

28. "Cubans Strong on Ball Playing," *Grand Forks Herald* (Grand Forks, North Dakota), February 27, 1912; Figueredo, *Cuban Baseball*, 98.

29. Lanctot, *Fair Dealing*, 38.

30. "New Grandstand for Old Park," *St. Louis Star and Times*, March 21, 1911; *Suburbanite Economist*, January 31, 1913; *Suburbanite Economist*, July 3, 1914; *Suburbanite Economist*, November 22, 1918; "American Giants Shy at Joining New Baseball League," *Waterloo Courier* (Waterloo, Iowa), February 12, 1921.

31. "Rube Foster Has a Word to say to the Baseball Fans," *Chicago Defender*, January 5, 1954, as reproduced in Lester, *Foster in His Time*, 153–154.

32. "American Giants Win, 7 to 3," *Chicago Daily Tribune*, May 31, 1912.

33. Layton Revel and Luis Munoz, *Early Pioneers of the Negro Leagues: Home Run

Johnson (Carrollton, TX: Center for Negro League Baseball Research, 2016), 28; Riley, 483.
34. "Lil' Arthur Wants to be Ballplayer," *Vancouver Province* (Vancouver, British Columbia), July 23, 1912.
35. McNeil, *Winter League*, 41.
36. Julius N. Avendouph, "Rube Foster and His American Giants Win Pennant in Winter League," *Chicago Defender*, April 5, 1913.
37. "Weird Game with Much Noise, Win by Giants," *San Diego Union*, November 17, 1912.
38. McNeil, *Winter League*, 40–42; *Fresno Morning Republican*, March 22, 1913.
39. McNeil, *Winter League*, 46.
40. Al C. Coy, "Giants Win from Beavers-M'Credie's Faith Unshaken," *San Francisco Examiner*, March 16, 1913.
41. *Fresno Morning*, March 22, 1913.
42. "Benefit Game Nets $300," *The Inter Ocean*, May 7, 1913; "Danger" Talbert Benefit," *Indianapolis Freeman*, May 17, 1913.
43. "American Giants Lose," *Chicago Defender*, July 5, 1913.
44. "Cubans Again Beaten," *Inter Ocean*, June 18, 1913.
45. "American Giants Coming Back," *Chicago Defender*, September 6, 1913.
46. Riley, *Encyclopedia*, 483; "Lincoln Giants Worlds Champs," *Chicago Examiner*, August 14, 1913.
47. "Thh [sic] Boys at Palm Beach Welcomes the Arrival of the Tribune," *Philadelphia Tribune*, January 31, 1914.
48. McNeil, *Out of Season*, 16–18; Riley, *Encyclopedia*, 695.
49. "Fatty Weakened and Portland Scored Four Runs," baseballhistorydaily.com/tag/portland-colts/. Accessed February 18, 2021.
50. "The Lew Hubbard Giants and the Lord of the Slums," https://shadowballexpress.wordpress.com/2020/03/02/the-lew-hubbard-giants-and-the-lord-of-the-slums/. Accessed January 26, 2021; "Will Entertain Giants," *Oregon Daily Journal*, April 11, 1914.
51. "Colts Beaten by Colored Giants in Wobbly Game," *Oregon Daily Journal*, April 13, 1914.
52. "American Giants at Gardens Tomorrow," *Anaconda Standard*, April 21, 1914.
53. Fay Albert Young, "The Sporting World," *Chicago Defender*, April 25, 1914.
54. "'Rube' Foster's Team Starving in Oregon." *Chicago Defender*. April 11, 1914.
55. "The Sporting World," *Chicago Defender*, March 21, 1914.
56. "Butlers Defeat Louisville, 5–1," *Chicago Daily Tribune*, September 21, 1914.
57. Frank A. Young, "Rube Foster Triumphs," *Chicago Defender*, June 6, 1914; "Giants in Close Tilt," *Chicago Defender*, June 13, 1914; "Irv Young," SABR Biography Project, https://sabr.org/bioproj/person/irv-young/. Accessed January 19, 2021; Frank A. Young, "Giants Make Clean Sweep; Grace Wins Too," *Chicago Defender*, September 12, 1914.
58. "News From Sunpsy," *Philadelphia Tribune*, February 6, 1915.
59. Alonzo Leath, "American Giants Pass Through the Mound City," *Chicago Defender*, March 6, 1915; "'Daylight Special' at Chicago Central Station," https://texashistory.unt.edu/ark:/67531/metapth28863/. Accessed December 1, 2020; Riley, 403–404.
60. Riley, *Encyclopedia*, 561.
61. Riley, *Encyclopedia*, 561; "Bill Monroe," SABR Biography Project, https://sabr.org/bioproj/person/bill-monroe/. Accessed November 13, 2021.
62. Frank A. Young, "American Giants Clean Up Along Western Front," *Chicago Defender*, April 17, 1915; "Schedule of the American Giants," *Chicago Defender*, February 20, 1915, American Giants Pass Through the Mound City," *Chicago Defender*, March 6, 1915; "American Giants Beat P. L. Champions," *Chicago Defender*, April 3, 1915; Riley, *Encyclopedia*, 296, 57, 626, 403.
63. "1915 Chicago American Giants," https://www.seamheads.com/NegroLgs/team.php?yearID=1915&teamID=CAG. Accessed November 8, 2021; "Stars Shut Out American Giants," *New York Age*, August 12, 1915; Riley, *Encyclopedia*, 485.

Chapter 5

1. "Rioters Hang Another Negro," *New York Times*, August 16, 1908.
2. "Second Lynching in Springfield Riots," *Washington Post*, August 16, 1908;

"$45,000 Paid For Race Riot," *Chicago Defender*, August 16, 1913; "Auto Escapade," *Decatur Herald* (Decatur, Illinois), August 15, 1908; "Loper is Willing to Compromise," *Streator Free Press* (Streator, Illinois), February 11, 1909.

3. "Illinois Jury is Busy," *Washington Post*, August 22, 1908; "Joan of Arc Suicide," *Baltimore Sun*, August 27, 1908, "Woman Rioter a Suicide," *New York Times*, August 27, 1908; "Antipathy to Blacks Pre-Natal in Woman," *Alton Evening Telegraph* (Alton, Illinois), August 28, 1908.

4. Roberta Senechal de la Roche, *In Lincoln's Shadow: The 1908 Race Riot in Springfield, Illinois*, reissue (Carbondale: Southern Illinois University Press, 2008), 19, 22, 163, 168.

5. Ibid., 169–173.

6. "Race War in Chicago," *Sun*, August 21, 1908.

7. Sophia Tarren, "1908 Race Riot Led to NAACP," *Atlanta Daily World*, August 14, 2008; "Late Literary News," *Afro-American*, August 6, 1911; For an example of her column, see "Book Chat," *New York Amsterdam News*, January 31, 1923.

8. "Birth of the NAACP." Pratt Library, https://eresource.prattlibrary.org:2106/HRC/Search/Details/5?articleId=158010&q=Birth%20of%20the%20NAACP. Accessed April 12, 2021.

9. "15 Negroes Hurt In Chicago Race Riot," *New York Times*, February 7, 1911.

10. "43rd Street Riot a Farce," *Chicago Defender*, February 11, 1913.

11. "Illinois is to Stop Race Ridicule," *Chicago Defender*, March 13, 1915; "History Making Week for Afro-Americans," *Chicago Defender*, May 22, 1915; "Jackson's Moving Picture Bill Is Lost by One Vote," *Chicago Defender*, June 26, 1915.

12. Frank A. Young, "American Giants Take Lead in World's Series," *Chicago Defender*, September 5, 1914. Fay no doubt chose the term "World Series" to hype the Series' importance and draw more people to the park. The first official World Series between the pennant winning teams of two recognized Negro Leagues would not be played for another ten years. That said, the Lincoln Giants and Brooklyn Royal Giants were the two of the best eastern teams at the time. The American Giants and Indianapolis ABC's were held in similar esteem in the Mid-West. (Ben Taylor, "Greatest Series Ever Played," *Afro-American*, February 19, 1927.)

13. "American Giants Beat Cubans Who Start Trouble." *Chicago Defender*, August 28, 1915; "Rube Wants Big Bonus to Come," *The Honolulu Advertiser*, September 13, 1915.

14. "American Giants in Fierce Riot at Hoosier City," *Chicago Defender*, July 24, 1915.

15. "Taylorites Humble the Red Sox Twice," *Chicago Defender*, August 19, 1916; "St. L. Giants Win Close Game From Wabadas," *Chicago Defender*, October 7, 1916.

16. "Fight Ends A.B.C. Game, *Chicago Defender*, October 30, 1915.

17. William Dismukes, "Winter Blasts and Summer Echoes," *Pittsburgh Courier*, December 28, 1923; Riley, 763, 406.

18. "Dismukes and Pat Ragan in Pitching Duel," *Chicago Defender*, October 23, 1915; "Pat Ragan Considering Offer," *New York Times*, December 29, 1913.

19. "Still Wants to Come," *Honolulu Advertiser*, November 29, 1915.

20. "American Giants Willing to Come," *Honolulu Advertiser*, October 10, 1915.

21. Riley, 839; "Wickware in a Three Hit, No Run Game," *Chicago Defender*, November 27, 1915.

22. "American Giants Top Winter League," *Chicago Defender*, January 1, 1916.

23. "American Giants Open To-Day," *Chicago Defender*, April 29, 1916.

24. "Fatty Weakened and Portland Scored Four Runs," Baseball History Daily (website), https://baseballhistorydaily.com/tag/portland-colts/. Accessed February 23, 2021.

25. McNeil, *Winter League*, 46.

26. "The Boys at Palm Beach Welcomes the Arrival of the Tribune," *Philadelphia Tribune*, January 31, 1914; Fritz Holland, "Recalls Mixed Games in Florida," *Afro-American*, March 27, 1954.

27. "Rube Foster Off for the Coast," *Chicago Defender*, January 22, 1916.

28. "Locals Take Series Four Out of Seven," *Vancouver Sun*, April 22, 1916.

29. "American Giants Win Uphill Game 10–8," *Chicago Defender*, April 27, 1916.

30. "American Giants Open Today." *Chicago Defender*, April 29, 1916.

Chapter 6

1. Lisa McGirr, *The War on Alcohol: Prohibition and the Rise of the American State* (New York: W.W. Norton, 2016), 10–12.
2. Daniel Okrent, *Last Call: The Rise and Fall of Prohibition* (New York: Scribner, 2010), 28.
3. *Ibid.*, 49.
4. Home Run, "E. Pluvis Is King," *Chicago Defender*, May 6, 1916; "Edgar 'Blue' Washington," SABR Biography Project, https://sabr.org/bioproj/person/edgar-blue-washington/. Accessed August 17, 2020.
5. "Rube Fires Tom Williams Outright," *Chicago Defender*, April 6, 1918.
6. Riley, *Encyclopedia*, 863.
7. "National League News," *Chicago Defender*, March 11, 1922; "Rogers Park Opens Season Against Rube," *Chicago Defender*, April 15, 1922; "State Normal Team to Play All Summer," *Pittsburgh Courier*, January 13, 1923.
8. William Dismukes, "Winters Blast and Summer Echoes," *Pittsburgh Courier*, December 29, 1923.
9. Al Monroe, "Speaking of Sports," *Chicago Defender*, October 12, 1935.
10. "Liquor—And the Havoc It Has Wrought in the Ranks of Baseball's Big Stars," *Pittsburgh Courier*, April 3, 1926.
11. "Home Run by Hill Helps Fosters Beat Cubans, 2–1," *Chicago Daily Tribune*, May 23, 1916.
12. Mr. Fan, "Rube Foster in Come Back Role," *Chicago Defender*, May 20, 1916.
13. "Rube Foster VS. George Millin," Chicago Defender, July 22, 1916.
14. Mr. Fan, "Too Much Mullin," *Chicago Defender*, July 29, 1916.
15. "Fay Says," *Chicago Defender*, August 13, 1955.
16. "Gunthers' Errors and Leland's 5–1 Win," *Chicago Examiner*, May 16, 1910, as cited in "Pete Hill," SABR Biography Project, https://sabr.org/bioproj/person/pete-hill/. Accessed June 29, 2020.
17. "No-Hit, No-Run Game to American Giants," *Chicago Defender*, September 9, 1916.
18. "Thousands Bet on Coming Series," *Chicago Defender*, October 21, 1916. "Once Over," *Chicago Defender*, September 9, 1916.
19. "Rube Foster Speaks," *Chicago Defender*, November 25, 1916.
20. "Thousands Bet on Coming Series," *Chicago Defender*, October 21, 1916.
21. Mr. Fan, "Rube Foster Tells A Few Things of Interest," *Chicago Defender*, November 11, 1916; "Rube Foster Speaks," *Chicago Defender*, November 18 and 23, 1916; Holway, *Complete Book*, 112.
22. Jeremy Beer, *Oscar Charleston*, 86–87; "American Giants Win Palm Beach Championship," *Chicago Defender*, March 31, 1917.
23. "Telegram," *Chicago Defender*, March 17, 1917.
24. "American Giants Still on Rampage," *Chicago Defender*, July 28, 1917; "Rube Foster Bats the American Giants to Victory," *Chicago Defender*, June 16, 1917; "Eighth Inning Rally Defeats Taylor's Nine," *Chicago Defender*, August 11, 1917.
25. Riley, *Encyclopedia*, 561–62; "Benefit Game for Moore Brings in a Neat Sum," *Chicago Defender*, July 7, 1917. https://drive.google.com/file/d/-0B1Wcncq5-bHdTFpXaWE0bjVNeFU/view?resourcekey=0-w3xedD4bhwvJb8mUbcmU2g. Accessed November 13, 2021.
26. "Am. Giants Again Beat Texas All-Star Team," *Chicago Defender*, August 4, 1917.
27. "Curtain Falls on Baseball," *Chicago Defender*, October 27, 1917.
28. "Chicago's Bathers Rout Policemen," *The Washington Post*, August 1, 1917; "Heat Kills 19 in Chicago," *The Baltimore Sun*, August 1, 1917.
29. "American Giants Arrive Safely in South; Turn Down Havana Trip," *Chicago Defender*, February 2, 1918.
30. Riley, *Encyclopedia*, 290, 325.
31. "American Giants at Palm Beach, Fla." *New York Age*, February 2, 1918.
32. "American Giants Arrive Safely," *Chicago Defender*.
33. "Breakers Win Game from Poincianas," *Chicago Defender*, February 16, 1918; Riley, 854, 654.
34. "Rube Wins Championship," *Chicago Defender*, March 23, 1918; "American Giants Have Completed Their Tour," *Chicago Defender*, April 13, 1918.

Chapter 7

1. Riley, *Encyclopedia*, 860–861; Mister Fan, "American Giants to Present New Line-Up for This Season," *Chicago Defender*, March 30, 1918.
2. Mister Fan, "Crowd Disappointed When Camp Grant Team Fails to Show," *Chicago Defender*, May 25, 1918.
3. "American Giants Face Hardest Test in History," *Chicago Defender*, July 20, 1918; "Giants Lose Both Games to Beloit," *Chicago Defender*, July 27, 1918.
4. Eliot Asinof, *Eight Men Out: The Black Sox and the 1919 World Series* (New York: Henry Holt, 2000), 61.
5. "Giants Get New Pitcher," *New York Times*, July 15, 1918; "Felsch Quits Sox to Take Job and Will Play Semipro Ball," *Washington Post*, July 2, 1918.
6. "Influenza Epidemic Grave," *Washington Post*, January 5, 1916.
7. "Dr. A. Wilberforce Williams Talks on Preventive Measures, First Aid Remedies, Hygienics and Sanitation," *Chicago Defender*, June 8, 1916.
8. Telephone interview with John M. Barry, August 11, 2020.
9. John M. Barry, *The Great Influenza: The Story of the Greatest Pandemic in History* (New York: Penguin, 2018) 167–174.
10. "Drastic Rule in Chicago," *New York Times*, October 4, 1918; "New Cases Decrease at the Army Camp," *New York Times*, October 17, 1918; Spanish Plague Raging in Chicago," *Chicago Defender*, October 19, 1918.
11. John M. Barry, *Great Influenza*, 337.
12. *Ibid*.
13. *Ibid*.
14. *Ibid*., 202, 211, 337, 339
15. *Ibid*., 201.
16. *Ibid*., 213.
17. *Ibid*., 213.
18. *Ibid*., 213.
19. *Ibid*., 201, 210–219.
20. "Dr. A. Wilberforce Williams Talks on Preventive Measures, First Aid Remedies, Hygienics and Sanitation," *Chicago Defender*, October 12, 1918.
21. "New Cases Decrease at the Army Camps," *New York Times*, October 17, 1918.
22. Barry, *Great Influenza*, 199–209.
23. "Red Cross Parades," *Washington Post*, May 12, 1918.
24. "Big Drive in Country," *Sun*, May 30, 1918.
25. "President Leads Red Cross Parade," *New York Times*, May 19, 1918.
26. "U.S. Directs Flu Fight," *Sun*, October 18, 1918.
27. "12,000 Nurses Parade in Loop," *Chicago Defender*, September 14, 1918.
28. "The Influenza Pandemic of 1918," https://virus.stanford.edu/uda/. Accessed June 23, 2020; Barry, *Great Influenza*, 391.
29. Gary Ashwill, "Black Baseball and the 1918 Pandemic," Agate Type blog, https://agatetype.typepad.com/agate_type/2020/06/black-baseball-the-1918-pandemic.html. Accessed August 17, 2020.
30. "American Giants Win Series from Hilldale," *Philadelphia Inquirer*, August 9, 1918.
31. "Bacharach Giants Win Again," *Philadelphia Inquirer*, July 31, 1918.
32. *Englewood Times*, September 6, 1918.
33. "American Giants Defeat A.B.C.'s in Washington," *Chicago Defender*, August 3, 1918; "Dizzy" Dismukes, "Dismukes Names His 9 Best Outfielders," *Pittsburgh Courier*, March 8, 1930.
34. "Draft Hits Rube Foster's Club Hard," *Chicago Defender*, July 27, 1918.
35. "Work or Fight 1918," http://recordsofrights.org/events/127/work-or-fight#:~:text=Work%20or%20Fight%20 1918,a%20%E2%80%9Cnecessary%E2%80%9D%20civilian%20occupation. Accessed June 24, 2020; "Twilight Ball," *Chicago Defender*, July 13, 1918; "ABCS Take Twilight Game," *Chicago Defender*, July 20, 1918.
36. "Giants to Go East," *Chicago Defender*, July 13, 1918; "14,000 See Williams Beat Donaldson," *Chicago Defender*, June 15, 1918; "10,000 Baseball Fans Rail at Umpire's Boner," *Chicago Defender*, September 21, 1918.
37. "Flu Epidemic Believed on Wane," *Baltimore Sun*, October 13, 1918.
38. "Influenza Epidemic Closes Baseball Season for American Giants," *Chicago Defender*, November 2, 1918.
39. Dave Wyatt, "American Giants Take Series from All-Star Big Leaguers," *Chicago Defender*, October 19, 1918.
40. No title, *Appeal* (Saint Paul, Minnesota), November 2, 1918.
41. "Influenza Epidemic Closes

Baseball Season for American Giants," Seamheads, https://www.seamheads.com/NegroLgs/team.php?yearID=1918&teamID=CAG&LGOrd=2. Accessed June 23, 2020.

42. "Jews Segregated at Royal Poinciana," *Afro-American*, March 3, 1919; "Bishop Hurst, Noted Prelate Dies Suddenly," *Philadelphia Tribune*, May 8, 1930.

43. Captain J.H. Smith, "20,000 See Cuban Stars and American Giants," *Chicago Defender*, June 7, 1919.

44. Barry interview.

45. "25,000 See Am. Giants Cop Double-Header," *Chicago Defender*, August 30, 1919; "American Giants Drop One Game; Win One," *Chicago Defender*, September 6, 1919.

Chapter 8

1. Winifred Conkling, *Votes for Women: American Suffragists and the Battle for the Ballot* (Chapel Hill, NC: Algonquin Young Readers, 2018), 30–37.

2. Okrent, *Last Call*, 15.

3. "Suffragists to Invade Halls of Congress and Deliver Messages from Home to Members," *Washington Herald*, April 7, 1903.

4. "More 'Antis' Organize," *Sun*, February 14, 1911.

5. Okrent, *Last Call*, 64.

6. "Braves Arctic Hazards, But Flees Suffragists," *Moline Dispatch* (Moline, Illinois), March 1, 1913.

7. "This Huge Women's March Drowned Out a Presidential Inauguration in 1913," History.com, https://www.history.com/news/this-huge-womens-march-drowned-out-a-presidential-inauguration-in-1913. Accessed September 19, 2020.

8. "Women to Storm Capitol with Big Petition Today," *Inter-Ocean*, April 7, 1913.

9. Conkling, *Votes for Women*, 165.

10. Okrent, *Last Call*, 66.

11. "Chicago Women Politicians in Riot," *Philadelphia Tribune*, April 10, 1915.

12. Ibid., 15.

13. "Chicago Crowds in Riot to Seize Suffragists' Anti-Wilson Banners," *Washington Post*, October 20, 1916.

14. "Militants in Riot: 13 Held for Trial," *Washington Post*, July 5, 1917; "Suffragists Go To Jail," *New York Times*, July 7, 1917; "White House Riot Broken up By Police," *New York Times*, July 5, 1917; Conkling, *Votes for Women*, 184.

15. Conkling, *Votes for Women*, 252.

16. Woodrow Wilson to Frederic Yates, September 5, 1908, in *The Papers of Woodrow Wilson*, vol. 18, ed. Arthur S. Link et al. (Princeton University Press), 417; Quoted in Victoria Bissell Brown, "Did Woodrow Wilson's Gender Politics Matter," in John M. Cooper (ed.), *Reconsidering Woodrow Wilson: Progressivism, Internationalism, War, and Peace* (Washington, D.C., Woodrow Wilson Center Press, 2008).

17. Conkling, *Votes for Women*, 257–9.

18. "Tennessee Attempt to Revoke Suffrage," *New York Times*, September 1, 1920.

19. *"Letter from President Woodrow Wilson to Carrie Chapman Catt, June 7, 1918."* Courtesy of Iowa State University Library Special Collections and University Archives. Accessed October 7, 2020.

Conkling, *Votes for Women*, 252–266.

20. Conkling, *Votes for Women*, 257.

21. "Antis Keep Up Their Battle on Suffrage," *Belvidere Daily Republican* (Belvidere, Illinois), August 23, 1920; "Seek to Advance Suff Suit," *The Sun*, October 4, 1920; "To Ask Withdrawal of Suffrage Ratification," October 20, 1920.

22. Jessica Bennett and Veronica Chambers, "Radical, Exciting and Relevant, Especially Now," *New York Times Supplement: How American Women Won the Right to Vote*, August 16, 2020.

23. "This Huge Women's March Drowned Out a Presidential Inauguration in 1913," History.com, https://www.history.com/news/this-huge-womens-march-drowned-out-a-presidential-inauguration-in-1913. Accessed September 19, 2020; Ida B. Wells, Alfreda M. Duster (Ed.), *Crusade for Justice: The Autobiography of Ida B. Wells* (University of Chicago Press, 2nd Ed., 2020), 10; See the Library of Congress' Records of the National Woman's Party (Group I, boxes 1–3) for correspondence on the role of African American women in the parade (MSS). See also Crisis, 5:6 (April 1913), p.267; reprint ed. (New York: Negro Universities Press, 1969); E185.5.C9 GenColl). For Wells Barnett, see the *Chicago Tribune*, March 4, 1913. Additional sources of material on African

American women and the march include the aforementioned records of the National Woman's Party and the National American Woman Suffrage Association (both collections are described in the Library's Manuscript Division's Women's Suffrage section).

24. "City Federation of Women's Clubs Meet," *Chicago Defender*, March 8, 1913.

Chapter 9

1. Riley, *Encyclopedia*, 443, 302, 331, 840, 860–61, 382.
2. Draft Cards, Ancestry.com. Accessed August 15, 2020.
3. Robert Charles Cottrell, *The Best Pitcher in Baseball*, 133–134, as cited in "Pete Hill," SABR Biography Project, https://sabr.org/bioproj/person/pete-hill/. Accessed June 30, 2020.
4. "Pete Hill," SABR Biography Project, https://sabr.org/bioproj/person/pete-hill/. Accessed October 22, 2020; Riley, 829, 545, 624, 253.
5. Richard Bak, *Turkey Stearnes and the Detroit Stars: The Negro Leagues in Detroit, 1999–1933* (Detroit: Wayne State University Press, 60), 1994.
6. "American Giants Open Sunday," *Chicago Defender*, April 12, 1919; Riley, *Encyclopedia*, 164.
7. Riley, *Encyclopedia*, 228.
8. "Giants' Recruits Work Hard," *Chicago Defender*, April 5, 1919.
9. "American Giants Open Sunday," *Chicago Defender*, April 12, 1919
10. "Detroit Stars Leave with Good Will of Chicagoans," *Chicago Defender*, April 19, 1919; Dave Wyatt, "Ready for Summer Sport," *Chicago Defender*, April 12, 1919; "American Giants Open Sunday," *Chicago Defender*.
11. "Sol White's Column of 'Baseball Dope,'" *Cleveland Advocate*, Vol. 5, Issue 47, March 29, 1919, 7.
12. "The Passing of Pete Hill," *Half-Century Magazine*, Vol. 6, No. 4, April 1919.
13. Bak, 57; "Tenny Blount, Late Baseball Mogul, Dies in Fall Downstairs," *Chicago Defender*, December 29, 1934.
14. Larry Lester, Sammy Miller, Dick Clark, *Black Baseball in Detroit* (Chicago: Arcadia, 2000), 77; "'Tenny' Blount Entertains Sports Writers," *Chicago Defender*, August 2, 1919; "$10,000 Marmon," *Chicago Defender*, August 20, 1921; "High Speed," *Chicago Defender*," August 27, 1921.
15. Bak, 16, 60–61.
16. "Captain Hill and Team Due Here Next Week," *Chicago Defender*, April 15, 1919.
17. "Detroit Stars Open at Mack's Park April 20," *Chicago Defender*, April 19, 1919.
18. Euella A. Nielsen, "Detroit Stars (1919–1931)," Black Past, https//www.blackpast.org/african-american-history/detroit-stars-1919-1931/. Accessed March 11, 2021.
19. "Capt. Pete Hill's Team Wins Second Victory," *Chicago Defender*, May 3, 1919.
20. "American Giants Book Attractions," *Chicago Defender*, May 31, 1919.
21. "Hill Writes the Defender," *Chicago Defender*, June 14, 1919.
22. Capt. James H. Smith, "American Giants Blank the Detroit Stars," *Chicago Defender*, June 21, 1919.
23. "Detroit Stars Capture Series," *Chicago Defender*, August 9, 1919.
24. Cottrell, 128–129.
25. Cameron McWhirter, *Red Summer: The Summer of 1919 and the Awakening of Black America* (New York: Henry Holt, 2011), 15.
26. McWhirter, 128.
27. *Emily Frankenstein Papers* [manuscript] 1915–1920, Chicago History Museum, 200–204; "Baby's Body in Stack," *Sun*, July 28, 1919: "Admits He Killed 6-Year Old Girl," *Washington Post*, July 28, 1919.
28. "Full Confession by Slayer of Janet," *Chicago Daily Tribune*, July 28, 1918.
29. Frankenstein Papers.
30. "This Boy's Death Caused Race Riot," *Chicago Defender*, August 30, 1919; "Riots Sweep Chicago," *Chicago Defender*, August 2, 1919.
31. Ragan's Colts Hand Fosterites a Loss," *Chicago Defender*, October 6, 1917; "DeMoss Stars as Giants Trim Ragans," *Chicago Defender*, October 20, 1917; Owen Forsyth, "Ragan's Colts—A Southside Chicago Gang," Irish Mob (website), theirishmob.com/Ragans-colts-a-southside-Chicago-gang/. Accessed March 30, 2021.

32. "Ragan's Colts Again," *Chicago Defender*, March 13, 1926.

33. "Two Killed, 50 Hurt in Furious Race Riots in Chicago," *New York Times*, July 29, 1919.

34. J. Wesley Jones, "West Side News," *Chicago Defender*, June 5, 1920; "2 Killed, 50 Hurt in Furious Race Riots in Chicago," *New York Times*, July 28, 1918; "Everything Reported Quiet in the Main Chicago Race Riot District," *New York Times*, August 9, 1919; "Free Officers," *Chicago Defender*, October 4, 1919.

35. Nettie George Speedy, "Four Rioters Get Prison Sentences," *Chicago Defender*, December 20, 1919.

36. Gary Ashwill, "White Racial Violence and the Negro Leagues: The Chicago Riots of 1919," June 14, 2020; "Claudio Manela," Agate Type blog, https://agatetype.typepad.com/. Accessed August 3, 2020.

37. "Fatal Rioting at Capital Resumed Despite Troops; President Wilson Acts," *The Sun*, July 23, 1919; "For Action on Race Riot Peril," *New York Times*, October 5, 1919.

38. Barbara Foley, *Specters of 1919: Class and Nation in the Making of the New Negro* (Urbana: University of Illinois Press, 2008), 13.

39. "Minutes of Meeting of Board of Directors," September 8, 1919, NAACP Papers, Part 1, Reel 1; *Papers of Francis Grimke*, "The Race Problem," Howard University, Moorland-Spingarn Center, Manuscript Division, Washington, D.C., as cited in McWhirter, 151.

40. David M. Kennedy, *Over Here: The First World War and American Society* (New York: Oxford University Press, 2004), 279, 281–282; "The Great Migration," History.com, https://www.history.com/topics/Black-history/great-migration. Accessed June 25, 2020.

41. Foley, 13.

42. "Detroit Stars Are After Pennant," *Chicago Defender*, September 20, 1919.

43. *Cincinnati Enquirer*; "Why is Cincinnati called the Queen City?" Cincinnati.com, https://www.cincinnati.com/story/news/2020/12/22/why-cincinnati-called-queen-city/4007103001/. Accessed March 11, 2021.

44. "Scoreboard Crowd Breaks Records," *New York Times*, October 5, 1919; "Richest World's Series in the History of the Game," *Sun*, October 10, 1919.

45. "Detroit Stars Ready for Next Season," *Chicago Defender*, February 14, 1920.

46. *Ibid.*

47. "Pete Hill Writes on Detroit Stars," *Chicago Defender*, January 10, 1920; Riley, 383.

48. "Second Battle Goes Same Way as Initial One," *Detroit Free Press*, June 9, 1919; "Stars Capture First in East," *Detroit Free Press*, July 17, 1919, as cited in "Pete Hill," SABR Biography Project, https://sabr.org/bioproj/person/pete-hill/. Accessed June 29, 2020.

49. "Would Avert Race Riot in Chicago," *Chicago Defender*, March 27, 1920.

50. "2 Dead, Many Hurt in Chicago Riot," *New York Times*, June 21, 1920; "Killing by Negro in Chicago Rumpus Starts Race Riot," *New York Times*, September 21, 1920.

Chapter 10

1. "Big Negro National Baseball League Formed," *Chicago Defender*, December 31, 1910; Lester, *Foster in His Time*, 60.

2. "To Break Nat Strong," *Afro-American*, February 11, 1921.

3. Cary B. Lewis, "Baseball Circuit for Next Season," *Chicago Defender*, October 4, 1919.

4. Larry Lester, *Baseball's First Colored World Series: The 1924 Meeting of the Hilldale Giants and Kansas City Monarchs* (Jefferson, NC: McFarland, 2006), 18–19.

5. Buck O'Neil, "YMCA Building Dedicated to Negro League Baseball Greats," *Atlanta Daily World*, March 5, 2000; Leslie Heaphy, "The Creation of a Negro National League," in Steven Geitschier (Ed.), *Replays, Rivalries, and Rumbles: The Most Iconic Moments in American Sports* (Champaign: University of Illinois Press, 2017), 27; David Conrads, "Felix Payne," Pendergast Years (website), https://pendergastkc.org/article/biography/felix-payne. Accessed July 22, 2020.

6. "Baseball Men Write League Constitution," *Chicago Defender*, February 21,1920.

7. Andrew ("Rube") Foster, "Pitfalls of Baseball," *Chicago Defender*, December 13, 1919.

Notes—Chapter 10

8. Larry Lester, *Colored World Series*, 11.
9. *Ibid.*, 115.
10. Ryan Nilsson, "Founder of the Negro Leagues Was Not Your Average Rube," *Chicago Sun Times*, July 12, 2020.
11. Al Monroe, "Negro Teams Thrive During War Years," *Chicago Daily Defender*, May 2, 1961.
12. "Baseball Magnates in Big Harmony Meeting," *Chicago Defender*, December 11, 1920.
13. Cottrell, *Best Pitcher*, 165.
14. "Bolden Challenges Foster to Debate," *Baltimore Afro-American*, February 16, 1923.
15. "'Rube' Foster Is No Czar of Baseball," *Baltimore Afro-American*, October 10, 1924.
16. "Rube Foster Has Pockets Picked on Streetcar," *Chicago Defender*, August 15, 1914.
17. "Imperial Art Club," *Chicago Defender*, June 26, 1915.
18. "City Federation of Womans' Clubs Meet," *Chicago Defender*, May 8, 1913; "The Young Matron's Club," *Chicago Defender*, May 31, 1913; "The Young Matrons' Culture Club," *Chicago Defender*, February 21, 1914; "Imperial Art Club," *Chicago Defender*, June 26, 1915; "Help Amanda Smith Home," *Chicago Defender*, September 14, 1918; "Mrs. Rube Foster Off for Mountains," *Chicago Defender*, August 18, 1917; *Britannica*, "Amanda Smith," https://www.britannica.com/biography/Amanda-Smith. Accessed August 29, 2020.
19. "Negro National League Standings (1920–1948)," Center for Negro League Baseball Research, www.cnlbr.org. Accessed July 12, 2020. Lester, *Colored World Series*, 11.
20. "Andrew Volstead: Tool or Dedicated Prohibitionist?" https://www.alcoholproblemsandsolutions.org/andrew-volstead/. Accessed September 8, 2020.
21. Daniel Okrent, *Last Call: The Rise and Fall of Prohibition* (New York: Simon and Schuster, 2010), 104–114.
22. "Andrew Volstead."
23. Okrent, *Last Call*, 308.
24. "Smuggle Booze to Camp Meeting in Milk Cans," *Chicago Defender*, August 10, 1918.
25. "Promises To Dry Up Chicago If He Is Given Co-operation," *Baltimore Sun*, October 18, 1920.
26. "Chicago: The Terrible Genna Brothers," 2017, https://www.nationalcrimesyndicate.com/chicago-the-terrible-genna-brothers/. Accessed October 28, 2021; Okrent, *Last Call*, 128.
27. "Chicago Jury Indicts 31 Under Volstead Act," *Baltimore Sun*, November 29, 1920; "People: Edward J. Brundage," https://peoplepill.com/people/edward-j-brundage/. Brundrage, the uncle of Olympic Chairman, Avery Brundrage, committed suicide over financial pressures after his term as Attorney General ended in 1925.
28. "Tells of Big Liquor Ring," *New York Times*, February 25, 1921.
29. *Ibid.*
30. Alistair Moray, *The Diary of a Rum-Runner* (London: Philip Allan, 1929), 25, as cited in Okrent, *Last Call*, 163.
31. Okrent, 163.
32. "Chicago Gets Soap Booze," *New York Times*, October 31, 1920.
33. "Whiskey Being Torpedoed Into U.S., Says Dalrymple," *Baltimore Sun*, April 21, 1920; "Blockade Runners Bringing In Liquor," *Washington Post*, August 16, 1920.
34. "Chicago is Wettest Spot, Detroit Greatest Entry Point for Liquor, in Nation," *Washington Post*, January 19, 1922.
35. Bak, *Turkey Stearnes*, 129.
36. Okrent, *Last Call*, 259.
37. *Ibid.*, 260.
38. *Ibid.*
39. "Chicago's Bootlegging Police To Be Trailed By Dry Sleuths," *Baltimore Sun*, September 26, 1921.
40. "The Infamous House Bootlegger Known as the Man in the Green Hat," https://history.house.gov/Historical-Highlights/1901-1950/The-infamous-House-bootlegger-known-as-the-%E2%80%9CMan-in-the-Green-Hat%E2%80%9D/. Accessed January 2, 2021; "The Man in the Green Hat," senate.gov/artandhistory/history/minute/The_Man_in_the_Green_Hat.htm. Accessed January 2, 2021; George L. Cassiday, "The Man in the Green Hat," *Washington Post*, October 27, 1930.
41. Okrent, *Last Call*, 125.
42. "Unintended Consequences of

Prohibition," pbs.org/kenburns/prohibition/unintended-consequences/. Accessed November 9, 2021.
 43. "Women's Rights Advanced During Prohibition," Mob Museum, https://themobmuseum.org/the-history/how-prohibition-changed-american-culture/womens-rights/. Accessed November 17, 2021.

Chapter 11

 1. "Detroit Stars Strong," *Chicago Defender*, May 8, 1920; "Detroit Stars," *Chicago Defender*, April 10, 1920; Riley, *Encyclopedia*, 190–91, 387.
 2. "Goes to Detroit," *Chicago Defender*, April 17, 1920; "Society," *Chicago Defender*, July 24, 1920.
 3. "Circuit Opens at Detroit," *Chicago Defender*, May 15, 1920; "Detroit Stars Win," *Chicago Defender*, April 17, 1920; "Stars Win Fourth Straight Victory," *Chicago Defender*, May 8, 1920.
 4. "Western Circuit Negro National League, *Chicago Defender*, May 15, 1920.
 5. "Detroit Stars," *Chicago Defender*, April 10, 1920; Dave Wyatt, "Big Crowd Sees Stars Battle, *Chicago Defender*, May 22, 1920.
 6. "Cuban Stars Win Two," *Chicago Defender*, May 29, 1920.
 7. "Cuban Stars Here," *Chicago Defender*, May 29, 1920.
 8. Dave Wyatt, "A.B.C. Triumph in First Home Games," *Chicago Defender*, May 8, 1920.
 9. "Monarchs Beaten in Slugging Bee," *Chicago Defender*, July 17, 1920; "Watching the Scoreboard," *Chicago Defender*, July 31, 1920.
 10. "Donaldson Masters Detroit," *Chicago Defender*, April 21, 1920; "Watching the Scoreboard," *Chicago Defender*, September 11, 1920.
 11. "Stars Stop Bacharachs," *Cleveland Gazette*, August 7, 1920.
 12. Marie Teasley, *Michigan Chronicle*, October 6, 1999.
 13. Bak, *Turkey Stearnes*, 57.
 14. "Blont [sic] and Hill Ready for Gong," *Chicago Defender*, February 19, 1921.
 15. Untitled notice, *Belvidere Daily Republican* (Belvidere, Illinois), November 10, 1920.
 16. "Detroit Stars Win From Creamery," *Chicago Defender*, May 7, 1921; "Force Beats Hagerman in Slab Duel," *Chicago Defender*, May 21, 1921,
 17. "Detroit Stars Beat Bacharach Giants 9 to 8," *Chicago Defender*, May 14, 1921; "Redding Pitches; Detroit Stars Taste Defeat," *Chicago Defender*, May 14, 1921.
 18. Roy L. Jackson; "Blount's Men Setting Hot Pace in League," *Chicago Defender*, July 2, 1921.
 19. Walter F. White, "Tulsa's Shame Due to Race Prejudice and Corrupt Rule," *New York Evening Post*, June 18, 1921.
 20. "N.Y. Messenger Warns of Riots," *Afro-American*, July 8, 1921; Bak, 124.
 21. "Future of American Negro to be Discussed in Detroit, *Philadelphia Tribune*, June 25, 1921.
 22. "Square Deal for Negro Demanded in Call to Nation," *Philadelphia Tribune*, July 6, 1921.
 23. "Future of American Negro to be Discussed in Detroit," *Philadelphia Tribune*, June 25, 1921.
 24. "Detroit Mob Tries to Lynch a Negro," *New York Times*, August 8, 1921.
 25. "Pete Hill's Bat Wins Two For Detroit Stars," *Chicago Defender*, July 16, 1921.
 26. "Detroit Stars Invade Chicago For Big Series," *Chicago Defender*, August 20, 1921.
 27. "American Giants Handed Shutout by Detroit Stars," *Chicago Defender*, August 27, 1921.
 28. "Hilldale Takes 5 Out of 6 From Detroit Stars," *Philadelphia Tribune*, September 17, 1921.
 29. "Display Ad 9," *Philadelphia Tribune*, September 3, 1921.
 30. Riley, *Encyclopedia*, 432–434; "19 Men Report to Chappie Johnson," *Philadelphia Evening Public Ledger*, April 1, 1922; "Knights Down Chappie's Men," *Schenectady Gazette*, July 19, 1922; "North Phils to Oppose Fletcher," *Philadelphia Evening Public Ledger*, July 31, 1922, as cited in "Pete Hill," SABR Biography Project, https://sabr.org/bioproj/person/pete-hill/. Accessed June 29, 2020.
 31. Gary Ashwill, "'Black Sox Players,' Nos. 1 & 2," Agate Type, December 11, 2006, https://agatetype.typepad.com/agate_type/2006/12/black_sox_playe.html, accessed June 4, 2022; "Johnson to

Manage Phila. Team," *New York Age*, February 11, 1922.
　32. "Display Ad 2," *New Journal and Guide*, September 23, 1922; "All Stars Will Play Richmond Giants," *New Journal and Guide*, September 23, 1922.
　33. "19 Men Report to Chappie Johnson," *Philadelphia Evening Public Ledger*, April 1, 1922; "All-Star Game Tomorrow," *Philadelphia Evening Public Ledger*, August 18, 1922; Riley, *Encyclopedia*, 676–77.
　34. "1922 Philadelphia Royal Stars," Seamheads Negro Leagues Database, http://seamheads.com/NegroLgs/team.php?yearID=1922&teamID=PRS&tab=fld_bypos. Accessed July 16, 2020; "Bridesburg vs, Shanahan," *Philadelphia Evening Public Ledger*, August 2, 1922.
　35. "Right Off the Bat," *Pittsburgh Courier*, April 7, 1923.
　36. "Milwaukee Stars vs. Cermacks," *Chicago Defender*, April 14, 1923; "Hillies Down Cubans in Milwaukee Opening," *Chicago Defender*, May 5, 1923; Riley, *Encyclopedia*, 41, 729.
　37. "American Giants Play Milwaukee 2 Games Sunday," *Chicago Defender*, May 5, 1923; "Milwaukee Stars 9-Heights 6," *Chicago Heights Star*, July 19, 1923; Riley, *Encyclopedia*, 267, 419.
　38. "Pete Hill is in Town; Will Pilot Milwaukee," *Chicago Defender*, April 7, 1923; Cliff Christi, "Gone, Not Forgotten," *Milwaukee Journal*, June 17, 1992.
　39. "Angola Drops Batting Bee to Wisconsin Nine," *Fort Wayne Journal-Gazette*, June 14, 1923; "Angola Loses to Milwaukee Bears, *Angola Herald*, June 29, 1923; "Lost the Ball Game," *Tipton Daily Tribune*, May 25, 1923.
　40. "League Standings," *Pittsburgh Courier*, June 9, 1923.
　41. "Indianapolis is Still Holding League Lead," *Chicago Defender*, May 16, 1923; "Detroit Takes Double Header from Milwaukee," *Pittsburgh Courier*, June 23, 1923; "Milwaukee Bears Find Birmingham Tough Pickens [sic]," *Chicago Defender*, July 28, 1923; "Fosters Play Milwaukee Two Games, Then Go South," *Chicago Defender*, August 18, 1923; Center for Negro League Baseball Research, www.cnlbr.org. Accessed April 9, 2020; "Milwaukee Stars This Evening," *Chicago Heights Star*, July 12, 1923; "Milwaukee Stars 9-Heights 6," *Chicago Heights Star*, July 19, 1923.

Chapter 12

　1. "Sox Will Start To Work April 1," *Baltimore Afro-American*, March 7, 1924.
　2. Riley, *Encyclopedia*, 91–92.
　3. Lanctot, *Fair Dealing*, 99.
　4. "Bogus Rum Permit Lands Man in Jail," *Baltimore Sun*, October 27, 1922; Riley, 734.
　5. "Amateur Ball Clubs," *The Sun*, March 25, 1906; "Gossip of Baltimore's Amateur Balltossers," *Sun*, September 4, 1914; "Colored Mittmen Collide Tonight," *Sun*, August 27, 1923.
　6. Untitled article, *Pittsburgh Courier*, May 17, 1924.
　7. John Holway, *Voices from the Great Black Baseball Leagues*, 66–67; "Rumors Indicate That Storm is Brewing Between the Owners and Players," *New York Age*, December 20, 1924; "Spedden Will 'Junk' Present Black Sox Club," *Baltimore Afro-American*, November 2, 1923.
　8. "Colored Baseball Players Receive Handsome Salaries," *Sun*, August 23, 1923.
　9. "Blackmon [sic] To Baltimore," *Pittsburgh Courier*, May 10, 1924; Riley, *Encyclopedia*, 87.
　10. "'Biz' Mackey and 'Nip' Winters Tell Gray's Manager They Will Join," *Pittsburgh Courier*, June 28, 1924; "Beckwith Released by Homestead Grays," *New Journal and Guide*, June 28, 1924.
　11. "Bus For Black Sox," *Baltimore Afro-American*, February 8, 1924.
　12. "Sox Prepare to Start East," *Afro-American*, March 21, 1924.
　13. Jules Tygiel, *Past Time: Baseball as History* (New York: Oxford University Press, 2001), 130.
　14. Bernard McKenna, *The Baltimore Black Sox: A Negro Leagues History, 1913–1936* (Jefferson, NC: McFarland, 2020), 83–84; "Sox Prepare to Start East," *Afro-American*, March 21, 1924.
　15. "Fay Says," *Chicago Defender*, February 16, 1924.
　16. "'Not Through as Player and Manager,' Says Pete Hill," *Pittsburgh Courier*, February 23, 1924.
　17. "Black Sox Team is Baltimore

Bound," *Baltimore Afro-American*, March 28, 1924.

18. "Holloway Better Jumper Than Frog: Hops to Baltimore," *Chicago Defender*, April 12, 1924.

19. John Holway, *Voices from the Great Black Baseball Leagues* (New York: Dodd Mead, 1975), 117.

20. McNeil, *Cool Papas*, 99.

21. Riley, *Encyclopedia*, 445–446; "Wade Johnson Blacklisted," *Chicago Defender*, April 19, 1924.

22. "Holloway Better Jumper Than Frog; Hops to Baltimore" and "Wade Johnson to Baltimore," *Pittsburgh Courier*, April 19, 1924.

23. Chester L. Washington, Jr., "'Sez Chez,'" *The Pittsburgh Courier*, May 6, 1931; Riley, 92.

24. "Black Sox Team Is Baltimore Bound," *Baltimore Afro-American*, March 28, 1924.

25. "5,000 See Sox In Opener," *Baltimore Afro-American*, April 18, 1924.

26. "Sox Lose Series to Bacharachs," *Baltimore Afro-American*, May 2, 1924; "Pete Hill Hero of Victory," *Baltimore Afro-American*, May 9, 1924.

27. "Sox in Double Win Over Lit Brothers," *Baltimore Afro-American*, July 11, 1924.

28. "Pete Punches with Bases Loaded," *Baltimore Afro-American*, June 20, 1924; Riley, *Encyclopedia*, 374, 529.

29. "8,000 See Sox and Hilldale Split Double Header Sunday, Sox Still in Second Place," *Baltimore Afro-American*, July 25, 1924.

30. W. Rollo Wilson, "Eastern Snapshots," *Pittsburgh Courier*, August 2, 1924.

31. "Big Shakeup Likely Soon in Baltimore Black Sox Lineup," *New York Age*, December 20, 1924.

32. Riley, *Encyclopedia*, 683.

33. "Orioles and Sox Will Not Play Series," *Baltimore Afro-American*, October 3, 1925.

34. Herbert A. Wilkinson, "Black Sox Split with Athletics," *Baltimore Sun*, October 13, 1924.

35. Pete Hill, "Kinky Questions," *Baltimore Afro-American*, May 23, 1924.

36. "Pete Hill Says K.C. Should Win 'On Paper,'" *Baltimore Afro-American*, October 3, 1924; Pete Hill, "Pete Hill Yet Confident K.C. Takes Series," *Baltimore Afro-American*, October 10, 1924; "Pete Hill Says 'I Told You So,'" *Afro-American*, October 31, 1924.

37. "Pete Hill to Again Manage Sox," *Baltimore Afro-American*, October 24, 1924; "Black Sox Manager to Winter in 'Chi,'" *Afro-American*, November 8, 1924; "Bolden to Head Eastern League," *Afro-American*, December 13, 1924; "Pete Hill, Business Mgr.," *Baltimore Afro-American*, December 20, 1924; "Harken to That Other Ancient," *Pittsburgh Courier*, April 25, 1925.

38. "Black Sox Triumph in Two Double Bills," *Baltimore Afro-American*, July 18, 1925.

39. "Sox and Giants to Lock Horns Sunday," *Baltimore Afro-American*, August 8, 1925.

40. Riley, *Encyclopedia*, 70.

41. Riley, *Encyclopedia*, 761, 763.

42. "New Sox Leader," *Baltimore Afro-American*, January 30, 1926; "Kansas City Again Leads Westerners," *Pittsburgh Courier*, August 22, 1925.

43. "Mirror: To Produce a Byrd," *Baltimore Afro-American*, December 5, 1925.

44. Riley, *Encyclopedia*, 49.

Chapter 13

1. 1940 Census.

2. 2 Riley, *Encyclopedia*, 434; Revel and Munoz, 40–41; "Pittsburgh Stars Win," *Buffalo Inquirer*, May 24, 1919.

3. "Oscar Bright Looks for Good Season," *Buffalo American*, March 18, 1920.

"Oscar Bright Looks for Good Season," *Buffalo American*, March 18, 1920; "Eight Teams in Semi-Pro League," *Buffalo Enquirer*, March 27, 1920.

4. "Bud Fowler," SABR Biography Project, https://sabr.org/bioproj/person/budfowler/. Accessed May 17, 2021; Endres' World War I Draft registration; "Black Rocks in the Field," *Buffalo Courier*, April 4, 1909; *Buffalo Inquirer*, May 7, 1909.

5. "Grant Homerun Johnson is to play with Baccarach [sic] Giants," *Buffalo Morning Express*, March 29, 1920; "Semi-Pro Teams, Too, Are Ready for Gala Opening," *Buffalo Courier*, April 23, 1920.

6. "Colored Stars to Take Southern Trip," *Buffalo Times*, January 20, 1921.

7. "3,700 See Stars Go Back To Top in

Semi-Pro Leagues," *Buffalo Inquirer*, July 22, 1918; J.H. Thomas, "Buffalo," *Chicago Defender*, September 14, 1918; "All Canada League Cities After the Famous Pittsburgh Stars of Buffalo for Exhibition Games," *Buffalo Commercial*, April 29, 1919; "Pittsburgh Stars Go On a Jamboree," *Chicago Defender News Service*, July 29, 1916.

8. Riley, 435–6; "Burlin White with the Big Steel City Giants Shows Form," *Philadelphia Tribune*, July 19, 1924; "Local News," *Buffalo American*, November 22, 1923.

9. "Up North," *Afro-American*, July 17, 1926.

10. "Sheridan Town Picnic," *Fredonia Censor*, July 23, 1926; "Spiders and Colored All Stars to Stage Duel at Ball Park Sunday," *Jamestown Evening Journal*, July 24, 1926; "Sheridan Picnic Has Fine Program," *Dunkirk Evening Observer*, July 23, 1926.

11. "Hill Stars Win at Lewiston, 10–1," *Buffalo Times*, August 3, 1926.

12. "Speaker McGinnis To Give Address at Sheridan Picnic," *Jamestown Evening Journal*, July 30, 1927,

13. "Cardinals Will Send Amato to Mound Against Pete Hill's Fast Colored Nine at Stadium Sunday," *Niagara Falls Gazette*, June 18, 1927.

14. "7th Old Home Week Breaks All Records," *Ellicottville Post* (Ellicottville, New York), August 24, 1927.

15. "Billy Webb," Chautauqua Sports Hall of Fame, https://www.chautauquasportshalloffame.org/billywebb.php. Accessed October 29, 2020.

16. "Jamestown," *Buffalo Times*, August 14, 1926, http://www.ibhof.com/pages/about/inductees/oldtimer/langford.html. Accessed December 5, 2020.

17. *Warren Tribune*, August 16, 1926.

18. "Sixth Annual Old Home Week Replete with Many Big Attractions," *Ellicottville Post* (Ellicottville, New York), August 11, 1928.

19. "Here Next Week," *Warren Tribune*, May 24, 1928.

20. "Fast Colored Team in City Thursday," *Lockport (N.Y.) Union-Sun and Journal*, July 19, 1932.

21. "Twilight Game Will See IM-COS Against Dusky Buffalo Club," *Lockport [N.Y.] Union-Sun and Journal*, August 18, 1932.

22. "Red Caps," Pratt Library, https://eresource.prattlibrary.org:2106/HRC/Search/Details/5?articleId=160391&q=%22Red%20Caps%22. Accessed June 30, 2020.

23. "County Fair Will Start Next Week," *Times Herald* (Orleans, New York), August 14, 1930; "Buffalo Red Caps Defeat Ludlow Wildcats 19–6," *Kane Republican* (Kane, Pennsylvania), July 21, 1930.

24. "Society," *Buffalo American*, October 25, 1925.

25. Letter to Mr. Michael R. Hill, Sr., from Linda Luckett, Public Affairs Specialist, Railroad Retirement Board, January 21, 2010; *Buffalo American*, October 29, 1925.

26. Eric K. Washington, *Boss of the Grips: The Life of James H. Williams and the Red Caps of Grand Central Terminal* (New York: Liveright, 2019) dust jacket, 100, 116–118; "Webster Accepts Terms," *Chicago Defender*, March 30, 1918; Riley, *Encyclopedia*, 825.

27. "Red Caps Close Season with Bacharach Giants," *Philadelphia Tribune*, October 14, 1916; "Red Cap League Opens at Hilldale," *Philadelphia Tribune*, July 4, 1935; "Watching the Scoreboard," *Chicago Defender*, June 4, 1921; "New York-Washington Red Cap Game," *Philadelphia Tribune*, September 11, 1915; "Station Porter Shows Oil Paintings," *New Journal and Guide*, November 5, 1949; "Wilmington Red Caps Reorganized," *Philadelphia Tribune*, March 31, 1938.

28. Chico Renfroe, "Let's Go Down Memory Lane," *Atlanta Daily World*, May 17, 1977.

29. "John P. Hill Estate Article," *Buffalo Courier Express*, March 20, 1952; "Man Stricken Fatally While Operating Auto," *Buffalo Courier Express*, December 20, 1951; John Preston Hill Death Certificate.

30. Monroe, October 1935.

31. "Rube Falters," *Inter-Ocean*, October 22, 1909.

32. Sam Lacy, "From A to Z," *Baltimore Afro-American*, May 17, 1951.

33. Russ J. Cowans, "Russ' Corner," *Chicago Defender*, May 13, 1950.

34. Wendell Smith, "Sports Beat," *Pittsburgh Courier*, October 2, 1948.

35. "Gary Gets First Negro Referee," *Chicago Defender*, February 7, 1948.

36. Fay, "Fay Says," *Chicago Defender*, December 29, 1951.

37. Frank Litsky, "Sam Lacy, 99, Fought Racism as Sportswriter," *New York Times*, May 12, 2003.
38. Sam Lacy, "Why Hall of Fame Doesn't Daze Me," *Baltimore Afro-American*, August 10, 1968.
39. Alex Holt, "Still No Cheering in the Press Box," Shirley Povich Center for Sports Journalism, https://povichcenter.umd.edu/still-no-cheering-press-box/chapter/Sam-Lacy/index.html. Accessed July 30, 2020.
40. Sam Lacy, "Wait Ends for Billy Williams," *Baltimore Afro-American*, January 24, 1987.
41. "Old Time Diamond Stars to Be Guests," *Baltimore Afro-American*, August 26, 1939.
42. "Pete Hill, Retired Ball Player Visits Soldier Son," *Chicago Defender*, December 12, 1942.
43. "Corporal Hill Visits," *Chicago Defender*, December 26, 1942; "Electrical School Bars Colored Vet," *Chicago Defender*, July 7, 1945.
44. "Coyne Electrical School Bias Hit," *Chicago Defender*, September 21, 1946.
45. "Breaks Vet School Bias," *Pittsburgh Courier*, September 14, 1946.
46. Indiana State Board of Health Medical Certificate of Death No. 76-008819.

Chapter 14

1. Ted Williams, with John Underwood, *My Turn at Bat: The Story of My Life* (New York: Simon and Schuster, 1969), 249.
2. "This Morning with Shirley Povich," *Washington Post*, July 26, 1966.
3. Bowie Kuhn, *Hardball: The Education of a Baseball Commissioner* (New York: Times, 1987), 110–111.
4. The letter's text was reprinted in Hunt Auctions, Inc., catalogue for an internet/phone auction closing December 9, 2005.
5. John Holway, "Blacks Losers Only at Hall of Fame," *Boston Globe*, August 4, 1978.
6. Telephone interview with Clifford Kachline, January 17, 2005.
7. Telephone interview with Monte Irvin, January 26, 2006.
8. Kuhn, *Hardball*, 109–110.

9. "Old-Time Negro Stars Get Hall of Fame Boost," *Michigan Chronicle*, August 16, 1969.
10. Irvin interview, June 2005; Joseph Durso, "Baseball to Admit Negro Stars of Pre-Integration Era into Hall of Fame," *New York Times*, February 4, 1971; "Place for Ex-Negro Stars in Shrine," February 13, 1971 (Clipping in Hall of Fame file); Kuhn, *Hardball*, 110.
11. Milton Gross, "Robinson Speaks Out," *New York Post*, February 4, 1971.
12. Stan Isaacs, "Why Doesn't Baseball Put Paige in Front of the Hall" *Newsday*, February 5, 1971; "Baseball's Front Door Opens to Satchel Paige," New York Times, July 8, 1971.
13. "Paige Enters 'Real' Baseball Hall of Fame," *Chicago Daily Defender*, July 10, 1971.
14. Frank H. Saunders, "Frankly Speaking," *Michigan Chronicle*, February 20, 1971; "Paige Receives Just Due Today," *Sun*, August 9, 1971.
15. Jim Overmyer, *Effa Manley and the Newark Eagles* (Metuchen, NJ: Scarecrow, 1993), 5, 73 as cited in Bob Luke, *The Most Famous Woman in Baseball: Effa Manley and the Negro Leagues* (Washington, D.C.: Potomac, 2011), 161.
16. Effa Manley to John Holway, June 17, 1977.
17. Bob Luke, *Willie Wells: "El Diablo" of the Negro Leagues* (Austin: University of Texas Press, 2007), 118–126; Riley, *Encyclopedia*, 316–18.
18. "Hall of Fame Inductions by Year," MLB.com, https://www.mlb.com/news/hall-of-fame-inductions-by-year. Accessed November 29, 2021.
19. Interview with Dale Petroskey, February 21, 2006.
20. "Hall of Fame Inductions by Year.".
21. Ira Berlow, "17 From Black Baseball Included in Hall at Last," *New York Times*, July 31, 2006; Descriptions of the Black inductees were taken from their entries in Riley, *Encyclopedia*, 1994.
22. "Hall of Fame Inductions by Year."
23. "Six Candidates Elected to Hall of Fame as Part of Class of 2022," National Baseball Hall of Fame website, https://baseballhall.org/news/sixcandidates-elected-to-hall-of-fame-as-part-of-class-of-2022. Accessed December 30, 2021; Riley, *Encyclopedia*, 499–500.

Epilogue

1. Kevin Kirkland, "Penn Hills Man Wins Battle with Baseball Hall of Fame for his Great-Uncle," *Pittsburgh Post-Gazette*, March 29, 2012; John Kikis, "Baseball Hall of Famer Pete Hill Gets a New Plaque," October 14, 2010, http://www.google.com/hostednews/ap/article/ALeqM5h5RxjUKUV2D2f-9fB4bmqN2W. Accessed August 3, 2020.

2. Ryan Whirty, "Remembering Pete Hill," *Art Voice*, May 6, 2011. An article in Hill's Hall of Fame file in Cooperstown, New York.

3. Karen E. Pride, "Negro League Players Gravesites Honored," *Chicago Defender*, September 27, 2004; Tara Kadioglu, "Ex-Burr Oak Cemetery Workers Convicted of Desecrating Bodies," *Chicago Tribune*, February 12, 2015.

4. "Negro Leagues Players Honored with Gravestones," NPR Weekend Edition, June 18, 2011.

5. Alan Schwarz, "For Players of Negro Leagues, Final Measure of Recognition," *New York Times*, July 1, 2010.

6. Zann Nelson, "Researcher Discovers Hill's Burial Site," *Culpeper Star Exponent*, November 9, 2010; Telephone interview with Dr. Jeremy Krock on July 19, 2020.

7. "Allegheny County Council Proclamation," November 10, 2010.

8. Virginia Department of Historic Resources Press Release, October 7, 2010.

9. Robert F. McDonnell to Ms. Elizabeth Ann Nelson, October 5, 2010.

10. Allison Brophy Champion, "Nelson Gets Award for Pete Hill Research," *Culpeper Star-Exponent*, August 1, 2010.

11. Ashwill had had to navigate an appeal process to convince the Social Security Administration that Hill was in fact dead. Ashwill's brief description of his efforts can be found in the October 12, 2010, entry of his Agate Type blog, https://agatetype.typepad.com/agate_type/2010/10/happy-birthday.html.

12. Donnie Johnston, "Culpeper Balks at Marker for Hill," *Freelancestar.com*, July 6, 2011; Allison Brophy Campion, "Board Approves Hill Marker, Issues of Race Still Linger," *Culpeper Star-Exponent*, September 7, 2011.

Bibliography

Books

Asinof, Eliot. *Eight Men Out: The Black Sox and the 1919 World Series*. New York: Henry Holt, 2000.

Bak, Richard. *Turkey Stearnes and the Detroit Stars: The Negro Leagues in Detroit, 1999–1933* Detroit: Wayne State University Press.

Barry, John M. *The Great Influenza: The Story of the Greatest Pandemic in History*. New York: Penguin, 2018.

Beer, Jeremy. *Oscar Charleston: The Life and Legend of Baseball's Greatest Forgotten Player*. Lincoln: University of Nebraska Press, 2019.

Bjarkman, Peter, Jr. *A History of Cuban Baseball, 1864–2006*. Jefferson, NC: McFarland, 2007.

Bruce, Janet. *The Kansas City Monarchs: Champions of Black Baseball*. Lawrence: University Press of Kansas, 1985.

Carroll, Brian. *When to Stop Cheering? The Black Press, the Black Community, and the Integration of Professional Baseball*. New York: Routledge, 2007.

Conkling, Winifred. *Votes for Women: American Suffragists and the Battle for the Ballot*. Chapel Hill, NC: Algonquin Young Readers, 2018.

Cottrell, Robert Charles. *The Best Pitcher in Baseball: The Life of Rube Foster, Negro League Giant*. New York: New York University Press, 2001.

DeBono, Paul. Indianapolis ABCs: History of a Premier Team in the Negro Leagues. Jefferson, NC: McFarland,1997.

De la Roche, Roberta Senechal. *In Lincoln's Shadow: The 1908 Race Riot in Springfield, Illinois*. Carbondale: Southern Illinois University Press, 2008.

Dickson, Paul. *The Dickson Baseball Dictionary: The Revised, Expanded, and Now Definitive Work on the Language of Baseball*. 3rd Ed. New York: W.W. Norton, 2009.

Dixon, Phil S. *Phil Dixon's American Baseball Chronicles*. Volume 3, *Great Teams: The 1905 Philadelphia Giants*. Bloomington, IN: Xlibris, 2010.

Figueredo, Jorge. *Cuban Baseball: A Statistical History 1878–1961*. Jefferson, NC: McFarland, 2011.

Foley, Barbara. *Specters of 1919: Class and Nation in the Making of the New Negro*. Urbana: University of Illinois Press, 2008.

Gietschier, Steven, ed. *Replays, Rivalries, and Rumbles: The Most Iconic Moments in American Sports*. Champaign: University of Illinois Press, 2017.

Heaphy, Leslie A., ed. *Black Baseball and Chicago*. Jefferson, NC: McFarland, 2006.

_____. *The Negro Leagues: 1869–1960*. Jefferson, NC: McFarland, 2003.

Henderson, Edwin Bancroft. *The Negro in Sports*. Washington, D.C.: Associated Publishers, 1939.

Holway, John B. *Baseball Stars: Negro League Pioneers*. New York: Mecklermedia, 1988.

_____. *The Complete Book of Baseball's Negro Leagues: The Other Half of Baseball History*. Fern Park, FL: Hastings House, 2001.

_____. *Voices from the Great Black Baseball Leagues.* New York: Dodd Mead, 1975.
Hornsby, Alton, Jr. *Chronology of African-American History: Significant Events and People from 1619 to the Present.* Detroit: Gale Research, 1991.
Krist, Gary. *City of Scoundrels: The Twelve Days of Disaster That Gave Birth to the Modern Chicago.* New York: Crown, 2012.
Kuhn, Bowie. *Hardball: The Education of a Baseball Commissioner.* New York: Times, 1987.
Lanctot, Neil. *Fair Dealing and Clean Playing: The Hilldale Club and the Development of Black Professional Baseball.* Jefferson, NC: McFarland, 1994. Reprinted Syracuse, NY: Syracuse University Press, 1994.
Lester, Larry. *Baseball's First Colored World Series: The 1924 Meeting of the Hilldale Giants and Kansas City Monarchs.* Jefferson, NC: McFarland, 2006.
_____. *Rube Foster in His Time: On the Field and in the Papers with Black Baseball's Greatest Visionary.* Jefferson, NC: McFarland, 2012.
Lester, Larry, Sammy J. Miller, and Dick Clark. *Black Baseball in Chicago.* Chicago: Arcadia, 2000.
_____. *Black Baseball in Detroit.* Chicago: Arcadia, 2000.
Luke, Bob. *Willie Wells: "El Diablo" of the Negro Leagues.* Austin: University of Texas Press, 2007.
Malloy, Jerry, ed. *Sol White's History of Colored Base Ball with Other Documents on the Early Black Game* 1886–1936. Lincoln: University of Nebraska Press, 1995.
McGirr, Lisa. *The War on Alcohol: Prohibition and the Rise of the American State.* New York: W.W. Norton, 2016.
McKenna, Bernard. *The Baltimore Black Sox: A Negro Leagues History, 1913–1936.* Jefferson, NC: McFarland, 2020.
McNeil, William F. *Black Baseball Out of Season: Pay for Play Outside of the Negro Leagues.* Jefferson, NC: McFarland, 2017.
_____. *The California Winter League: America's First Integrated Professional Baseball League.* Jefferson, NC: McFarland, 2000.
_____. *Cool Papas and Double Duties: The All-Time Greats of the Negro Leagues.* Jefferson, NC: McFarland, 2001.
Miller, Patrick B., and David K. Wiggians, eds. *Sport and the Color Line: Black Athletes and Race Relations in Twentieth Century America.* Philadelphia: Routledge, 2003.
Motley, Bob, with Byron Motley. *The Negro Baseball Leagues: Tales of Umpiring Legendary Players, Breaking Barriers, and Making American History.* New York: Sports Publishing, 2007.
Okrent, Daniel. *Last Call: The Rise and Fall of Prohibition.* New York: Simon & Schuster, 2010.
Overmyer, James E. *Black Baseball and the Boardwalk: The Bacharach Giants of Atlantic City.* 1916–1929. Jefferson, NC: McFarland, 2014.
Peterson, Robert. *Only the Ball Was White: A History of Legendary Black Players and All-Black Professional Teams.* New York: Oxford University Press, 1992.
Reichler, Joseph L., ed. *The Baseball Encyclopedia.* 7th ed. New York: Macmillan, 1988.
Revel, Layton, and Luis Munoz. *Early Pioneers of the Negro Leagues: Walter "Slick" Schlichter.* Carrollton, TX: Center for Negro League Baseball Research, 2016.
Riley, James A. *The Biographical Encyclopedia of the Negro Baseball Leagues.* New York: Carroll & Graf, 1994.
_____. *Of Monarchs and Black Barons: Essays on Baseball's Negro Leagues.* Jefferson, NC: McFarland, 2012.
Robertson, James I., Jr. *General A.P. Hill: The Story of a Confederate Warrior.* New York: Vintage Illustrated, 1992.
Rosenberg, Howard W. *Cap Anson 4: Bigger Than Babe Ruth.* Arlington, VA: Tile, 2006.
Tygiel, Jules. *Past Time: Baseball as History.* New York: Oxford University Press, 2001.
Washington, Eric K. *Boss of the Grips: The Life of James H. Williams and the Red Caps of Grand Central Terminal.* New York: Liveright, 2019.
Wells, Ida B., and Alfreda M. Duster, ed. *Crusade for Justice: The Autobiography of Ida B. Wells.* 2nd Ed. Chicago: University of Chicago Press, 2020.

Williams, Ted, with John Underwood. *My Turn at Bat: The Story of My Life*. New York: Simon & Schuster, 1969.

Archival Sources

A. Bartlett Giamatti Research Center, National Baseball Hall of Fame, Cooperstown, NY.
The Library of Congress, Washington, D.C.
The Lincoln Library, Springfield, Illinois.
Woodrow Wilson House, Washington, D.C.

Newspapers

Alton Evening Telegraph (Alton, Illinois)
Anaconda Standard (Anaconda, Montana)
The Appeal-Democrat (Marysville, California)
Atlanta Daily World
Baltimore Afro-American
Baltimore Sun
Belvidere Daily Republican (Illinois)
Boone County Republican (Belvidere, Illinois)
Boston Globe
Buffalo American
Buffalo Commercial
Buffalo Courier Express
Buffalo Inquirer
Buffalo Morning Express
Buffalo Times
Burlington Free Press (Vermont)
Chicago Daily Tribune
Chicago Examiner
Chicago Heights Star
Chicago Inter-Ocean
Cleveland Gazette
The Courier (Waterloo, Iowa)
Culpeper Star-Exponent
Decatur Herald (Decatur, Illinois)
Detroit Free Press
Detroit Tribune
The Dispatch
Dunkirk Evening Observer (Dunkirk, New York)
Englewood Economist (Illinois)
Eugene Guard (Oregon)
Fennimore Times (Wisconsin)
Franklin's Paper the Statesman (Denver)
Fredonia Censor (Chautauqua, NY)
Fresno Morning Republican
Grand Forks Union (North Dakota)
Harrisburg Daily Independent
Honolulu Advertiser
Honolulu Star-Bulletin
Indianapolis Freeman
Jamestown Evening Journal (New York)
Kane Republican (Kane, Pennsylvania)
Lockport Evening Sun and Journal (New York)
Los Angeles Herald
Los Angeles Record
McClatchy-Tribune Business News (Pittsburgh)
Michigan Chronicle
Milwaukee Journal
Mineral Point Tribune (Wisconsin)
New Journal and Guide (Virginia Beach, Virginia)
New York Age
New York Evening Post
New York Times
Niagara Falls Gazette
Oregon Daily Journal
Palm Beach Daily News
Philadelphia Evening Item
Philadelphia Evening Public Ledger
Philadelphia Inquirer
The Philadelphia Item
Philadelphia Tribune
Pittsburgh Courier
Pittsburgh Post-Gazette
The Post (Ellicottville, NY)
The Province (Vancouver, British Columbia)
Republican-Northwestern (Belvidere, IL)
St Louis Post-Dispatch
St Louis Star and Times
San Diego Union
San Francisco Call
Schenectady Gazette
Scranton Tribune
Scranton Truth
Sporting News
Standard Union (Brooklyn, New York)
The Statesman (Denver)
Suburbanite Economist (Chicago)
Times Herald (Orlean, New York)
Union Sun and Journal (Lockport, New York)

Vancouver Sun
The Warren Tribune (Warren, Ohio)

Washington Herald (D.C.)
Washington Post

Interviews

John Barry
Ron Hill
Monte Irvin

Clifford Kachline
Jeremy Kroch
James "Red" Moore

Index

Numbers in ***bold italics*** indicate pages with illustrations

Abbott, Robert S. 23
Acme Colored Giants 6
Addams, Jane 108
Afro-American, Baltimore 13, 18, 148, 150, 156, 159
Agate Type blog *see* Ashwill, Gary
alcohol 80–82, 101, 102, 104
Alexander, Grover Cleveland 24
Alfa Suffrage Club 108
All-Nations team 10–11; *see also* Wilkinson, J. Leslie
Allegheny County Council 173
Almendares (Cuban team) 34, 35, 40–41, 51–52, 57
American Association 5
American Brewing Company 74
American Giants: after Foster's death 179n8; alcohol and 80–81; All-Nations team against 10; among best midwestern teams 187n12; barnstorming 55, 60, 62, 64, 77–78, 84; California Winter League and 60–61; *Chicago Defender* coverage of 24; Chicago riots and 116–7; Cuban Stars against 56–57; Detroit Stars against 113, 119, 135, 138; gentlemanly behavior off the field by 62; Hill's playing for 6, 12–13; Indianapolis ABCs against 83–84, 97; Johnson and Hill on 24; Leland Giants renamed as 45; Lincoln Giants against 59–60; major leaguers and 88–89; Milwaukee Bears against 141; Omaha All Professionals against 74; outdrawing White teams 7; postwar roster 109; racial conflict during game 73; roster (1919), Detroit Stars and 110; Schorling's Park and 55, 59; "Smokey" Joe Williams and 54; in Vancouver, Canada ***78***; Wisconsin Fairs and 56; *see also* Foster, Andrew "Rube"
American Giants Garage, Chicago 123
American Medical Association (AMA) 91
American Series 29–30, 34, 51–52
Ames, J.R. 136
Amundsen, Roald 102

Anderson, Bud 64
Andrew, John A. 16
Anson, Cap and Anson's Colts 37, 41
Anthony, Susan B. 108
Antis (against women's suffrage) 102, 104, 107
Anti-Saloon League 79
Argentina, Blacks playing baseball in 9
Argyle Hotel team, Babylon, Long Island 27
Army's 86th Division team 88–89
Ashenback, Edward 32
Ashwill, Gary: Culpeper County marker for Hill and 176; on Hall of Fame's inaccuracies for Hill 169; on Hill's home runs 119; on Hill's start in baseball 18; on Philadelphia Royal Stars 140; roadside sign honoring Hill and 174; Seamheads Negro Leagues database and 3; Social Security Administration on Hill and 199n11
Asian-American women, voting rights for 108
Asinof, Eliot 89, 129
Association Opposed to Woman Suffrage, Baltimore 102
Atlantic City *see* Bacharach Giants, Atlantic City
Atlantic Park 120
Auburn Park 46, 54; *see also* Leland Giants
Augustine, Leon 141

Babe Ruth All Stars 157
Bacharach Giants, Atlantic City: American Giants against 97; Baltimore Black Sox against 147; Cannonball Redding joins 109; Chappie Johnson and 154; Chicago riots and 116–7; Detroit Stars against 119, 135, 136; Hill pinch hitting against 148–9; NNL formation talks and 122; Pennsylvania Red Caps against 158; players in Palm Beach from 86
Bahamas, Prohibition and 128
Baker, J.D. 116
Baldwin, Jesse 45

205

206 Index

Ball, Walter 42
Ballard, Clergy 70
Baltimore: managed professional Black teams in 1; Spanish flu and restraints on games in 98
Baltimore All-Stars 144
Baltimore Black Sox: Beckwith as manager 150, 151-2; challenging White teams 149-50; Hill as manager 12, 18, 143, 145-6, 147-8, 152; at Maryland Park 145; 1924 season 147-9; Philadelphia Baseball Association and 139; team photo *148*, *151*
Baltimore Orioles 149
Baltimore Sun 39, 114, 165
Bancroft, Dave 60
Banks, Nathanial 16
Barbour, Jess 57, *75*
Barnes, Everett D. "Eppie" 164
Barnes Colored Americans, Pittsburgh 19
barnstorming: American Giants and 55, 60, 62, 64, 77-78, *78*, 84; in California and the Northwest 77; Chicago Giants and 54; Leland Giants and 38-39; Page Fence Giants and 19; *see also* California Winter League; Florida, hotel teams
Barrow, Ed 29
Barry, John M. 90
Bartley, Bill 32
Baseball Hall of Fame: correcting inaccuracies for Hill at 169; Early Baseball Era Committee 167; Hill as least known of early Black players in 1-2; Hill's corrected plaque postcard by *171*, 172; Hill's inaccurate plaque postcard by *170*; Hill's induction into 162; on Hill's start in baseball 18; induction requirements 162-3; Kansas City Monarchs and 11; Kuhn's Committee on Negro Leagues and 163-5; Lacy's nominations of Hill to 159-60; McGinnity and Alexander in 24; Negro Leaguer inductions (2006) 166-7; "Smokey" Joe Williams and 54
Baseball Writers Association 159-60
Battle, Samuel "Jesse" 158
Bauchman, Harry 66, *78*
Baum, Allen T. 77, 79
Beckwith, John 145, 149, 150, 151-2, *151*
Beer, Jeremy 12
Bell, James "Cool Papa" 11, 12, 165
Beloit, Wisconsin, (White) team 89
Belvidere Daily Republican 35
Biden, Joe 138
Billy Webb's Spiders 156-7
Birmingham Black Barons 141, 152-3
Birmingham Giants 39, 41
Birth of a Nation 37, 72
Bjarkman, Peter 31
Black baseball: alcohol and 80-82; in Buffalo, New York 154; Burr Oak Cemetery, Illinois and 172; early, legacy of 177; the games 7; motivation and pay for 8-9; overview 5-6; playing conditions 6-7; Spanish flu and 96-97; weekday game start times for 97-98; *see also* Negro League teams
Black Bronchos of San Antonio, Texas 39
Black Panthers 27
Black Sox Scandal 2, 89, 118-9
Black troops, Civil War and 16
Blackman, Henry 144-5
Blackof, John 103
Blacks, early movie depictions of 37
Bloomer Girls, Kansas City team 10
Blount, John T. "Tenny" 111-2, 116, 122, *134*, 135, 136, 138
Blue, Rupert 89, 90
Bolden, Ed 143, 147
Booker, James 34, 44
Booker, Pete *30*
Boston Braves 157
Bowman, Emmett "Scotty" *30*, 33
Bowser, Thomas 74
boxing 64, 157; *see also* Johnson, Jack
Brady, Hugh 71
Brazelton, Clarkson (possibly) *78*
Breakers Hotel, Palm Beach, Florida *27*
Breakers Hotel team 25, 44-45, 63, *75*, 86, 87
Bright, Oscar 154, 155
Brisco Motors (White) team 136
Britt (or Britton), George *148*, *151*
Brooklyn Dodgers 6, 162
Brooklyn Royal Giants: American Giants and 55, 65; Breakers Hotel team and 44-45; Buffalo's Black Rocks (White) against 154; in Cuba (1908) 38; National Association of Colored Baseball Clubs of the United States and Cuba and 33; as one of best eastern teams 187n12; players in Palm Beach from 86; playoffs (1905) and 29
Brown, Mordecai "Three Finger" 43
Brown, Ray 166
Brown, Willard 11, 166
Brundage, Edward J. 126-7, 193n27
Bryson, George 176
Buffalo, New York 12, 24, 154, 155-7
Buffalo American 154
Buffalo Enquirer 155
Buffalo Giants 154, 155
Buffalo Red Caps 157-9
Buffalo Semi-Pro League 154
Buffalo Steel Giants 154
Buffalo's Black Rocks (White) 154
Burn, Harry T. 107
Burns, Ken, baseball documentary 167
Burns, Lucy 105-6
Burr Oak Cemetery, Alsip, Illinois 172
Burton, Scott 70
Bush, Donie "Ownie" 73
Busse, Fred A. 47
Buxton, Byron 11

Index

California, managed professional Black teams in 1
California Winter League (CWL) 24, 52–54, 60, *61*, 62–63, 74–75
Callahan, Daniel 114, 116
Cameron, Lucille 50
Camp Grant (Army base) 88–89, 90, 93–94, *93*
Campanella, Roy 163
Canada, Prohibition and 128, 130
Capone, Al 115, 131
Carnegie, Andrew 17
Carnegie Elks, Pittsburgh 148, 151
Carr, Wayne *148*
Carter, George E. 99
Cassiday, George L. 130–1
Cedar Mountain, Buena, Virginia, Civil War battle at 16
Cermacks, Chicago 140
Chacon, Pelayo 86
Champion, Allison Brophy 15
Chance, Frank 42–43
Charleston, Oscar: Florida Hotel League and 84; Hall of Fame and 165; Lacy on 160; Malarcher on 12; as pitcher 97; racial conflict on the field and 73; raiding Midwest teams 147; replacing Hill with Giants 110; as teetotaler 82
Chase, Bill 176
Chateau de la Plaisance (House of Pleasure) 44
Chicago: election of 1916 and 104–5, *105*; managed professional Black teams in 1; Prohibition in 126–7, *127*, 129; proposed Negro League and 121; race riots 71, 85–86, 113–7, 120; racial tensions 37, 72; Red Cross nurses march in 95–96, *96*; Spanish flu and restraints on games in 98; Spanish flu in 90–91; *see also* American Giants; Leland Giants
Chicago Broad Ax 57, 59
Chicago City League 37, 45, 46
Chicago Cubs 7, 10, 42, 51
Chicago Daily Tribune 41
Chicago Defender: on All-Nations team against American Giants 10; on American Giants 60–61, 63, 65, 83; on Auburn Park 46; on Blacks in Hall of Fame 162; on charity game for Moore 85; on Detroit Stars 112, 118; Dr. Williams as health expert for 90; Foster and 59, 84; on Foster and Leland Giants' reception/banquet 51; on Grand Central Redcaps 158; on Hill 140, 146; Hill's letters to 13, 119; on Leland Giants Park opening 44; on racial conflict/tensions and discrimination 72, 73, 161; on Ragen's Colts and 1919 riots 115–6; Wyatt as sportswriter for 24; Young as sportswriter for 64
Chicago Giants 23, 45, 52–54, 56, 62, 119, 122, 134–5
Chicago Gunthers 37, 38, 41, 46, 56, 65, 83
Chicago Heights Star 141–2
Chicago Logan Squares 37
Chicago Star 161
Chicago Tribune 162
Chicago Union Giants 22, 23
Chicago Unions 23
Chicago West Ends 37, 59
Chicago White Sox 2, 7, 54–55, 83, 118–9
Cincinnati Reds 2, 118–9
Civil War, battle of Cedar Mountain and 16
Clark, Dick 166
Clark, Jane Forbes 166
Clark, Morten 81–82
Clarke, Robert *151*
Cline-Cline nine, Los Angeles 74–75
Coast Guard, Prohibition and 128, *128*
Cobb, Lorenza 122
Cobb, Ty "Georgia Peach" 1, 11, 51–52
Coconut League 25
Cohen's Speakeasy, Detroit 130
Colby, Bainbridge 107
Colored Sanders of Buffalo 157
Colored World Series 150
Columbus, Ohio, proposed Negro League and 121
Columbus Buckeyes 138
Comiskey, Charles 28, 47, 54, 62, 83, 85, 89
Comiskey, John Louis 54
Comiskey Park 160
Committee on Negro Leagues 163–5
Conner, John W. 55
Cooper, Andy "Lefty" 11, 119, 133, *134*, 135, 136, 138, 166
Cooperstown *see* Baseball Hall of Fame
Corey, Ed 115
The Courier, Waterloo, Iowa 59
Couzens, James J. 134, 137
Cowans, Russ J. 159
Cowpers (Chicago) 133
Coyne Electrical School, Chicago 161
Crawford, Sam 73, 110
Creighton, James A. 70
The Crisis 71
Crowe, Robert 114
Crutchfield, Jimmie 172–3
Cuba: Blacks playing baseball in 1, 9, 24, 29, 57, 77; Platt Amendment and 31
Cuban American Series 19, 52
Cuban Fés 34, 35, 52, 57
Cuban Giants 27, 38, 48, 122, 133–4, 154
Cuban Giants of New York 33
Cuban League 35
Cuban Stars: American Giants and 56–57, 63, 65, 97, 99; Buffalo's Black Rocks (White) against 154; Detroit Stars against 119; Hill with Leland Giants and 41; Milwaukee Bears against 141; NNL formation talks and 122; players in Palm Beach from 86; racial conflict and 73

Cuban Stars of Havana 33
Cuban X-Giants: in Cuba 30; Florida hotel teams and 25; Foster and 22, 23, 24; Hill's nickname and 19–20; National Association of Colored Baseball Clubs of the United States and Cuba and 33; 1906 playing season and 32; Philadelphia Giants and 21, 28–29; reserving seats for Whites and 39
Culpeper County, Virginia, roadside sign honoring Hill in 173–4, *174*
Culpeper Sports Complex, plaque honoring Hill at *175*, 176–7
Culpeper Star-Exponent 169

The Daily Tropical Sun 66
Dalrymple, A.V. 126, 129
Dandridge, Ray 9
Darrow, Clarence 130
Davis, Harry 29
Day, Connie 145, *148*, *151*
Day, Leon 8–9, 165
Dayton Marcos 99, 119, 122, 125
dead ball era 11, 12, 180n27
Declaration of Sentiments 101
Decoration Day 172
Delavan and Ohio Railroad 157–8
Delaware Lackawanna and Western Railroad 157
DeMoss, Elwood "Bingo" 73, 84, 110
Deneen, Charles S. 69
Derby Truck Company team 133
Detroit: professional Black teams in 1; Prohibition and 126, 129–30; racial tensions 137–8; Spanish flu in 90
Detroit Creamery (White) team 136
Detroit Free Press 116
Detroit Stars: American Giants against 113; Hill managing 12, 119–20; as new Foster team 110, 111; NNL formation talks and 122; Opening Day events 112–3, 133–4, 136; second year for 133–4, *134*, 135; Wickware and 109
Detroit Tigers 51–52, 116
Dickson, Paul 180n27
Diggs, Gordon 35
Dihigo, Martin 165
Dismukes, William "Dizzy" 81, 82
Dixon, Steven *78*
Donaldson, John 10, 110, 135, 173
Donnegan, William 68
Dougherty, Pat 42, 43, 44, 57
Doyles, California Winter League and 52–53
Drake, C. St. Claire 91
DuBois, W.E.B. 71
Duggan, Larry 64
Duncan, Frank 44, 46, *78*, 110
Dunn, Jake 149
Dyckman Oval, New York City 100
Dyer, Leonidas C. 138

Eastern Colored League (ECL) 2, 57, 125, 143, 145–6, 147, 153
Eastland Hotel team, Hot Springs, Arkansas 28
Eckert, Spike 164
Eight Men Out (Asinof) 89
Embry, William "Cap" 141
Emmett Till Anti-lynching Act 138
Endres, Henry 154
Engleman, Larry 129
Englewood Economist 46
Englewood Times 97
Estill, C.W. 155
Evans, Billy 30

Federal League 73
Feency, Dominick 114
Fellows, Samuel E. 80
Felsch, Oscar "Happy" 89
Fennimore's Two Big Days (Wisconsin) 56
Ferguson, James E. "Pa" 104
fights, at Black baseball games 7
Figueredo, Jorge 19
Fitzgerald, Thomas 114–5
Fitzmorris, Charles 130
Flagler, Henry Morrison 25, 26, 77
Fleetwood, Moses 37
Florida: hotel teams 24, 25; professional Black teams in 1; segregation in 66; *see also* Breakers Hotel team; Royal Poinciana Hotel team
Florida Hotel League 84
Florida League 25
Forbes, Frank 163–4
Force, Bill *148*, *151*
Fort Worth Giants 39, 55
Foster, Andrew (father) 22
Foster, Andrew "Rube": on alcohol 80–81; on American Giants in Palm Beach 87; as American Giants manager 179n8; at American League Park 97; Anson and 38; Blount and 138; California Winter League and 52, 62–63; championship and 32, 83–84; Chicago riots and 116; colored umpires for NNL and 141; Cuban Fés and 34, 35, 57; Cuban Stars and 56; Cuban X-Giants vs. Philadelphia Giants and 28; Detroit Stars as second team of 110, 111; Florida hotel teams and 25, 44–45; in formal attire *23*; Hall of Fame and 165–6; on Hill as finest all-round baseball man 160; as Hill mentor 1–2, 12, 21–24, 140, 143; Hill's playing for 6; on Hill's short bunt play 11; injuries to 64; Jack Johnson and 48, 49; league for Midwestern Black teams and 121–2; Leland Giants Park opening reception and 44; as Leland Giants' player/manager 37–38, 41–43; Leland's relationship with 45–46; letter making arrangements for a game *76*; on losing to Lincoln Giants 60; Moseley

Index

and 43; Negro National League and 34, 122–4; New York Giants and 182*n*48; news of Schorling's 50-50 arrangement with 57, 59; on pay raise 33; Philadelphia Giants and 21, *30*; as pitcher 64, 65, 82–84, 85, 159; playoffs (1905) and 29; private Pullman car for players 6–7; reception/banquet for Leland Giants and 51; Schlichter lures to Philadelphia Giants 28; Schorling's Park and 55; Scranton Miners game and 32; stealing second 77; Talbert's medical care and 62; Umpire Goeckel dispute with 98; *see also* American Giants
Foster, Christina 22
Foster, Earl Mack 22, 124
Foster, Evaline 22
Foster, Johnson 22
Foster, Sarah "Smoochie" 22, 124
Foster, Sarah Watts 22, 108, 124
Fowler, Bud 5, 19, 154, 167
Francis, Bill *75*
Frankenstein, Emily 114, 115
Frankenstein, Victor 115
Freihofer, William F. and Freihofer Cup 32
Fresno Morning Republican 61
Frick, Ford 162
Fuqua Giants 35

Gans, Judy "Jude" *75*, *78*, 97, 109
Gatewood, "Big" Bill 42, 53, *134*, 173
Genna Brothers (Mike, Angelo, Peter, Tony, Sam, and James) 126
Giants, in African Americans team names 39
Gibson, Bob 163
Gibson, Josh 1, 162, 165
Giles, George 165
Glasser, Ira 165
Goeckel, Ed (umpire) 82, 98, *175*
Golden Slides 19
Gonzalez, Gervacio 86
Gottlieb, Ed 164
Grand Central Redcaps, Williamsbridge, New York 158
Grant, Charles 21, 28, *30*
Grant, Frank 5, 167
Grant, Leroy 57, *75*, 97, 109
The Great Influenza: The Story of the Deadliest Pandemic in History (Barry) 90
Great Migration 117
Green, Joe 62, 122, 134–5
Griffith, Clark 97
Griggs, Sam 138
Groesbeck, Alex J. 137
Gumbel, Bryant 3
Gunther, Charles 38
Gunthers *see* Chicago Gunthers

Habana team 34, 35, 51, 57, *58*
Hagadorn, Charles 93, 94

Haiti, Blacks playing baseball in 9
Half a Man (Ovington) 71
The Half Century 111
Hall, Perry 141
Hallam, Mrs. Earl 69
Harding, Warren G. 130
Harris, Nate 34
Harrisburg Daily Independent 6
Harrisburg Giants 152
Harrisburg Stars 147
Hatch, Frank 70
Havana Giants 39
Hawaii, Foster on games in 74
Hawkins, Louis 71
Heaphy, Leslie A. 9, 123
Hearn, Bunny 89
Henderson, Arthur "Rats" 148–9
Hernandez, Ricardo *58*
Hewitt, Joe *134*
Higgins, Robert 5
Hill, A.P. 16
Hill, Elizabeth "Lizzie" Seals 15, 17
Hill, Gertrude "Gerty" Lawson 35, 133, 135–6, 160, 161
Hill, Gwen 133
Hill, "Ike" 180*n*1
Hill, Jerome Bryant 15, 18
Hill, John (son) 36
Hill, John Preston "Pete": Allegheny County Council honors 173; American Giants and 55, 88; as Baltimore Black Sox business manager 150–1, *151*; as Baltimore Black Sox manager 12, 18, 143, 145–6, 147–8, *148*, 152; on baseball (1942) 160; batting averages 30, 34, 35–36, 37, 38, 41, 46, 52, 57, 61; Birmingham Black Barons and 152–3; Brooklyn Royal Giants and 38; Buffalo baseball and 155–7; Buffalo Red Caps and 157–9; California Winter League and 52, 60, *61*; catching, sensational 41, 56, 136, 143; *Chicago Defender* on 10, 118, 140, 146; childhood 15–16, 18; in civilian dress *152*; Cline-Cline nine against 75; Cuban Fé team and 34; Cuban Stars and 57, 63; Culpeper Sports Complex plaque honoring *175*; death of 159; as "Demon Hill" in the press 67; Detroit Stars and 110, 112, 119–20, *134*, 136–7; double plays 41, 83, 136; early baseball days 18–20; extra bases 29, 31–32, 38, 41, 52, 57, 65, 75, 118, 136, 148, 151; Florida hotel teams and 25, 45, 63, *75*, 84; Foster as mentor 21–24; Foster on alcohol and 81; grave of 172–3; Habana team and 39–41, 51, 57, *58*; Hall of Fame and 1, 167, 169, *170*, *171*, 172; hitting by 141–2, 146, 147–8, 151; "Home Run" Johnson as mentor 21, 24; home runs by 29, 112, 118, 119–20, 135, 138; Jim Crow in Oregon and 64; Lacy on 160; Leland Giants and 34, 37, 43, 44, 46–47; marriage

34–35, 135–6; Milwaukee Bears and 12, 140–1, 142; nickname 19–20, 155–6; Omaha All Professionals and 74; Philadelphia Athletics and 31–32, 33; Philadelphia Giants and 20, 21, 28, 29, *30*, 35–36; Philadelphia Royal Stars and 139–40; playing conditions for 6–7; profile 11–13; racial conflict on the field and 73; roadside sign honoring 173–4, *174*; as sportswriter 150; Tacoma Tigers and 78; in Vancouver, Canada *78*; Virginia Department of Historic Resources' roadside sign honoring *174*; World War I and 109
Hill, John Preston, Jr. 13
Hill, Johnson 119
Hill, Kenneth Preston 13, 133, 159, 160–1
Hill, Ron 15, 169, 173, 176
Hill, Ruben (Reuben W.) 15, 180n1
Hill, Walter Vaughn 15
Hilldale Club, Darby, Pennsylvania: Bolden as owner of 143; Detroit Stars against 119, 138; Eastern Colored League and 125; Hill as sportswriter about 150; NNL formation talks and 122; Pennsylvania Red Caps against 158; raiding Midwest teams 147; Specks Websters and 158
Hill's Stars, charity game for Moore and 85
Hobby, William Pettus 104
Hogan, Larry 166
Holland, Bill 36, 133, *134*, 136
Holloway, Christopher "Crush" or "the frog" 146, *148*, *151*
Holway, John 19, 146, 165
Holy Sepulchre Cemetery, Alsip, Illinois 172
Homestead Grays 11, 12, 99, 157
Honolulu Advertiser 73, 74
Hoover, Herbert 125–6
Hopkins, Albert J. 47
Hopkins Brothers Sporting Goods team, Kansas City 10
Hot Springs, Arkansas: American Giants in 55; Eastland Hotel team of 28
Howard, Kate 69, 70
Hubbard, Lew 64
Hughes, Charles Evan 105
Hurst, John 99
Huston-Tillotson University (was Samuel Huston College), broadside for game at 39, *40*
Hutchinson, Fred 44

Illinois Chronicle 24
Independent League 32
Indianapolis ABCs: All-Nations team against 10; American Giants against 85, 97, 99; championship series with American Giants 83–84; first NNL game and 134–5; Milwaukee Bears against 141; name of 74; NNL formation talks and 122; as one of best midwestern teams 187n12; racial conflict on the field and 73
Indianapolis Freeman 24
Inlet Ball Park, Atlantic City 28–29
integration: California Winter League and 52–54; *see also* segregation
Inter-City Association, Chicago 46
International League 5
Iron and Oil Leagues 6
Irvin, Monte 1, 12, 163, 165
Irvingtons, Baltimore 147
Isaac, Stan 164

Jackson (Michigan) Independents 133
Jackson, Major Robert R. 43, 44, 45–46, 72, 116, 118
Jackson, Reggie 163
Jackson, Roy 136–7
James, Joe 70
James, William "Knucks" *75*
Jamestown, New York, Petey Hill's Colored All Stars and 156–7
Jamestown Evening Journal 156
Jamison, Caesar 141
Jeffords, Jim 20
Jeffries, Edward J. 130
Jeffries, Harry *151*
Jeffries, Jim (Black) *151*
Jeffries, Jim (White) 48–49
Jenkins, Fergie 163
Jews, Royal Poinciana discrimination against 99
Jim Crow 64, 66, 99, 108; *see also* segregation
Johnson, Dicta *75*, 110
Johnson, George "Chappie" 45, 139, 140, 153, 157–8
Johnson, Grant "Home Run": Brooklyn Royal Giants and 36, 38; Cuban Fés and 34, 35; Cuban X-Giants and 19; Florida hotel teams and 25; Habana team and 40, 51, 52, 57, *58*; Hill in Buffalo with 153, 154; as Hill mentor 24; Kokomo Red Sox and 83; Leland Giants Park opening reception and 44; Philadelphia Giants and 21, 28, *30*
Johnson, Jack 20, 21, 47, 48–50, *49*, 60
Johnson, James Weldon 117
Johnson, Judy 163–4, 165
Johnson, Robert Wood, II 129
Johnson, Tom *78*, 83, 109, 113
Johnson, Wade "Heavy" 146, *148*, *151*
Johnson, Walter 1, 52
Jones, Randall 174
Journal of the American Medical Association (JAMA) 91
Coy, Al C. 62
The Jungle (Sinclair) 79–80

Kachline, Clifford 163
Kansas City, Kansas, proposed Negro League and 121

Index 211

Kansas City, Missouri, proposed Negro League and 121
Kansas City Giants 41, 45
Kansas City Monarchs 10–11, 80, 122, 135, 146, 150, 162
Keating, Dennis S. 114
Kelly, John 18
Kelly, Neill 73
Kennard, Dan 84
Kerr, Clara 48
Kerr, Paul 162-3, 164
Kilpatrick, Kathleen S. 173-4
Kimbro, Arthurs 96-97
Knights of Columbus team 113
Knox, Elwood C. 122
Kokomo Red Sox 82-83
Krock, Jeremy 172-3
Krusen, Wilmer 95
Ku Klux Klan 37, 137
Kuhn, Bowie 163-4, 165

La Porte, Indiana (White) team, American Giants against 82
Lacy, Sam 159-60, 164
Lake Michigan, Prohibition and 129
Lamar, E.B., Jr. 28
Lancaster (Pennsylvania) Athletic Club 20
Landis, Kenesaw Mountain 89, 114-5, 119
Langford, Sam, the "Boston Tar Baby" 157
Lawson, John, Jr. 35, 135-6
Lawson, Lulu 35
Lee, Robert E. 16
Leiber, Molly 161
Leland, Frank 23, 43-44, 45-46, 122
Leland Giants: Anson and 38; barnstorming 38-39; *Chicago Defender* coverage and 24; Foster as manager of 34, 37; Hill and 24, 41; Johnson and 24; Leland as manager for 23; outdrawing White teams 7; postseason in Florida and Cuba 51; Royal Poinciana Hotel team and 44-45; *see also* American Giants
Leland Giants Baseball and Amusement Association 43-44
Leland Giants Park 44
Leland Giants Rooters Club 44
Leonard, Buck 1, 152, 165
Lerner, Michael 131
Lester, Larry 121, 166, 173
Lewis, Cary B. 122, 124
Lewis, J. Hamilton 95
Lewiston, Idaho, American Giants playing in 64
Liberty Loan parade, Philadelphia, Spanish flu and 95
Lincoln Giants 57, 59-60, 63, 86, 147, 187n12
Lit, Samuel and Jacob and Lit Brothers team 151
Literary Digest 91
Litzinger, Edward R. 83

Lloyd, John Henry "Pop": American Giants and 65; beer on 12; Breakers Hotel team and 63, **75**; Brooklyn Royal Giants and 88; Habana team and 39-40, 51, 52, 57, **58**; Hall of Fame and 165; "Home Run" Johnson as predecessor of 24; Leland Giants and 42, 46; Leland Giants Park opening reception and 44; Lincoln Giants and 57; on motivation to play 9; in Vancouver, Canada **78**
Lloyd's Stars, charity game for Moore and 85
Lockport (N.Y.) Union Sun and Journal 157
Logan Squares, Chicago 140
London, Jack 80
Long, Dan 76-77
Long, Fred **134**
Loper, Harry 69-70
Lorimer, William 47-48
Los Angeles Herald 52-53
Louis, Joe 81
Louisville, Kentucky, proposed Negro League and 121
Lundy, Dick 165
lynchings 68, 70, 113, 137-8; *see also* race riots, conflict or tensions
Lyons, Jimmie 81, **134**

Mack, Connie 31-33, 149
Mack Park, Detroit 112, 120, 133-4
Mackey, "Biz" 165, 166
Mackey, G.L. 18
Maddox, Nick 144
Magrinat, J.H. **58**
Majestics (Illinois) 35
Major League Baseball (MLB) 8, 166; *see also* Baseball Hall of Fame
major leaguers, American Giants and 88-89
Malarcher, Dave 12
Malloy, Jerry 19
Manfred, Rob 3
Manhattans of Washington, DC 27
Manley, Effa 165, 166
Mann Act 49
Mantle, Mickey 160
Maple Park Cemetery, Bluefield, West Virginia 15
Marion, Kitty 106
Marshall, Bobby 42
masks, Spanish flu and 91, **92**, 93, 94
Mathewson, Christy "Matty" 24
Matthews, John 122
Maxwell Internationals 112
Mays, Willie 160, 163
McAlister, James 162
McClellan, Danny 21, 29, **30**, 36
McClure, Robert "Big Boy" 148, **151**
McCormicks 52, 54, 61
McCoy, Bill 129
McCredie, Walter Henry "Judge" 61, 62, 64, 77

Index

McDonald, Webster *134*
McDonnell, Robert F. 175
McGinnity, Joe "Iron Man" 24
McGraw, John "Muggsy" 10, 11, 21, 24, 28, 30, 61
McIver, Stuart 25–26
McKinny, J.L.T 22
McMahon, Jess 57
McNeil, William F. 60, 61
Means, Lewis 12
Memphis Giants 39
Mendez, José 10, 56, 109, 110, 111, 167
Merchants of the Commercial League 85
Merkle, Fred 60
Mexico, Blacks playing baseball in 9
Michigan-Ontario League 155
Michigan Semi-Pro Championship Tournament 135
middlemen, ball parks and 121–2
Mills, Florence 35
Milwaukee Bears 12, 140–1
Milwaukee White Sox 37, 66
Mineral Point Fair, Wisconsin 56
Minneapolis Millers 38
Mobile, Alabama, proposed Negro League and 121
Mongin, Sam *75*
Monroe, Al 81, 159
Monroe, Bill 21, *30*, 34, 35, 66–67
Moore, Henry/Harry "Mike" 21, *30*, 34, 85
Moore, James "Red" 9
Moran, Carlos *58*
Morgan, Charles 106
Moseley, Beauregard F. 43–44, 45, 62, 121
Mosquito Fleet 130
Mott, Lucretia 101
Mullin, George 82–83
Murphy, J.H. 99
Murray Hills team 22
Myers, Chief 60

Nagle, Walter 60; *see also* Tufts-Lyons team
Nation, Carry 104
National Association for the Advancement of Colored People (NAACP) 2, 71–72, 137–8
National Association of Baseball Players 5
National Association of Colored Baseball Clubs of the United States and Cuba 33–34
National Association of Professional Base Ball Players 5
National League 5
National League of Colored Baseball Clubs 23
National Retail Liquor Dealers 102
National Women's Party 105
Native American women, voting rights for 108
Nebelcamp, N.D. 126

Negro American League 2, 153
Negro League teams: Foster as father of 22; Hall of Fame induction requirements and 162–3; Kuhn's Committee on Negro Leagues and 163–4; Lester's newsletter on 173; Major League Baseball and records of 8; major leagues signing Black players and 162; research and literature on 166; Seamheads Negro Leagues database and 3; use of term 2; *see also* Black baseball
Negro Leagues Museum, Kansas City 167
Negro National Baseball League, proposed 121–2
Negro National League (NNL): blacklisting jumpers 146; championships before formation of 57; Detroit Stars and 133; East-West (all-star) game 160; Foster and formation of 2, 34, 122–4; Hill's retirement from 153; Milwaukee Bears and 140–1; opens for business 134–5; player raids and 147; stability of 125
Nelson, Zann 169, 173–5
Neuman's Fighting Phoenix team 155
New Continental Baseball League 59
New Orleans, proposed Negro League and 121
New Orleans Creoles 39
The New York Age 19
New York Amsterdam News 71
New York Central Railroad 157–8
New York Giants 32, 61, 182*n*48
New York Lincoln Giants 54; *see also* Lincoln Giants
New York Lincoln Stars 67
New York Sun 22
New York Times 26, 30, 48, 94, 162, 164
Newark International League Team 29
Newark Little Giants 38
Newarks (Baltimore team) 147
newspapers, Black baseball stories in 7–8
Niagara Falls Gazette 156
19th Amendment 101, 106–7, 108
Norfolk All-Stars, Philadelphia 139
Normal Park, Chicago 46, 54
Norway Motors team, Michigan 112–3

Occidental colored club 52
O'Farrell, Bob 85
Okrent, Daniel 125
O'Neil, Buck 167
Only the Ball Was White (Peterson) 8
Orange & Alexandria Railroad 16
Oregon, Jim Crow in 64
Oriole Park, reserved-for-Whites seats in 39
Orions of Philadelphia 27
Otsego, Michigan, Foster pitching for local team of 23
Ovington, Mary White 71

Pacific Coast League 60
Padron, Luis *58*

Index

Page Fence Giants 19
Paige, Leroy "Satchel" 1, 9, 11, 52, 86, 162–3, 164–5
Palm Beach *see* Breakers Hotel team; Royal Poinciana Hotel team
Palm Beach Daily News 45
Palm Beach News 63
Pantages (San Diego) 75
parades, Spanish flu and 95–96, **96**
pay, for Black baseball 8–9
Payne, Andrew "Jap" 34, 42, 44, 121, 122
Pennsylvania Red Caps 158
Pete Hill's Elite Colored Elks 156
Peterson, Robert 8, 19, 166
Petey Hill's Colored All Stars 155–6
Petroskey, Dale 166
Pettus, Bill 45, **75**, 139
Petway, Bruce: California Winter League and 52; as catcher 82; Detroit Stars and 110, **134**; funeral for brother Howard 98; Habana team and 51, 52, 57; Hill's throw and tag by 83; injuries to 64; Leland Giants and 46; Leland Giants Park opening reception and 44; World War I and 109
Philadelphia: managed professional Black teams in 1; Spanish flu and 95
Philadelphia Athletics 10, 31–32, 51, 149–50
Philadelphia Baseball Association 139–40
Philadelphia Giants: in Cuba 35; Cuban X-Giants and 28–29; Florida hotel teams and 25; founding of 20; *Harrisburg Daily Independent*'s reporting on 6; Hill and 19, 20–21, 24, 181n23; Home Run Johnson and 24; Jack Johnson and 48; Lawson and 35; National Association of Colored Baseball Clubs of the United States and Cuba and 33; in 1905 29, **30**; 1906 playing season and 31–32
Philadelphia Inquirer 28, 29
Philadelphia Keystones 27
Philadelphia News Item 20, 21
Philadelphia Royal Stars Baseball Club 139
Philadelphia Tribune 20, 26, 32, 104, 137
Pierce, Bill 57, 60
Pine Ridges, Buffalo (White) team 155
Pittsburgh Colored Stars, Buffalo 154
Pittsburgh Courier: on alcohol and playing baseball 81–82; All-Time-Negro League All-Star Team (1952) 12; on Hill 140, 152–3, 159; Lizzie Hill's death announcement in 18; "Posey's Points" column in 12; Wilson on Schlichter's pay for players 33; Wyatt as sportswriter for 24
Pittsburgh Crawfords 11, 157
Pittsburgh Daily Post 19
Pittsburgh Keystones 18–19, 181n23
Plank, Eddie 33
Platt, Orville and Platt Amendment 31
Poles, Spottswood 57, **75**
Pompez, Alex 164, 166
Portland Beavers 61, 62, 64
Portland Coast League (PCL) 61, 77
Portland Colts 64
Posey, Cumberland "Cum" 11–12, 145, 166–7
Posey, Seward Hayes "See" 12
Povich, Shirley 162
Powell, Adam Clayton, Jr. 158
Prohibition: Bahamas and 128; Canada and 128, 130; in Chicago 126–7, **127**, 129; in Detroit 126, 129–30; "drys" and "wets" and 126; George Rossiter's Sea Food House and 144; Hill's career and 2; House and Senate and 130–1; ineffectiveness of 131–2; seeds of 79–80; women's suffrage movement and 104
proposed Negro National Baseball League 121–2
Providence Grays 5
Provident Hospital, Chicago, charity game benefiting 47
Pryor, Andrew 141–2
Pryor, Wes 44
Pullen, O'Neal **148**
Pullman Colored Giants 157
pushmobile races, Schlichter and 20

race riots, conflict or tensions: American Giants and 116–7; in Chicago 37, 71, 72, 85–86, 113–6; in Detroit 137–8; on the field 72–74; NAACP birth and 71–72; off the field 68–71; Red Summer of 1919 117; in Springfield, Illinois 68–70; in Tulsa, Oklahoma 137; women's suffrage movement and 108
racism: Anson and 37–38; Black baseball and 6; Coyne Electrical School, Chicago and 160–1; Florida hotel teams and 25–26; lynchings 68, 70, 113, 137–8
Radcliffe, Theodore Roosevelt "Double Duty" 9
Ragen, Frank and Ragen's Colts 115
railroads: barnstorming and 39; Black baseball travelers and 6–7; bus travel replacing 145; Civil War and 16; Prohibition and 126, 128, 130; Red Caps for 24, 157–9; spring training and 66; *see also* Red Caps teams
Raymer, Abraham 70
record keeping: of African Americans in late 1800s 15; American Giants and 67; American Giants and Chicago riots 116; attendance after Spanish flu 99; Babe Ruth's home runs 119; of base running 11; of Black peoples' graves 173, 180n1; Chappie Johnson's pitching 139; Culpeper County, Virginia on Hill and 176; Detroit Stars' first season 119; Foster on 1908 Leland Giants and 38; Foster's challenge on Leland Giants and 43; Hall induction and 162–3; Hill's marriage and 136; Leland

Giants and 41, 47; Lincoln Giants and 57; Milwaukee Bears and 141, 142; Petey Hill's Colored All Stars 156; Royal Poinciana Hotel team and 29; of spectators 155; sporadic, Negro League teams and 7–8; *see also* Seamheads Negro Leagues database
Red Caps teams 157–9
Red Cross 91, 94, 95
Red Summer (1919) 117
Redding, Dick "Cannonball" 57, **75**, 85, 86–87, 109, 155
Reichler, Joe 164
Reinsdorf, Jerry 173
Relay Athletic Club, Baltimore 144
Republican National Convention (1908) 38
Republican-Northwestern, Belvidere, Illinois 34–35
Reynolds, John T. 18
Richardson, George 69
Richmond Giants 139, 140
Rickey, Branch 6
Riley, James A. 11, 42, 139–40
Rixey, Eppa 174, 176
Roberts, Nan Butler 176
Robertson, John Dill 91, 96
Robeson, Paul 158
Robinson, Al 45
Robinson, Jackie 6, 11, 160, 162, 163, 164
Rock, Patrick 169
Rockefeller, John D. 25
Roesink, John A. 112, 135, 136
Roesink S & S Team 112, 135
Rogan, Wilber "Bullet" or "Bullet Joe" 11, 52, 165
Rogers Park (White) team 99
Rojo, Julio **151**
Rommel, Eddie 149
Rosenwald, Julius 122
Rossiter, George 143, 144, 147, 150–1, 153
Royal Giants *see* Brooklyn Royal Giants
Royal Poinciana Hotel, Palm Beach, Florida 25–26, **26, 27**, 77, 99
Royal Poinciana Hotel team 25, 29, 84, 86
Royal Rooters Club 133
Runyan, Damon 9
Ruth, Babe 1, 9, 29, 42, 119, 120

St. Louis Giants 122
St. Louis, proposed Negro League and 121
St. Louis Stars 11, 63
St. Louis Times and Star 55
St. Paul Gophers 41, 42, 45
Samuel Huston College (now Huston-Tillotson University), broadside for game at 39, **40**
San Antonio Black Broncos 53
San Diego Bears 52, 53, 60, 61
San Francisco Examiner 62
San Francisco's Panama Fair 67
Sanchez, Gonzalo **58, 175**

Santop, Louis 12, 57, 63, **75**, 167
Saunders, Frank H. 164–5
Scanlon, Jimmy 73
Schlichter, H. Walter "Slick" 20, 28–29, **30**, 32, 33–34; *see also* Philadelphia Giants
Schorling, John M. 54, 57, 59
Schorling's Park, Chicago: American Giants at 10, 56, 63, 65; building of 54–55; Hill's homers in 82, 84–85; riots (1919) and 116–7
Schrieber, Belle 49
Schulte, Frank 43
Scott, Elisha 122
Scranton Miners 32
The Scranton Truth 32
Seamheads Negro Leagues database 19, 67
segregation: barnstorming and 39; birth of NAACP and 71–72; Chicago City League and 37; Florida hotels and 25–26, 77, 99; Hill's career and 68; Jim Crow 64, 66, 99, 108; Leland Giants Baseball and Amusement Association and 44; Long on organizational baseball and 76–77; Mason-Dixon Line and 139; race riots and 68–71; West Palm Beach ferry to Palm Beach and 66
17th Amendment, passage of 48
Shaw, Robert Gould 16
Sheppard, Morris 79
Shillay, John R. 120
Simpson, A.L. 106
Sinclair, Upton 79–80
Sinnott, Richard 114, 116
Skaw, Chris 6–7
Slaughter, John 66
Smith, Chino 12
Smith, Harry 20
Smith, Hilton 11
Smith, Thomas B. 95
Smith, Wendell 159, 164
Smith (Amanda) Orphanage and Industrial Home for Abandoned and Destitute Colored Children 124–5
Snaer, Lucien 141
Snodgrass, Fred 60
Social Security Administration 199n11
Society for American Baseball Research (SABR) 18–19, 173, 175
Sol White's History of Colored Baseball 19
Southern California Winter League 52; *see also* California Winter League
Southern Negro League 2
Spanish-American War 31
Spanish flu: at Army bases 93–94; Black baseball and 96–97; deaths 88, 94; early reports of 89; Hill's career and 2; in large cities 90–91; masks and 91, **92**, 93; parades and 95–96, **96**; restraints on games and 98–99; on the wane 100
Speaker, Tris 1, 11
Spedden, Charles 143, 144–5, 147, 152, 153

Springfield, Illinois race riot 68–70, **69**
Stack, Ed 163, 165
Standard Times, New Bedford, Massachusetts 129
Standard Union, Brooklyn 56
Stanton, Elizabeth Cady 101
Stanton, Henry 101
Stars, Buffalo, New York 154–5
Stars of Cuba 46
statistics, Seamheads Negro Leagues database and 3
Stauber, George 114, 116
Stearns, "Turkey" 52, 165
Steel City Giants 155
Stengal, Casey 11
Stovey, George 5, 38
Strong, Joe **148, 151**
Strong, Nat 22, 121–2
Strothers, Tim 44
Suburban Economist 54, 55, 59
Susan B. Anthony Amendment 106–7
Sutter, Bruce 167
Suttles, "Mule" 52, 166

Tacoma Tigers 77–78
Taft, Charles 38
Taft, William Howard 38
Talbert, Dangerfield "Old Reliable" 34, 42, 62
Tate, George and Tate's Stars, Cleveland 140
Taylor, Ben 146, 152, 167
Taylor, C.I.: alcohol policy 81; American Brewing Company and 74; at American League Park 97; championship series and 83–84; charity game for Moore and 85; NNL and 122, 123, 134–5; *see also* Indianapolis ABCs
Taylor, James "Candy Jim" 12, 173
Taylor, "Steel Arm" Johnny 45
The Tennessee Ten 35
Terrell, Robert H. 97
Texas Stars 85
Thompson, Frank 27
Thorn, John 8
Till, Emmett 138, 172
Tillman, Benjamin 47–48
Tipton Legion, Angola, Indiana team 141
Toledo Blue Stockings 5, 37
Torriente, Cristóbal 10, 12, 65, 73, 166
Triplett, Norman 97
tuberculosis 62, 67
Tufts-Lyons team 60, 61
Tulsa, Oklahoma race riots 137
Tygiel, Jules 145

umpires: Beckwith slugging 152; for Black baseball 7; championship series and 83, 84; colored 141, 147; proposed Negro League and 121; racial conflict on the field and 72–73

United States Brewers Association 102
U.S. House of Representatives 130–1
U.S. Public Health Service 95
U.S. Senate 131

Valdes, Camilo **58**
Vancouver, Canada, American Giants playing in 77–78, **78**
Vancouver Beavers 77
Venezuela, Blacks playing baseball in 9
Victoria, British Columbia 62
Victory, George M. 158
Vincent, Fay 173
Virginia House of Delegates Resolution, honoring Nelson 175
Virginia Midland Railroad 16
Volstead Act (1921) 2, 125; *see also* Prohibition
Voting Rights Act (1965) 108

W & D Diners team, Silver Creek, New York 156
Waco Yellow Jackets 23
Waddell, "Rube" 22, 33
Wagner, Honus 1, 148
Walker, Dolletha Steep 159
Walker, Frank 121
Walker, Moses Fleetwood "Fleet" 5
Walker, Seth M. 107
Walker, Welday 5
Wallace, Dick 66, **75**
Wallace, Steve 176
Walling, William English 71
War to End All Wars 2; *see also* World War I
Ward, Geoffrey C. 48, 49–50
Warfield, Frank **134**
Warren Tribune 157
Warrington, Noah 66
Washington, Chester L., Jr. 147
Washington, Dinah 172
Washington, Edgar "Blue" **78**, 80
Washington, Kenneth 80
Washington, Tom **30**
Washington, D.C., suffragists in 103, **103**, 105–6
Washington Post 114, 162
Washington Potomacs 147–8
Webb, Billy 156–7
Webster, Pearl Franklin "Specks" 96, 158
Welch, William Henry 91
Wells, Willie 1, 52, 165
Wells-Barnett, Ida B. 108
Wesley, Edgar 110, **134**, 135
West Baden Sprudels 63
Westinghouse, George 17
White, Harry 41
White, Sol 19, 20, 27, **30**, 33, 111, 167
White, William Edward 5
White-on-Black riots 68–71; *see also* race riots, conflict or tensions

White Park Owners Association 46
White Sox Park, Giants–Gunther benefit game for Provident Hospital at 47
Whites: NAACP founding and 71–72; seats reserved for 39, *40*
Whitworth, Richard 83, 113, 147
Wickware, Frank 44, 74–75, 81, 97, 109, 110
Wilkinson, Herbert 150
Wilkinson, J. Leslie 10–11, 122, 123, 167
Wilkinson, Janet 114
Williams, A. Wilberforce 90, 94
Williams, Bobby "Rawhide" 88, 97, 109
Williams, Clarence 28
Williams, "Cyclone" Joe (later "Smokey" Joe): Breakers Hotel team and 63, *75*, 86, 87; California Winter League and 52; Chicago Giants and 53–54; Habana team and 57; Lincoln Giants and 57
Williams, Daniel Hale 90
Williams, Eugene 114
Williams, Frank 111
Williams, James H. 158
Williams, Phil 18–19
Williams, Ted 162
Williams, Tom 80–81
Williams, Wesley 158
Williamson, Ned 5–6
Wilson, Andrew 141–2
Wilson, Jud "Boojum" 144, *148*, *151*, 160, 166
Wilson, W. Rollo 33, 48, 144
Wilson, Woodrow: on Blacks and communism 118; Liberty Loan parade and 95; race riots (1919) and 117; suffragists and 102–3, 104–5, *105*, 106; Volstead Act vetoed by 125

Winder, Charles S. *17*
Winters, Jess "Nip" 139
Wisconsin Fairs 56
Woman's Christian Temperance Union 102
women, Prohibition and 132
women's suffrage: Antis against 102; election of 1916 and 104–5, *105*; Hill's career and 2; Jim Crow and other impediments to 108; marches and demonstrations for 88; 19th Amendment on 101, 106–7; Prohibition and 104; racial tensions and 108
Wood, C. Bernice (possibly) *78*
Woods, "Window Washer" 111
World Series: Black Sox Scandal and 118–9; Colored 150
World War I 10, 88
Wright, George 34
Wright, J.H. 56
Wyatt, David "Dave": Detroit Stars' Opening Day and 136; with Foster in Otsego, Michigan 23; NNL and 122, 124, 134–5; as sportswriter 23–24, 98; on "war in Negro baseball" 45

Yancey, Bill 163–4
Yates, Frederic 106
Young, Dick 163, 164
Young, Frank A. "Fay" 64, 65, 73, 146, 159, 187*n*12
Young, Irv "Young Cy" 65
Young, Robert J. 99

Zimmer, Don 173